narr STUDIENBÜCHER

Paul Skandera / Peter Burleigh

A Manual of English Phonetics and Phonology

Twelve Lessons with an Integrated Course
in Phonetic Transcription

2nd completely revised edition

Peter Burleigh, MSt is Lecturer in English Language and Linguistics at Basel University.
Dr. Paul Skandera is Professor of English at the University of Applied Sciences in Innsbruck.

Bibliografische Information der Deutschen Nationalbibliothek

Die Deutsche Nationalbibliothek verzeichnet diese Publikation in der Deutschen Nationalbibliografie; detaillierte bibliografische Daten sind im Internet über <http://dnb.d-nb.de> abrufbar.

© 2011 · Narr Francke Attempto Verlag GmbH + Co. KG
Dischingerweg 5 · D-72070 Tübingen

Das Werk einschließlich aller seiner Teile ist urheberrechtlich geschützt. Jede Verwertung außerhalb der engen Grenzen des Urheberrechtsgesetzes ist ohne Zustimmung des Verlages unzulässig und strafbar. Das gilt insbesondere für Vervielfältigungen, Übersetzungen, Mikroverfilmungen und die Einspeicherung und Verarbeitung in elektronischen Systemen.
Gedruckt auf chlorfrei gebleichtem und säurefreiem Werkdruckpapier.

Internet: http://www.narr-studienbuecher.de
E-Mail: info@narr.de

Satz: CompArt, Mössingen

Printed in the EU

ISSN 0941-8105
ISBN 978-3-8233-6665-2

Contents

A note to students and instructors IX

LESSON ONE: THE PRELIMINARIES 1
What is linguistics? 1
    Prescriptivism and descriptivism 1
    Parole vs. langue and performance vs. competence 1
    The four core areas of linguistics 1
    Other branches of linguistics 2
What are phonetics and phonology? 3
    Phonetics 3
    Phonology 5
Whose pronunciation are we describing? 6
    The notion of a standard variety 6
    Received Pronunciation: An accent 6
How do we write down spoken language? 7
    Traditional spelling 7
    Phonetic transcription 7
    The International Phonetic Alphabet 8

LESSON TWO: THE DESCRIPTION OF SPEECH SOUNDS 9
Phonetic features 9
    Loudness 9
    Pitch 10
    Tone of voice 10
    Duration and length 10
    Air-stream mechanism 11
    Voicedness and voicelessness: The state of the glottis 12
Phonologically relevant features: Distinctive features 12
    Intensity of articulation I: Lenis and fortis 12
    Place of articulation I 13
    Manner of articulation I 14
Exercises 15

LESSON THREE: CONSONANTS 19
    The phoneme 19
The English consonant phonemes 20
    Place of articulation II 20

Manner of articulation II	22
The consonant table	25
The problem cases	25
Of semi-vowels, contoids, and vocoids ...	25
... and more terminological confusion	26
Exercises	27

LESSON FOUR: VOWELS — 31

The description of vowels	31
Manner of articulation III	32
The vowel chart I	33
The cardinal vowels	33
The English vowel phonemes	35
Long vowels	35
Short vowels	36
The vowel chart II	37
Intensity of articulation II: Lax and tense	37
Diphthongs and triphthongs	38
The shortening of vowels, nasals, and the lateral	40
Exercises	41

LESSON FIVE: ALLOPHONIC VARIATION — 43

The allo-/-eme relationship	43
Allophone vs. phoneme	43
The two allophone criteria	44
Allophones in free variation	45
Allophones in complementary distribution	45
Devoicing	46
Fronting and retraction	47
Two (or three) types of phonetic transcription	49
Phonetic transcription proper	49
Phonemic transcription	49
Broad phonetic transcription: An intermediate type	50
Unstressed *i*- and *u*-sounds	50
A brief excursion into morphophonology	51
The regular plural, the possessive case, and the third-person singular morphemes	52
The regular past tense and past participle morphemes	52
The pronunciation of the letter sequence <ng>	53
Exercises	54

Contents

LESSON SIX: CONNECTED SPEECH — 57

Linking — 57
- Liaison — 57
- Linking *r* and intrusive *r*: Two cases of liaison — 58
- Non-rhotic and rhotic accents — 59
- Juncture — 60

Exercises — 63

LESSON SEVEN: THE SYLLABLE — 65

- A phonetic approach to the syllable — 65
- Phonotactics — 67
- A phonological approach to the syllable — 67
- Syllabic consonants — 68
- Stressed and unstressed syllables vs. strong and weak syllables — 71
- Stress patterns in polysyllabic words — 73

Exercises — 76

LESSON EIGHT: STRONG AND WEAK FORMS — 79

- What are strong and weak forms? — 79
- Grammatical words — 80
- The distribution of strong and weak forms — 80
- The forms — 81

Exercises — 85

LESSON NINE: CONNECTED SPEECH, CONTD. — 87

Rhythm — 87
- What is rhythm? — 87
- Two types of rhythm — 87

Assimilation — 89
- What is assimilation? — 89
- Various types of assimilation — 90
- The opposite of assimilation: Dissimilation — 94

Elision — 94
- What is elision? — 94
- Various types of elision — 95
- The opposite of elision: Intrusion — 97

Exercises — 99

Lesson Ten: Allophonic Variation, contd. — 101

- Aspiration — 101
- Secondary articulation — 103
- Main types of secondary articulation — 104
- Exercises — 107

Lesson Eleven: More Allophones — 109

- *t*-sounds — 109
- *r*-sounds — 112
- *l*-sounds — 115
- Exercises — 118

Lesson Twelve: Intonation — 119

- What is intonation? — 119
- Pitch — 120
- The tone unit — 120
- Intonation patterns — 121
- Tone unit structure — 122
- Functions of intonation — 123
- Exercises — 125

Appendix I: Solutions to the exercises — 127
Appendix II: Glossary of linguistic terms — 151

A note to students and instructors

This book is a manual of English phonetics and phonology intended for students of English in undergraduate university courses in the German-speaking region. It deals mainly with British English, but makes references to American English where appropriate and occasionally also to other varieties. The book is motivated by the fact that there is currently no textbook which satisfactorily combines an introduction to the theory of phonetics and phonology with the practice of transcription even though at nearly all universities both fields are mandatory subjects of study. Thus the book has been designed to be used either as seminar material in the classroom or for self-study.

The book is tailored to the workload of one semester, spanning twelve weeks or more. Its breadth, therefore, does not compete with other, more extensive introductions to phonetics and phonology. In fact, the spirit of the book is revealed in the word *manual*: Our introduction is a compendium, a handbook that can be worked through from cover to cover, giving the pedagogic gratification of completeness and achievement, and avoiding the recurrent questions of which chapters or sections from a longer work are relevant to a course, or rather an exam.

The manual is entirely self-explanatory and requires absolutely no prior knowledge of linguistics. The first lesson begins, then, with the basic question of what linguistics is. It gives a short overview of the various branches of linguistics, and locates phonetics and phonology in this broad context. This approach is especially advantageous for students who begin their English studies with phonetics and phonology before taking other, more general linguistics courses. As the manual progresses, terminology and knowledge are advanced in a carefully staged manner, with each lesson building on previous lessons. Complementary exercises in a separate section at the end of each lesson give students the opportunity to put the theory they have learnt into practice.

Technical terms that are introduced appear first in bold (or sometimes in italic) type, and are often followed by common alternative terms and a gloss in German. Thus new terms and concepts can be clearly identified, which facilitates progression in the course, and is useful for revision and exam preparation. The alternative terms are given because it is one of the aims of this manual to prepare students for the array of (sometimes confusing and contradicting) terminologies used in other textbooks, which they will be reading in more advanced courses. This aim can only be achieved by acquainting the readers with a variety of different terms for the same concept, and, conversely, with different definitions of the same term. At the same time, this approach pre-empts the widely held expectation that, in technical jargon, there must be a one-to-one correspondence between concept and term. While this would certainly be desirable, it is far from the academic reality. A glossary of most of the technical terms is provided at the end of the manual.

Most importantly, the exercises in the separate sections constitute a fully integrated course in phonetic transcription, including annotated model solutions at the end of the book. They develop in a carefully graded way from the transcription of simple written texts to the more difficult transcription of naturally spoken dialogue. All spoken texts are provided on the accompanying CD. The exercises are meant to be done parallel to each lesson, thus steadily building students' confidence and skill in transcription.

The authors worked together for several years in the Department of English at the University of Basel, and the manual is based on teaching material developed for the Introduction to English Phonetics course taught there. Special thanks are therefore due, first and foremost, to Professor D. J. Allerton, whose lecture shaped the subject matter of our manual. Thanks are also extended, however, to the large number of students who contributed to the development of the exercises and model solutions over the years.

Finally, the authors express their gratitude to Dr. James Fanning of the University of Greifswald for his detailed critique of the first edition of this book, which was indispensable in the preparation of this second edition.

Paul Skandera, Innsbruck
Peter Burleigh, Basel

LESSON 1
THE PRELIMINARIES

What is linguistics?

Prescriptivism and descriptivism

From ancient times until the present, language purists have believed that the task of the grammarian is to *pre*scribe (rather than *de*scribe) correct usage that all educated people should use in speaking and writing. **Prescriptive** language scholars have laid down rules that are often based on Latin and Greek, on a classical canon of literary works, on the origin of particular words, on logic, or simply on their personal likes and dislikes. Prescriptivists have been criticised for not taking sufficient account of ongoing language change and stylistic variation. By contrast, the aim of linguistics is to *de*scribe language objectively and systematically. **Descriptive** linguists observe and analyse language as it is used naturally in any given speech community [*Sprachgemeinschaft*], and they attempt to discover the rules and regularities of the underlying language system, or code.

Parole vs. langue and performance vs. competence

In order to separate the two meanings of the word *language* implied in the last sentence of the previous paragraph, the Swiss linguist Ferdinand de Saussure (1857–1913) proposed the French terms **parole** to refer to actual language use (i.e. to concrete utterances) and **langue** for a speech community's shared knowledge of a language (i.e. for the language system).

A similar dichotomy was put forward by the American linguist Noam Chomsky (b. 1928), who used the terms **performance** and **competence** to refer to largely the same concepts. Chomsky, however, put more emphasis on the individual nature of language. Performance, then, is the actual language use of an individual speaker, and competence is that individual speaker's knowledge of the language. Chomsky later replaced these terms with **E(xternalised)-language** and **I(nternalised)-language**, but the new terms are rarely used.

The four core areas of linguistics

The system or structure of a language (langue or competence) can be described at four different levels, which form the core areas of linguistics, sometimes called *microlinguis-*

tics: **(1) Phonetics** and **phonology** deal with pronunciation, or, more precisely, with speech sounds and the sound system. **(2) Morphology** covers the structure of words. **(3) Syntax** explains sentence patterns. (Morphology and syntax, often combined into *morphosyntax*, have traditionally been referred to as *grammar*.) **(4) Lexicology** and **semantics** describe the vocabulary, or lexicon, and explore different aspects of meaning.

Other branches of linguistics

Utilising the core areas are various other branches of linguistics, sometimes referred to as *macrolinguistics*. Most of these are interdisciplinary fields because they overlap with other sciences. The first four branches are concerned with language variation, and are therefore often subsumed under the label *variational linguistics*: **(1) Dialectology** is at the interface between linguistics and geography. It is the study of regional variation within a language. **(2) Sociolinguistics** connects linguistics with sociology. It is concerned with language variation according to age, sex, social class, etc. **(3) Ethnolinguistics** overlaps with anthropology and investigates language variation and the role language plays in ethnic groups. These three branches study the way language is used in different speech communities. They are therefore often referred to as *sociolinguistics*, which is then used in a broader sense as a superordinate term. The language variety [*Varietät*] spoken in a particular speech community is referred to as a *lect*. Thus we speak of *dialects*, *sociolects*, and *ethnolects*. The characteristic speech of an individual person is called an *idiolect*.

(4) Discourse analysis, text linguistics, and **stylistics** are closely related disciplines that also deal with language variation. Unlike the first three branches, however, they do not look at the way language is used in different speech communities, but rather at the language characteristics of different text types, especially beyond the sentence level. The language of these text types is communicated either through the medium of speech (e.g. personal conversations, broadcast discussions, lectures) or through the medium of writing (e.g. personal letters, newspaper articles, academic papers). And even though many linguists tend to be primarily interested in spoken language, one important field of study, which connects linguistics with literary science, is the characteristic use of language in works of literature.

The next four branches of linguistics are not concerned with language variation: **(5) Contrastive linguistics** describes the similarities and differences between two or more modern languages, especially in order to improve language teaching and translation. **(6) Psycholinguistics** overlaps with psychology and explores mental aspects of language, such as language learning. **(7) Neurolinguistics** overlaps with medical science and investigates the connection between language and the nervous system. It is especially interested in the neurological processes necessary to produce speech sounds and in language disorders [*Sprachstörungen*]. **(8) Computational linguistics** [*Computerlinguistik*] overlaps with artificial intelligence. Some of its concerns are machine translation, automatic speech recognition, and speech simulation.

The four core areas and all the other branches of linguistics mentioned so far extend their insights to various other domains. The practical application of linguistic findings, for example to the field of foreign language teaching, is called **(9) applied linguistics**. This term is contrasted with **general** or **theoretical linguistics**, which denotes a more theoretical orientation.

In the four core areas and in branches (1) to (4) above, linguists usually study the state of a language or variety at one particular period of time (e.g. present-day English or English at the time of Shakespeare). This approach is called **synchronic linguistics** [from Greek *sún khrónos*, 'together with time']. But linguists may also study and compare the states of a language or variety at different points in time. This approach is called **(10) historical** or **diachronic linguistics** [from Greek *diá khrónos*, 'through time']. It connects linguistics with history and is concerned with language change and with the origin of words. Diachronic linguistics overlaps with **(11) comparative linguistics**, which also compares the states of languages or varieties at different points in time, but uses its findings to study the historical relations between different languages.

Finally, it is important to note that the various linguistic disciplines can hardly be kept apart, and that the borders between them are often blurred. If, for example, we were doing a study of the use of the *'s*-genitive (as in *the girl's father*) and the *of*-genitive (as in *the father of the girl*) in working-class speech in London over the past two hundred years, we would be doing morphology, syntax, sociolinguistics, dialectology, and historical linguistics at the same time.

All the different branches of linguistics are recapitulated in Figure 1.

What are phonetics and phonology?

We have already learnt that phonetics and phonology are concerned with speech sounds and the sound system. We also know that linguists analyse actual language use (parole or performance), and then try to infer the underlying language system (langue or competence).

Phonetics

Phonetics first of all divides, or segments, concrete utterances into individual speech sounds. It is therefore exclusively concerned with parole or performance. Phonetics can then be divided into three distinct phases: (1) articulatory phonetics, (2) acoustic phonetics, and (3) auditory phonetics.

(1) Articulatory phonetics describes in detail how the speech organs, also called vocal organs or articulators [*Sprechwerkzeuge*], in the vocal tract [*Mundraum*] are used in order to produce, or articulate, (specific) speech sounds. **(2) Acoustic phonetics** studies the physical properties of speech sounds, i.e. the way in which the air vibrates as sounds pass from speaker to listener. A spectrograph is a machine that measures the soundwaves [*Schallwellen*] and depicts them as images, called spectrograms or sonograms, showing the duration, frequency, intensity, and quality of the sounds. **(3) Auditory phonetics** investigates the perception of speech sounds by the listener, i.e. how the sounds are transmitted from the ear to the brain, and how they are processed.

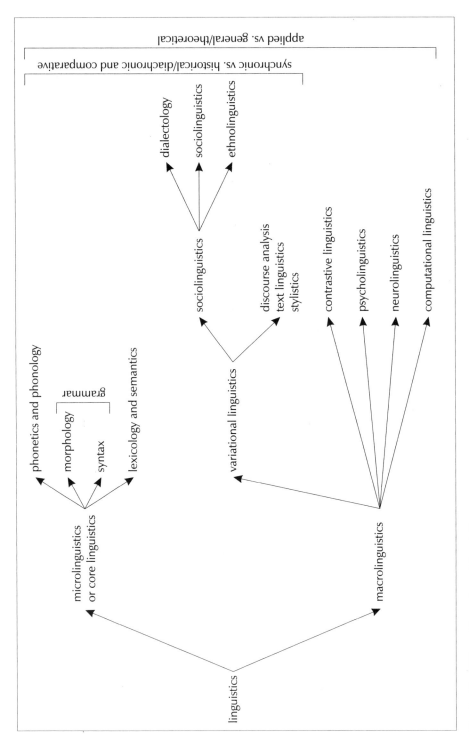

Fig. 1 The different branches of linguistics.

Owing to its close association with physics (and also with medicine), phonetics is sometimes considered a natural science, rather than a branch of linguistics (which belongs to the humanities) in the narrow sense. But no matter how we classify it, phonetics is an indispensable prerequisite for phonology, and is therefore an integral part of all introductions to linguistics. In the language departments of most universities, however, the study of phonetics is largely restricted to articulatory phonetics because of its applications to the learning and teaching of pronunciation. For that reason, this manual, too, will only be concerned with articulatory phonetics, and phonology.

Phonology

Phonology deals with the speakers' knowledge of the sound system of a language. It is therefore exclusively concerned with langue or competence. (Phonology, then, is not the study of telephone manners, as one student once jokingly suggested.) Phonology can be divided into two branches: (1) segmental phonology and (2) suprasegmental phonology.

(1) Segmental phonology is based on the segmentation of language into individual speech sounds provided by phonetics. Unlike phonetics, however, segmental phonology is not interested in the production, the physical properties, or the perception of these sounds, but in the function and possible combinations of sounds within the sound system. **(2) Suprasegmental phonology**, also called **prosody**, is concerned with those features of pronunciation that cannot be segmented because they extend over more than one segment, or sound. Such features include stress [*Betonung*], rhythm, and intonation (also called pitch contour or pitch movement [*Tonhöhenbewegung*]).

The three phases of phonetics and the different spheres of phonetics and phonology are illustrated by the speech chain in Figure 2.

TIP   It is often not easy for students beginning the study of linguistics to understand the difference between phonetics and phonology. It is therefore advisable to return to the above explanations from time to time as you work through this manual.

Fig. 2 The speech chain.

Whose pronunciation are we describing?

The notion of a standard variety

In all linguistic research, we have to define the language variety that we are concerned with by delineating the speech community and/or the text type. For example, we can investigate the Manchester dialect, the language used in e-mail messages, or the speech of children in conversations with their peers.

In language teaching, on the other hand, it is customary to use a more idealised **standard variety**, or simply **standard** [*hochsprachliche Variante*], as a model. A standard variety is the form of a language that is generally associated with educated speakers. And even though it may have a regional base, we regard it as regionally neutral in that it can be found anywhere in a country. A standard is therefore a sociolect, rather than a dialect. The standard variety of English in Great Britain is called *Standard British English* (popularly referred to by such non-linguistic terms as *King's English*, *Queen's English*, *BBC English*, or *Oxford English*). The standard variety spoken in the United States is called *General American (English)* or *Standard American English*.

Received Pronunciation: An accent

A standard variety has a fixed grammar and vocabulary, but its pronunciation may vary according to the regional origin, social group, or ethnicity of the speaker. We use the term **accent** to refer to the way a variety is pronounced. It is quite possible, then, that a standard variety is spoken in different accents. One of these accents usually carries the most prestige, and is used as a model in the teaching of pronunciation. The most prestigious accent of Standard British English, for example, was first called *Public School Pronunciation* and renamed **Received Pronunciation**, or simply **RP**, in the 1920s. There is no widely used term for the most prestigious accent of General American, but it is sometimes referred to as *Network Standard* or *Network English*.

Received Pronunciation is associated with the dialect spoken in the south-east of England. The word *received* may seem awkward in this construction, but it is used here in the sense 'generally accepted as proper'. RP was initially described by the British phonetician Daniel Jones (1881-1967) in the first edition of his *English Pronouncing Dictionary* in 1917. And although RP is probably the most discussed accent around the world, it is important to note that it is a minority pronunciation unlikely ever to have been used by more than 3 to 4 per cent of the British population. Most educated speakers of British English speak a modified RP or near RP.

In this manual, we use RP, or near RP, as our model to illustrate English phonetics and phonology. RP is also the accent used in practically all British dictionaries and introductory textbooks.

How do we write down spoken language?

Traditional spelling

In order to describe somebody's individual pronunciation or the sounds of a language variety, we need a method of writing down sounds as accurately as possible. The first method that comes to mind is the traditional alphabetical spelling system, also called **orthography**. It does, after all, relate speech sounds to letters. In most languages, however, the relationship between speech and writing is not very consistent. In English, one particular sound may be represented by different letters or combinations of letters. The second sound in the word *he*, for example, is represented differently in *see*, *sea*, *seize*, *people*, *key*, *Caesar*, *believe*, *amoeba*, *machine*, and *silly*. Conversely, the same letters may indicate different sounds, such as the *a* in *dad, father, many, call, village*, and *Dame*. According to a statistical analysis conducted by Godfrey Dewey (reported in his book *English Spelling: Roadblock to Reading* from 1971), there are 13.7 different spellings per sound, and 3.5 sounds per letter. And some letters, like the *b* in *debt*, have no sound at all in certain words.

The rather confusing nature of English spelling can be explained by the long tradition of printing in England. When in 1476 William Caxton, who had learnt the art of printing in Cologne, set up the first printing house just outside London, the orthography became less variable, and many subsequent sound changes were not accompanied by changes in the spelling. The spellings of many words in English today are therefore based on the pronunciation used in the time from Chaucer to Shakespeare. One example is the word *knight*, which in modern English is pronounced like the word *night*, but used to be pronounced similar to the German word *Knecht*, from which it originated. Another factor that contributed to the discrepancy between sound and spelling is the unusually high number of loanwords which have entered the English language throughout its history and retained their original spelling. On the other hand, one study suggests that there are fewer than 500 words in English whose spelling is significantly irregular. If this is true, it seems that many of these words are among the most frequently used words in the language.

Attempts to eliminate spelling irregularities can be traced back to the 16th century. **Spelling reform** has been promoted by such illustrious people as Benjamin Franklin, Charles Darwin, Alfred Lord Tennyson, Andrew Carnegie, Theodore Roosevelt, and George Bernard Shaw, in addition to numerous language professionals. In Britain, the Simplified Spelling Society advocates changes in the spelling system, as does the Reformed Spelling Association in the United States. So far, however, no attempt to change English orthography has shown any sign of success.

Phonetic transcription

If we want to write down speech sounds as accurately as possible, we cannot depend on traditional spelling. We need a method that relates sounds to letters or symbols more systematically: Each sound must be represented consistently by the same symbol, and, conversely, there must be a separate symbol for each distinctive sound. Such a one-to-one correspondence between speech and writing is referred to as a **phonographic** relationship. The symbols that we use to represent speech sounds in this manner are **phonetic symbols**. A whole set of them form a **phonetic alphabet**. Marks that we can add to indicate slight alterations to the usual value of a phonetic symbol are called **diacritics** [*diakritische Zeichen*]. The term **phonetic transcription** [from Latin *transcriptio*, 'writing over'; *phonetische Umschrift*, *Lautschrift*] refers to the process of writing down spoken language in phonetic symbols as well as to the resultant written text.

The International Phonetic Alphabet

The most widely used phonetic alphabet, and one that provides suitable symbols for the sounds of any language, is the **International Phonetic Alphabet**, or **IPA**. This is the phonetic alphabet used in this manual. It was first published in 1888 by the International Phonetic Association in France, and has since then been revised and corrected in various ways, most recently in 2005. It was initially developed by a group of French and British language teachers from a concept proposed by the Danish linguist Otto Jespersen (1860-1943). (The abbreviation *IPA* stands for both the alphabet and the association. The association's German name, *Weltlautschriftverein*, is almost never heard.) The International Phonetic Alphabet is used, with minor modifications and some unwelcome variation and inconsistencies, in almost all English-language dictionaries, except for American publications. The IPA does not, however, provide the means for a **prosodic transcription**, i.e. it cannot indicate suprasegmental features [*Suprasegmentalia*, *Prosodeme*] like rhythm or intonation. Apart from a mark to indicate stress, there is no generally agreed system for writing down the prosody of speech.

While some IPA symbols have been specially devised, quite a few of them look like ordinary Roman letters. They have probably been included for purely practical reasons, such as the facilitation of the printing process, but their inclusion has one serious disadvantage: The Roman letters used in the IPA may be misleading because they do not always represent the sounds that a speaker of English or German would expect. When memorising the symbols of the IPA and the corresponding sounds, it is therefore not advisable to be guided by your knowledge of the conventional ABC. Learn every symbol as though you had never seen it before!

In order to distinguish phonetic symbols from letters, phonetic symbols are enclosed either in square brackets, [ ], if they are used to represent a concrete utterance (parole or performance), or in slashes, //, when they indicate speech sounds as part of the sound system (langue or competence). Letters are enclosed within pointed brackets, <>, or they appear in single quotation marks, or in italics. Thus [p] represents an actual sound, /p/ indicates an abstract sound and our shared knowledge of its function within the sound system, and <p>, 'p', or *p* is an ordinary letter. Those IPA symbols that represent English sounds are listed on the inside front cover of this book.

LESSON 2
THE DESCRIPTION OF SPEECH SOUNDS

If we want to describe the pronunciation of a particular speaker or a speech community, we begin by describing all the individual sounds that occur in the lect of that speaker or speech community. In this manual, we count nine features that are relevant to the description of speech sounds, even though the exact number may vary in different linguistic textbooks. These nine features fall into two broad categories: The first category contains those characteristics that are relevant if we want to describe the physical aspects of English sounds as precisely as possible. They usually have no (or little) bearing on the function of the sounds within the sound system of RP or any other English accent. These features are therefore mainly phonetically relevant. They have no (or little) relevance to the segmental phonology of English. The second category contains those features that are both phonetically and phonologically relevant in English. For example, they explain the difference between the final sounds in word pairs like ca<u>b</u> and ca<u>p</u> or ser<u>ve</u> and sur<u>f</u>. The features in the second category, then, can distinguish meaning and are therefore called **distinctive** or **relevant features** [*distinktive* oder *relevante Merkmale*]. They are relevant to the function of sounds within the sound system.

Phonetic features

Loudness

Loudness is one of the main phonetic properties of spoken language and of individual sounds. It is related to the breadth, or amplitude, of the vibration of the **vocal folds**, or, to use an older term, the **vocal cords** [*Stimmbänder, Stimmlippen*]. The vocal folds are located behind the Adam's apple in the **voice box**, also called the **larynx** [*Kehlkopf*], at the top of the **windpipe**, or **trachea** [*Luftröhre*]. The greater the amplitude of the vibration, the louder the sound.

As a suprasegmental feature, or prosodic feature, loudness *can* distinguish meaning: It is one component of **stress** (together with pitch [*Tonhöhe*], duration, and sound quality), and thus contributes to the distinction between the noun *record* and the verb *record*, for example. It can also convey an emotional state such as anger. In the segmental phonology of English accents, however, it cannot distinguish meaning: The function of an individual sound within the sound system does not change with the loudness of its pronunciation. Loudness is therefore not a distinctive feature.

Pitch

Pitch is also an important phonetic characteristic. It is related to the frequency of the vibration of the vocal folds: The faster the vocal folds vibrate, the higher the pitch.

Like loudness, pitch can distinguish meaning at a suprasegmental level: It is a component of **stress**, and it shapes the intonation of connected speech. Stress and pitch movement tell us, for example, whether a sentence like *She speaks English* is meant to be a statement or a question. Pitch cannot, however, change the function of an individual sound within the sound system of English. By contrast, in over half the languages of the world, a change of pitch *can* change the function of a sound, i.e. the basic meaning of a word can be changed simply by varying the pitch of one of its sounds. These languages are called **tone languages**. Many Asian and native American languages are tone languages, and there are more than 1,000 tone languages in Africa alone. English belongs to the **non-tone languages**. Pitch is therefore not a distinctive feature in the segmental phonology of RP or any other English accent.

Tone of voice

We must distinguish between *sound quality* and *tone of voice*. We use the term **sound quality** to refer to the quality that is characterised by the distinctive features, listed in the second category below. This means that the final sound in the word *see*, for example, has the same quality irrespective of the loudness, pitch, or duration with which it is pronounced. **Tone of voice**, also called **voice quality, tonal quality**, or **timbre**, refers to the difference in "colour" that we hear between two voices when they produce a sound with otherwise exactly the same phonetic (including distinctive) features. This can be compared with the difference that we hear between two musical instruments. The different tones of voice are produced by different patterns of vibration of the vocal folds, which, in turn, cause different combinations of soundwaves that nevertheless result in the same sound quality.

Tone of voice, like loudness and pitch, is a feature of spoken language as well as of the pronunciation of individual sounds. Because it is less important in the communication of meaning, however, it is not usually considered a suprasegmental feature. By contrast, some linguists call it a **paralinguistic feature**. The tone of voice makes us characterise the voice of a speaker as female, feminine, male, masculine, harsh, breathy, murmured, creaky, or thin, for example. It enables us to recognise a particular speaker or to describe the speaker as female or male, young or old, angry or exhausted, etc. But the tone of voice does not change the function of individual speech sounds. Like the other characteristics in this category, it is not a distinctive feature in the segmental phonology of English accents.

Duration and length

Duration and length (sometimes also referred to as *sound quantity*) both refer to the span of time during which a sound is sustained. The term **duration** is usually restricted to phonetics, and is used for the absolute or actual time taken in the articulation of a sound. The final sound in the word *see*, for example, can be held for different spans of time depending on the speaker, on the emphasis that is given to the word in the particular utterance, and on a number of other chance factors. Even though it is usually considered a long sound, it can actually be given a rather short pronunciation. The difference here is one of duration. It is a purely phonetic concept because the function of the sound, and with it the sound quality, remains the same.

The term **length** is usually restricted to phonology. It refers to the relative time a sound is sustained as perceived by the listener. For example, the middle sounds in the words *fool* and *full* are commonly described as a long *u* and short *u*, respectively. The difference here is one of length. It can be seen as a phonological concept because the long *u* and short *u* have different functions within the English sound system. In other words, the difference in length can distinguish meaning, or at least it can help to distinguish meaning. Many linguists therefore count length among the distinctive features.

Why, then, do we not regard length as a distinctive feature in this manual, and list it with the phonologically relevant features below? If we listen carefully to the way the words *fool* and *full* are pronounced, we realise that it is not just the length that distinguishes the two middle sounds, but also their quality. A difference in length is almost always accompanied by a difference in sound quality, and it appears that the different quality is much more significant for our different perception of the sounds. In fact, it is quite possible to pronounce the long *u* in *fool* shorter than the short *u* in *full*. Labels like "long *u*" and "short *u*" can therefore be misleading. Thus, in this manual, we count length among the features that are mainly phonetically relevant.

Air-stream mechanism

All speech sounds are made with some movement of air. The majority of sounds used in the languages of the world are produced with air that is pushed up from the lungs through the **windpipe**, or **trachea**, and leaves the body through the mouth and sometimes through the nose. This movement of air is called an **egressive pulmonic air-stream** [*egressive*, 'outwards'; *pulmonic*, 'of the lungs']. Virtually all English sounds are produced by such an egressive pulmonic air-stream mechanism. The air-stream mechanism is therefore not a distinctive feature in English.

The egressive pulmonic air-stream mechanism is the only air-stream mechanism that uses lung air. All languages make use of it, but many languages additionally also have sounds that are produced by a different air-stream. In those languages, the air-stream mechanism may well be a distinctive feature. Three other air-stream mechanisms which are encountered in many languages, especially in Africa, use the air in the mouth, rather than lung air, to produce speech sounds: If air is pushed up from the space between the vocal folds, known as the **glottis** [*Stimmritze*], we speak of an **egressive glottalic** air-stream mechanism. A sound produced in this way is called **ejective**. If the glottis makes the air move inwards, we speak of an **ingressive glottalic** air-stream mechanism, and a sound produced in this way is called **implosive**. If air is sucked in as a result of movements against the back part of the roof of the mouth, known as the **velum** or **soft palate** [*weicher Gaumen*], we speak of an **ingressive**

velaric air-stream mechanism. A sound produced in this way is called **click**, and a language that has click sounds is often referred to as a **click language**.

Voicedness and voicelessness: The state of the glottis

All sounds that are produced by an egressive pulmonic air-stream mechanism, and therefore all English sounds, are made with air that passes through the **glottis**, which we have defined as the space between the vocal folds, located behind the Adam's apple in the voice box, or larynx.

If the glottis is narrow, i.e. if the vocal folds are together, the air-stream forces its way through and causes the vocal folds to vibrate. Sounds produced in this way are called **voiced** [*stimmhaft*]. You can check whether a sound is voiced either by placing a finger on either side of the larynx or by closing your ears with your fingers while you speak. When you say the word *zeal*, for example, you should be able to sense the vibration of the vocal folds for the entire time that you take to pronounce the word because all three sounds are voiced.

If the glottis is open, i.e. if the vocal folds are apart, the air passes through without causing the vocal folds to vibrate. Sounds produced in this way are called **voiceless** [*stimmlos*]. When you use the two tests to check which sounds in the word *seal* are voiced and which are voiceless, you will find that you do not sense any vibration of the vocal folds on the first sound, and that the vibration sets in on the second sound. This means that the first sound in *seal* is voiceless, and the other two are voiced. When we whisper, we are making all speech sounds voiceless, even the sounds in *zeal* and the final two in *seal*.

A third possibility is that the glottis is closed, i.e. the vocal folds are firmly pressed together, and the air-stream is stopped completely. Such a **glottal closure** [*Kehlverschluss*] can produce only one sound, which is called a **glottal stop** or **glottal plosive** [*Kehlkopfverschlusslaut, (Kehlkopf)knacklaut*]. Strictly speaking, the glottal stop is of little importance in the description of RP as it is usually associated with a non-standard London accent. It seems to be spreading in educated speech, however, and we therefore occasionally include it in our discussion.

The difference in meaning between *zeal* and *seal* can be solely attributed to the difference between their initial sounds, and it appears that the only difference between these two sounds is one of voicing. In this particular case, the voiced/voiceless contrast certainly distinguishes meaning, or at least it helps to distinguish meaning. Some linguists therefore consider the voiced/voiceless contrast a distinctive feature in English. The reason why we list it among the mainly phonetic features is that the voiced/voiceless contrast cannot always distinguish meaning, as we shall see shortly.

Phonologically relevant features: Distinctive features

Intensity of articulation I: Lenis and fortis

The voiced/voiceless contrast discussed above is usually accompanied by a difference in the force with which the air-stream is pushed up. English voiced sounds are usually made with a relatively weak breath force, or little muscular tension. This is called a **lenis** articulation [Latin, 'soft'; *ungespannt*]. English voiceless sounds, on the other hand, are made with more force, or higher tension. This is called a **fortis** articulation [Latin, 'strong'; *gespannt*]. You may occasionally hear the terms "soft" and "hard" in popular usage to describe speech sounds or their articulation (as in "soft *s*" or "hard *s*"), but they have been abandoned in linguistics.

The symmetrical relationship between voiced/voiceless and lenis/fortis does not always hold. Whereas fortis sounds are indeed always voiceless in English, lenis sounds, which are usually voiced, may also occur as voiceless variants, i.e. they can be **devoiced**. We have already seen one example in the discussion of *zeal* and *seal* above. We said that apparently the only difference between these two words is the voiced/voiceless contrast of their initial sounds, and that we are making all speech sounds voiceless when we whisper. Why, then, do we still perceive a difference between *zeal* and *seal* even when the words are whispered? The answer is that the voiced/voiceless contrast is *not* the only difference between the two words, or their initial sounds. There is another difference, namely the intensity with which the initial sounds are articulated: Although the initial sound in *zeal* is made voiceless when whispered, it retains its lenis articulation. In other words, the first sound in *zeal* is always articulated with a weaker breath force than the first sound in *seal*, no matter whether the words are whispered or not.

Some lenis sounds can also be devoiced in certain environments. For example, they are partly devoiced in word-initial position, and almost entirely devoiced word-finally, as in the words *cab* and *serve*. The final sounds, here, are devoiced, but we still perceive them as the same (voiced) sounds because of their lenis articulation. We still hear the words *cab* and *serve*. If, however, we increase the breath force, or muscular tension, when producing the final sounds, i.e. if we pronounce these sounds with a fortis articulation, we hear the words *cap* and *surf*. All this suggests that it is not really the voiced/voiceless contrast, but the lenis/fortis contrast that can distinguish meaning and must therefore be considered a distinctive feature.

Place of articulation I

You already know that virtually all English sounds are made with air that is pushed up from the lungs. In the production of approximately two thirds of these sounds, the air-stream is obstructed in the throat, technically called the **pharyngeal cavity** or **pharynx** [*Rachenraum, Rachen*], or in the vocal tract before it leaves the body through the mouth or nose. Sounds that are produced by an obstruction of air are called **consonants**. An important feature for the description of consonants is the exact place where the air-stream is obstructed. The place of articulation [*Artikulationsstelle, Artikulationsort*] names the speech organs that are primarily involved in the production of a particular sound.

To produce a consonant, there is usually one active, mobile, lower speech organ that moves and makes contact with a passive, immobile, upper speech organ. For example, in the articulation of the last sound in the word *surf*, the air-stream is obstructed by the contact of the lower lip with the upper teeth. This sound is therefore called a "labiodental consonant", or simply a "labiodental" [from Latin *labialis*, 'of the lips', and *dentalis*, 'of the teeth']. You will find a diagram showing all the speech organs referred to in this manual on the inside front cover.

Manner of articulation I

Another important feature for the description of speech sounds is the type or degree of closure of the speech organs involved. Thus the manner of articulation [*Artikulationsart*] refers mainly to the degree to which the air-stream is obstructed at the place of articulation of consonants. When pronouncing the last sound in *surf*, for example, the gap between the lower lip and the upper teeth is narrowed to the point where friction is caused as the air passes through. The resultant consonant is therefore called a "fricative". If we wanted to describe this sound using all three distinctive features, we would say that it is a "fortis labiodental fricative". There is no other sound in the English sound system that fits this description.

The places and manners of articulation will be discussed in greater detail in the next lesson, and we shall return to the intensity of articulation in Lesson Four.

EXERCISES

These discovery exercises are designed to help you discover the way the sounds of English are made, and how some of the features discussed in this lesson contribute to the distinction of word meaning. Exercises 2.1, 2.2, and 2.3 focus on purely phonetic features whereas exercises 2.4, 2.5, and 2.6 focus on the distinctive features, following the same order as in the text. Try the exercises at least twice to really familiarise yourself with the feature that is being considered.

2.1 Loudness and pitch

2.1a Loudness and pitch, as has already been mentioned, are components of stress. If you place stress at the beginning of some words, or alternatively towards the end, their meaning changes. Try the words below, noting whether they are verbs or nouns according to where the stress is placed. Can you identify any regularity?

refuse	rebel	produce
contract	conflict	compact
extract	project	conduct

2.1b Try varying the loudness and pitch movement when you say the phrases below, so that they sound like neutral statements, questions, or expressive utterances.

She did it.
Have you finished?
It's your turn to pay.
Actually, I don't like whisky.
We're not going there again.

These exercises illustrate the function of loudness and pitch as suprasegmental features. Although they can change meaning, it is important to realise that this occurs on a suprasegmental, and not a segmental, level.

2.2 Length

From the list of words below, match those that sound similar into pairs, for example *cheap* and *chip*. In each pair, identify which word has the longer middle sound. In the example just given, it is *cheap*. Now try to reverse the lengths. So make the middle sound in *cheap* short, and the one in *chip* long. Does the swapping of length swap the meaning of the words, or is the difference in the quality of the middle sounds the cue which distinguishes these aberrant forms from each other?

| long | who'd | ship | seat | pot | wheel | cooker | boon | did |
| deed | sit | port | lawn | will | cougar | hood | book | sheep |

2.3 Voicedness and voicelessness

Use the tests mentioned in this lesson – placing your finger and thumb around the larynx or closing your ears with your fingers – to match pairs of words with similar sounds that are either voiced or voiceless. There are two sets of words focusing on either the sound at the beginning or the sound at the end of the word. For example, the initial sound in *do* is voiced whereas the one in *to* is voiceless; the final sound in *bag* is voiced whereas the one in *back* is voiceless.

initial:
pat	this	dill	zed	zoo	that
fat	cream	fine	shed	bat	vat
thin	thank	Sue	green	till	vine

final:
mat	lop	leave	of	mad	cop
lob	bet	bed	cloth	tooth	pluck
off	cob	leaf	plug	teethe	clothe

2.4 Intensity of articulation: Lenis and fortis

Try saying the following pairs of words while holding your hand in front of your mouth, or placing a small, light, flat object, such as a dried leaf or a feather, on the palm of your hand held near your mouth: *bad/pad*, *van/fan*, *this/thin*, *zoo/shoe*, *gap/cap*. You will notice, by either feeling the air or seeing the object move, that with each of the pairs "extra" air is forced out at the underlined initial sound of one of the words compared with the other. Which ones are they? This difference can still be noticed even when you whisper the words. This exercise demonstrates the difference in the intensity of the articulation, i.e. the difference between lenis and fortis sounds. Remember that the lenis/fortis distinction also occurs between other pairs of sounds in English.

2.5 Place of articulation

Try the exercises below, and notice where there is an obstruction in the flow of air through the mouth.

2.5a Prepare to pronounce the first sound in the word *pan*, but do not actually say anything. Notice how there is a build-up of air pressure in the mouth. Which parts of your mouth are doing the most work to hold back the pressure? When you release the sound and say the word, which parts move? Try the same with *tan* and *can*.

2.5b Now repeat the exercise with the words *fat*, *other*, and *cash*, this time concentrating on the first, middle, and final sounds, respectively, trying to prolong them. Notice where the sound is made in your mouth. Where do you feel a stream of air passing through?

2.5c Again trying to prolong the initial sounds, say the words *might, light, right*. Compare this with the prolonged final sounds in *ram, ran, rang*. Think about the places where you can feel the sounds being made. What parts of the vocal tract are in contact or close proximity?

These three exercises show you some of the variety of place of articulation. There are many other places of articulation, which we shall discuss in the next lesson.

2.6 Manner of articulation

2.6a Try saying the initial sounds in the words *pad* and *mad*, the middle sounds in *utter* and *usher*, and the final sounds in *thing* and *thick*. Notice with each set that the sounds are made in approximately the same place, but your mouth is doing different things, i.e. the sounds are articulated in a different manner. Can you describe – even if only impressionistically – what is happening in these different articulations? Think about whether the articulators are in contact, or are close together. Where is the air-stream flowing through?

2.6b Prepare to say the initial sounds in *mood, nude, lewd*, and *rude*. Now hold your articulators in these positions, and try to blow out some extra air without either opening or closing your mouth. You should notice that the air in the words *mood* and *nude* passes through the nose, while in *lewd* and *rude* it passes through the mouth. In fact, with the latter pair, you can also feel that the air passes over the side of the tongue in *lewd*, and over the centre of the tongue in *rude*.

In the next lesson, we shall discuss how these and other articulations can be described formally, and give them their technical names.

Lesson 3
Consonants

The phoneme

Those speech sounds that we have so far rather elaborately referred to as "having a function within the sound system", or as "part of the speakers' langue or competence", are called **phonemes** [from Greek *phṓnēma*, 'sound']. The phoneme is a concept used in phonology, which is why the subdiscipline is sometimes called *phonemics* in the US. We saw in Lesson Two that a single phoneme can distinguish the word *cab* from *cap*, *serve* from *surf*, *fool* from *full*, and *zeal* from *seal*. A phoneme can therefore be defined as the smallest distinctive, or contrastive, unit [*kleinste bedeutungsunterscheidende Einheit*] in the sound system of a language. To put it in other words, a phoneme contrasts meaningfully with other speech sounds. We also saw in Lesson Two that the contrast between two phonemes lies solely in those characteristics that are phonologically relevant, and that it is therefore sufficient to describe phonemes only in terms of their distinctive features. Thus a phoneme has also been defined as a bundle of distinctive features (illustrated nicely by labels such as "fortis labiodental fricative"). The various definitions emphasise different aspects of the phoneme, but they all mean more or less the same thing.

It is important to remember that phonemes are abstract, idealised sounds that are never pronounced and never heard. Actual, concrete speech sounds can be regarded as the realisation of phonemes by individual speakers, and are referred to as **phones** [from Greek *phōnḗ*, 'voice']. The phone, then, is a concept used in phonetics. You learnt in Lesson One that phonetic symbols which represent phonemes are enclosed in slashes, //. Strictly speaking, they are then **phonemic symbols**, rather than phonetic symbols, but this terminological distinction is not always observed (and is not always clear). Phones, the true phonetic symbols, occur in square brackets, [ ].

If we want to establish what phonemes there are in a sound system, also called a **phonemic system** or **phoneme inventory** [*Phoneminventar*], we need to find pairs of words that differ in meaning and in only one sound. Linguists do this, for example, when they record a previously unknown language. Each of the two contrasting sounds in such a **minimal pair** [*Minimalpaar*] is a distinct phoneme. We have shown, then, that the final sounds in *ca<u>b</u>* and *ca<u>p</u>* are phonemes because the two words are a minimal pair. The same is true of the final sounds in *ser<u>ve</u>*/*sur<u>f</u>*, the middle sounds in *f<u>oo</u>l*/*f<u>u</u>ll*, and the initial sounds in *<u>z</u>eal*/*<u>s</u>eal*. Note that orthography is absolutely irrelevant here: The words *write* and *rhyme*, even though very different in their spelling, contrast only in their final sounds and are therefore also a minimal pair. The spelling of *week* and *weak*, on the other hand, differs in only one letter, but the two words are pronounced identically and are therefore *not* a minimal pair.

Every language has its own phoneme inventory, of course, but the phonemes sometimes also vary from dialect to dialect or from accent to accent. The phoneme inventory of most American English accents, for example, does not include the sound that most British speakers pronounce as the second sound in the word *sh*o*p*. Instead, American speakers usually use sounds with the quality of the second sound in *f*a*ther* or the second sound in *s*a*w*.

The English consonant phonemes

You already know that consonants are sounds that are produced by an obstruction of an air-stream either in the pharynx or in the vocal tract. There are 24 consonant phonemes in RP and in most other accents of English. The aim of this lesson is to describe these consonant phonemes to a point where there is only one phoneme in the sound system of English that fits each description, as we did with the final sound in *surf* in Lesson Two. You have learnt that loudness, pitch, tone of voice, and duration are suitable criteria to describe concrete speech sounds, or phones, but these features cannot distinguish phonemes. Length and voicing have proved to be rather unreliable features, and since all English sounds are made with egressive pulmonic air, the air-stream mechanism is not a suitable criterion either. For the description of English consonant phonemes, we therefore use only the distinctive features: the intensity of articulation, the place of articulation, and the manner of articulation.

Place of articulation II

There are thirteen possible places of articulation in the languages of the world, but not all of them are utilised in English. They are usually labelled according to the immobile, upper speech organ used in their production. The mobile, lower speech organ always lies directly opposite. In this section, all the places of articulation, progressing from the lips to the glottis, are briefly described, and the relevant English consonant phonemes for each category are given as IPA symbols. The underlined letters in the example words illustrate the sound a symbol represents. Remember that there is a list of all the phonetic symbols used in this manual and a diagram showing all the relevant speech organs on the inside front cover.

(1) **Bilabial** sounds are produced with both lips. There is only one fortis bilabial in English, namely /p/ as in *p*each, whereas there are two lenis bilabials, /b/ as in *b*anana and /m/ as in *m*ango.

(2) **Labiodental** sounds are produced by a movement of the lower lip against the upper teeth. There is one fortis labiodental in English, /f/ as in *f*ilm, and one lenis labiodental, /v/ as in *v*ideo.

The bilabials and labiodentals form one larger group, the **labials**, because they all make use of the lips.

(3) Dental, or **interdental**, sounds are made with the tongue tip and rims between the upper and lower teeth or against the upper teeth. The two dentals in English are often popularly called "teeaitch" because of their spelling. They are the fortis /θ/ as in t̲h̲in and the lenis /ð/ as in t̲h̲is.

(4) Alveolar sounds are made with the tongue tip coming near or touching the bony ridge behind the upper teeth, called the alveolar ridge [*Zahndamm, Zahnfächer, Zahnfortsatz*]. The two fortis alveolars are /t/ as in t̲iger and /s/ as in s̲nake. The four lenis alveolars are /d/ as in d̲olphin, /z/ as in z̲ebra, /n/ as in n̲ightingale, and /l/ as in l̲eopard.

(5) Postalveolar sounds are made with the tongue tip approaching or touching the rear of the alveolar ridge or the area just behind it. There is only one postalveolar in English, namely the lenis /r/ as in r̲ed.

(6) Retroflex sounds [from Latin *retrôflexus*, 'bent backwards'] are produced when the tip of the tongue is curled back to approach or make contact with the front part of the roof of the mouth, called the hard palate [*harter Gaumen, Gaumendach*], just behind the alveolar ridge. There are no retroflex phonemes in RP or any other accent of English. There is, however, a retroflex pronunciation variant (pertaining to parole or performance) of the /r/ phoneme in most American accents, in Irish English, and in accents of south-west England in words like wo̲r̲se and ha̲r̲d. This retroflex /r/ is phonetically transcribed as [ɻ].

The dentals, alveolars, postalveolars, and retroflex sounds all involve the tip of the tongue, and are therefore grouped together as **apical** sounds [from Latin *apex*, 'point'].

(7) Palatoalveolar sounds are made with the tongue tip touching the alveolar ridge, and with a simultaneous raising of the blade of the tongue [*Zungenblatt*] towards the hard palate. They therefore belong to the group of **laminal** sounds [from Latin *lamina*, 'thin plate']. The two fortis palatoalveolars in English are /tʃ/ as in c̲h̲eese and /ʃ/ as in s̲h̲erry. The two lenis palatoalveolars are /dʒ/ as in g̲in and /ʒ/ as in mea̲s̲ure.

(8) Palatal sounds are produced when the body of the tongue comes near or touches the (hard) palate. The lenis /j/ as in y̲es is the only palatal in English. An example from another language is the final sound in the High German pronunciation of the word i̲c̲h̲, transcribed as [ç].

(9) Velar sounds are made by placing the back of the tongue [*Hinterzunge*] against or near the velum, or soft palate [*weicher Gaumen, Gaumensegel*]. There is one fortis velar in English, namely /k/ as in C̲anada, whereas there are three lenis velars, /g/ as in G̲reenland, /ŋ/ as in E̲n̲gland, and /w/ as in W̲ales. An example from another language is the last sound in the High German word a̲c̲h̲, transcribed as [x].

The /w/ phoneme is different from the other English velars in that it is labialised, which means that it is pronounced with rounded lips. The lips, then, are a secondary place of articulation. The /w/ phoneme is therefore more specifically described as a labiovelar. A place of articulation which adds some quality to the main articulation is called **secondary articulation**. Some linguists speak of **coarticulation** or **double articulation**, but these terms are usually reserved for the simultaneous use of two places of obstruction of equal importance, which hardly ever occurs in English.

(10) Uvular sounds are made by moving the root or back of the tongue against the uvula [*Gaumenzäpfchen*], which is the appendage that hangs down from the velum. There are no uvular phonemes in English.

(11) Pharyngeal, also **pharyngal**, sounds are made when the root of the tongue is pulled back in the pharynx. There are no pharyngeal consonant phonemes in English.

The palatal, the velar, the uvular, and the pharyngeal sounds are grouped together as **dorsal** sounds because they all use the body of the tongue [from Latin *dorsalis*, 'of the back'].

(12) Epiglottal sounds are produced by a movement of the epiglottis [*Kehldeckel*] against the lower pharynx. Such sounds do not exist in English.

(13) Glottal sounds are produced in the larynx when air passes through the glottis. The only English phoneme that is articulated in this way is the fortis /h/ as in *hat*. The glottal stop, [ʔ], which we briefly discussed in Lesson Two, would also belong in this category, but it is not an English phoneme. In some non-standard British accents, it is a pronunciation variant of the /t/ phoneme in certain phonetic environments, as in the words *better* and *butter*.

Manner of articulation II

The manner of articulation, as you learnt in Lesson Two, refers to the type or degree of closure of the speech organs. There are eight different manners of articulation that use an egressive pulmonic air-stream mechanism, plus an additional one that has become a conventional category in the description of some languages, including English. In this section, we look at all nine categories, progressing from total closure of the speech organs to a fairly wide opening between them.

(1) Plosives, or **stops** [*Verschlusslaute*], are sounds for which the speaker makes a complete closure at some point in the vocal tract, builds up the air pressure while the closure is held, and then releases the air explosively through the mouth. English has three fortis plosives, namely /p/ as in *peach*, /t/ as in *tiger*, and /k/ as in *Canada*. The three lenis plosives are /b/ as in *banana*, /d/ as in *dolphin*, and /g/ as in *Greenland*. The glottal stop, [ʔ], is a fortis plosive, but we have already noted that it is not an English phoneme.

(2) Affricates [*Affrikata*] are sounds that consist of two elements. The first element is a plosive. This means that affricates, too, require a complete closure in the vocal tract, but the air is released slowly enough to produce friction, which we hear as a hissing *s*-like sound. The second element is articulated in the same place, i.e. with the same speech organs, as the preceding plosive. We therefore say that the two elements are **hom-**

organic sounds. There are two affricates in English: the fortis /tʃ/ as in *cheese* and the lenis /dʒ/ as in *gin*. (An affricate, then, is represented by one symbol consisting of two characters.)

Affricates are the additional category mentioned above. There is no compelling reason why we should analyse the two elements of an affricate as a single phoneme. The sequences /tr/ and /dr/, for example, are also homorganic sounds, but only very few linguists would recognise them as independent phonemes. Nevertheless, this analysis is usual for /tʃ/ and /dʒ/, so that the word *judge* consists of three phonemes, rather than five.

(3) Nasals [*Nasale*] have a closure in the vocal tract as well. They stand out from all other English phonemes, however, in that the velum, or soft palate, is lowered, so that air escapes through the nose. In the production of English nasals, usually *all* the air escapes through the nose. Other languages have nasals where some air also passes through the mouth, as in the final sound in the French word *bon*. The three English nasals are all lenis sounds: /m/ as in *mango*, /n/ as in *nightingale*, and /ŋ/ as in *England*.

All other English phonemes are usually produced with the velum raised, so that the passage to the nasal cavity [*Nasenraum*] is blocked, and the air escapes only through the mouth. In order to distinguish them from nasals, these sounds are sometimes called **orals**. We cannot actually feel our velum moving, but there is a simple test that shows us whether the velum is lowered or raised, and the effect that the position has on the sound quality: While you are pronouncing one of the three English nasals, stop your nose and release it again. You will hear how the quality changes when the air-stream through the nose is blocked. Try the same with any other English sound and you will find that the sound quality does not change a bit. Why? Because in oral sounds, the passage through the nose is already blocked at the velum.

Another terminological distinction that is sometimes made and that we should mention at this point is the contrast between non-continuant and continuant sounds. **Non-continuants** are produced with a complete closure of the speech organs. Plosives and affricates are non-continuants because the passage through both the mouth and the nose is blocked. By contrast, all other speech sounds, including nasals, are made without a complete closure of the speech organs, and are therefore called **continuants** [*Dauerlaute*]. (Some linguists count English nasals among the non-continuants, however, because the passage through the mouth is always closed.)

(4) Rolls, or **trills** [*gerollte Laute, Schwinglaute, Vibrationslaute*], involve an intermittent closure of the speech organs in the vocal tract. Rolls are produced when one articulator vibrates against another. There are no rolled phonemes in RP or any other accent of English, but some dialects have a rolled pronunciation variant of the /r/ phoneme. The typical Scottish /r/, for example, is produced by a vibration of the tongue against the alveolar ridge. Such an alveolar roll sometimes also occurs in stylised speech, for example on stage. The phonetic symbol for this pronunciation variant is the same as the one for the underlying phoneme, namely [r].

(5) Flaps, or **taps** [*ein-schlägige Vibrationslaute, geschlagene Vibrationslaute*], involve a single flap by one articulator against another. There are no flapped phonemes in English, but there are some pronunciation variants that are produced in this way. For example, in some accents of British English, including RP, the /r/ phoneme in words like ve*r*y is sometimes realised as a single flap of the tongue tip against the alveolar ridge. It sounds almost like a very fast [d]. Such an alveolar flap, transcribed as [ɾ], is also very common in American English, where it is a pronunciation variant of the /t/ and /d/ phonemes in words like la*tt*er and la*dd*er, which are then pronounced identically.

(6) **Fricatives** [*Reibelaute*] are made when air forces its way through a very narrow gap between two speech organs, thereby producing audible friction. The fricatives fall into two subcategories, slit fricatives and groove fricatives, according to the width and depth of the air passage.

There are four **slit fricatives** [*slit*, German 'Schlitz'] in English: the fortis /f/ as in *f*ilm and /θ/ as in *th*in, and the lenis /v/ as in *v*ideo and /ð/ as in *th*is. The fortis /h/ as in *h*at is usually also grouped together with the slit fricatives, but is best described as a **cavity fricative** as it has no point of narrowing.

Groove fricatives are made by forming a groove [German 'Rinne, Furche'] along the front part of the tongue [*Vorderzunge*]. They are made with more intensity than the slit fricatives, and have a sharper, s-like sound. They are therefore also called **sibilants** [from Latin *sibilans*, 'hissing']. The four groove fricatives in English are the fortis /s/ as in *s*nake and /ʃ/ as in *sh*erry, and the lenis /z/ as in *z*ebra and /ʒ/ as in mea*s*ure. Because of their fricative element, the two English affricates, /tʃ/ and /dʒ/, can also be regarded as groove fricatives.

(7) **Lateral fricatives** [*lateral*, German 'seitlich'] are made with air that escapes around the sides of a partial closure of the speech organs. There are no lateral fricative phonemes in RP or any other accent of English.

(8) **Laterals**, or more specifically **lateral approximants** [*Laterale, laterale Approximanten*], are also made with air that escapes around the sides of a partial closure of the speech organs, but the air passage is not quite as narrow as in lateral fricatives. English has only one lateral, namely the lenis /l/ as in *l*eopard, where the tip of the tongue touches the centre of the alveolar ridge.

(9) **Approximants** [*Approximanten*] are generally made with a wider gap between the speech organs than is the case in the production of fricatives. The speech organs approach each other, but they do not touch each other. The three English approximants are all lenis phonemes: /r/ as in *r*ed, /j/ as in *y*es, and /w/ as in *W*ales.

It should be noted here that no other consonant phoneme of English is as variable in its actual pronunciation as the /r/ phoneme. It has several different realisations, three of which we have already encountered in this lesson. Only one of these three, the retroflex [ɻ], is also an approximant, like the underlying phoneme. The manner of the articulation of the other two pronunciation variants is *not* the same as that of the underlying phoneme: As you already know, [r] is a roll, and [ɾ] is a flap.

Lateral approximants and approximants are grouped together and referred to as **frictionless continuants** [*geräuschlose Dauerlaute*] because none of them involves audible friction.

The consonant table

We can now use the three distinctive features to describe all English consonant phonemes. It is easier, however, if we first arrange the relevant phonetic symbols in a coordinate system with the places of articulation on the horizontal axis, the manners of articulation along the vertical axis, fortis sounds positioned on the left side of the grid squares, and lenis sounds on the right. You will find such a table containing all English consonant phonemes on the inside back cover of this manual.

If we now look at the consonant table, we can easily see that the /f/ in *surf* is a fortis labiodental fricative, as you have already learnt in Lesson Two, or that /n/ is a lenis alveolar nasal, and /r/ a lenis postalveolar approximant. But the table reveals much more than that. It shows that sixteen consonant phonemes form pairs within which the only distinguishing feature is the intensity of the articulation. For example, /p/ and /b/ are both bilabial plosives, and the only difference between them is that /p/ is produced with fortis articulation, and /b/ with lenis articulation. Similarly, the only difference between /t/ and /d/, /k/ and /g/, /tʃ/ and /dʒ/, /f/ and /v/, /θ/ and /ð/, /s/ and /z/, and /ʃ/ and /ʒ/ is that the first phoneme within each pair is fortis, and the second is lenis. There is also only one difference between /b/ and /m/, for example, but here the difference lies in the manner of articulation: Both sounds are lenis bilabials, but /b/ is a plosive whereas /m/ is a nasal. Furthermore, the consonant table makes it easy to see that other sounds are differentiated by *two* distinctive features. For example, /ʃ/ and /z/ are both groove fricatives, or sibilants, but they differ in the place as well as in the intensity of articulation. Finally, the table also shows that there are sounds that do not share a single distinctive feature. For example, /f/ and /d/ differ in place, manner, and intensity.

The problem cases

Of semi-vowels, contoids, and vocoids ...

All consonants generally have two things in common: (a) They are made with an obstruction of air, and (b) they typically occur at the margins of syllables. By contrast, the sounds that (a) are produced without any obstruction of air, and (b) usually occur at the centre of syllables are called **vowels**. The English frictionless continuants, i.e. the lateral approximant, /l/, and the approximants, /r, j, w/, however, do not fit neatly into the consonant category nor into the vowel category. We have so far regarded them as consonants because they always appear at the margins, and never at the centre, of syllables. This can be illustrated by words like *lot*, *car*, *yes*, and *wax*, and by the fact that *tlp* or *trp*, for example, are not possible words in English. You learnt in Lesson One that phonology, more precisely segmental phonology, is concerned with the function and possible combinations of sounds. We see, therefore, that the frictionless continuants are consonants from a phonological point of view. On the other hand, they are produced with almost no obstruction of air. In the case of /j/, for example, the obstruction is only great enough to cause audible friction after /p, t, k/ at the beginning of a syllable, as in the words *pupil*, *tune*, and *queue*. In the case of /w/, we hear friction only after /t, k/, as in *twin* or *quite*. From a purely phonetic point of view, then, the frictionless continuants are (almost) vowels.

In order to reflect their intermediate status, all frictionless continuants may be regarded as **semi-vowels** [*Halbvokale*] (or semi-consonants, of course, but this term is hardly ever used). They are sometimes also called **glides** [*Gleitlaute*] because, when articulating these sounds as parts of actual words, the tongue moves in gliding fashion either towards or away from a neighbouring vowel. Most linguists, however, refer only to /j, w/ as semi-vowels, or glides.

Alternatively, we can reserve the traditional terms *consonant* and *vowel* to refer only to the phonological properties of sounds. This would mean that we refer to those sounds that typically occur at the margins of syllables as **consonants**, and to those that usually occur at the centre as **vowels**. In order to refer to the phonetic properties, we then need another set of terms. We can call sounds that are produced with an obstruction of air **contoids** (rather than consonants), and those that are produced without any obstruction **vocoids** (rather than vowels). Thus all consonants except the frictionless continuants are contoids, all frictionless continuants are vocoids, and so are all vowels. We should note, however, that this terminology has not been universally adopted. Most linguists use the concept of semi-vowel, or glide, and subsume this category under the broader consonant category, as we did above.

... and more terminological confusion

This section would be unnecessary if it were not one of the aims of this manual to acquaint you with as many different terms for the same concept as possible, or, conversely, with different definitions of the same term. This is done in order to make it easier for you to read a wide range of linguistic texts with varying theoretical and terminological approaches. It is important to be aware that not all linguists use all the terms introduced in this lesson in the same way.

In connection with **groove fricatives**, or **sibilants**, note that some linguists regard only /z, s/ as belonging in this category whereas here we also include /ʒ, dʒ, ʃ, tʃ/.

Some linguists restrict the group of **approximants** to /l, j/, others to /j, w/. In a broader sense, the term sometimes covers the same group of sounds that we call frictionless continuants, i.e. /l, r, j, w/. Very few linguists also include the three nasals, /m, n, ŋ/, in this group because the nasals can, in certain phonetic environments, sound continuously without audible friction.

You have learnt that **semi-vowels**, or **glides**, encompass either all frictionless continuants or, more commonly, only /j, w/. Occasionally, /h/ is also put in this category.

Finally, /l, r/ are sometimes referred to as **liquids** [from Latin *liquidus*, 'flowing, clear'] because of their "flowing" sound quality. It is a traditional term that is not often used anymore, and should best be avoided.

Exercises

EXERCISES

3.1 Intensity of articulation

As in exercise 2.4 from the previous lesson, say the pairs of words below with your hand in front of your mouth. Pay attention to the sensation of the "extra" air forced out as you say the sounds represented by the underlined letters.

zoo, Sue	maze, mass	lose, loose
measure, mesh	treasure, trash	pleasure, lash
gin, chin	midge, match	judge, church

You will notice that with the sounds [s, ʃ, tʃ] you feel extra air forced out compared with the sounds [z, ʒ, dʒ]. The first word in each pair has a lenis fricative, with less intense articulation. Pairing of the words, and thus comparing individual sounds in those words, demonstrates the difference in intensity of articulation between lenis and fortis sounds. Remember that the lenis/fortis distinction also occurs in other consonant sounds in English.

3.2 Place of articulation

By keeping two of the three distinctive features of English consonants constant, we can discover the effect of the third. In exercise 3.2a, the sounds all have a plosive articulation and their intensity is fortis; we thus focus on the place where these sounds are articulated. In exercise 3.2b, the sounds all have fricative articulation and their intensity is lenis; again, place is the feature which varies.

3.2a Prepare to pronounce a [p] as in the word *pin*, but do not actually say anything. Notice how there is a build-up of air pressure in the mouth. Which parts of your mouth are doing the most work to hold back the pressure? When you do release the sound and say the word? Which parts move? Try the same with [t] in *tin* and [k] in *king*. These will show you how the place where an obstruction is made varies. Describe the places of articulation of these three sounds.

3.2b Try saying a long [v] as in the word *very*. Where do you feel a stream of air passing through? Try saying the sounds [ð] as in *the*, and [z] as in *zip*. Where do you feel the stream of air now? This again shows variation in place of articulation. Describe the place of articulation of these three sounds.

3.3 Manner of articulation

In this exercise, although intensity and place of articulation do vary, try to consider only the manner of articulation. Group the sounds represented by the underlined letters in the words below according to the degree of obstruction, using the terms you have learnt in this lesson.

door	shore	saw	jaw	nor	chore	war	gore
four	more	paw	law	raw	bore	core	your
vote	tore	zoom	think	sing	there	horse	treasure

3.4 Combining distinctive features

Taking the sound groups from exercise 3.3, arrange them from left to right with the sounds articulated closest to the front of the mouth on the left, and those articulated furthest back on the right. When you have completed this task, compare your arrangment with the solution at the end of this manual, and then with the English consonant table on the inside back cover.

3.5 Relating IPA symbols to sounds

3.5a Consider how the sounds represented by the underlined letters are made in the following pairs of words. Which features (intensity, place, or manner) distinguish the sounds and hence the words from each other? Write the IPA symbol for each of these sounds.

ro<u>p</u>e	ro<u>b</u>e
ri<u>ght</u>	ri<u>d</u>e
ho<u>m</u>e	ho<u>p</u>e
lin<u>k</u>	si<u>ng</u>
lea<u>v</u>e	lea<u>p</u>
<u>w</u>ord	<u>b</u>ird
<u>th</u>ink	<u>z</u>inc
<u>y</u>east	<u>f</u>east

3.5b In the next two sets of words, the distinctive differences between the sounds represented by the underlined letters are even greater. Think about how the sounds differ and write the IPA symbol for the sounds. Can you think of any other sets of minimal pairs which show how sounds contrast meaning?

<u>h</u>ome	<u>R</u>ome	<u>c</u>omb	
<u>r</u>ice	<u>v</u>ice	<u>n</u>ice	
<u>y</u>our	<u>f</u>our	<u>j</u>aw	
<u>sh</u>ip	<u>h</u>ip	<u>l</u>ip	
<u>th</u>in	<u>sh</u>in	<u>ch</u>in	
<u>s</u>ource	<u>f</u>orce	<u>c</u>ourse	<u>h</u>orse
<u>t</u>ap	<u>m</u>ap	<u>n</u>ap	<u>g</u>ap

3.6 IPA symbols

Write only the consonants and semi-vowels that occur in the following words as IPA symbols. For example, *dogs* should be transcribed [dgz]. Do a set, then check your answers before you do the next set.

3.6a

dot	top	hot	path	log	post	girl
cat	age	stop	able	sport	thumb	break
few	vine	waste	north	song	zebra	wash
measure	bottle	mum	itch	than	five	wrong

Exercises

3.6b

even	leave	very	cuff	fine	tough	awful
this	brother	choir	thin	seen	easy	breathe
ozone	witches	ducks	hens	foxes	bus	bust
weather	away	sow	pure	faith	mouth	morning

3.6c

new	thank	rabbit	car	kite	tablet	judge
church	switch	gin	dreamed	atlas	logging	stick
unit	ache	smash	treasure	ice	pleasure	eyes
finger	singer	cure	other	thought	broth	the

Lesson 4
Vowels

The description of vowels

We briefly introduced the notion of the vowel [from Latin *vocalis*, 'vocal'] in Lesson Three. Thus you already know that, (a) phonetically, vowels are produced without any obstruction of air, and, (b) phonologically, vowels usually occupy the centre of a syllable. Even though most languages have over twice as many consonants as vowels, in a way, vowels can be seen as predominant: They carry most of the loudness, pitch, and tone of voice that we perceive in concrete utterances, and since their sound quality varies considerably from region to region, vowels make up most of the characteristics that distinguish different accents of the same language. Different accents may even have different vowel systems. The typical Scottish pronunciation of English, for example, has only 10 vowel phonemes whereas RP has 12. The predominance of vowels is also reflected in the origin of the word *consonant*: It comes from the Latin word *consonans*, which means 'sounding together'. This implies that consonants do not comfortably occur alone. They usually sound together with vowels.

What are the criteria that we use to describe English vowel phonemes? We noted in Lesson Two that loudness, pitch, tone of voice, and duration are suitable criteria to describe concrete speech sounds, or phones, but these features cannot distinguish phonemes. Length has proved to be a rather unreliable feature, and so has voicing. It is important to note, here, that all English vowels are typically voiced, so that voicing would not count as a distinctive feature anyway. The same is true of the air-stream mechanism since all English sounds are made with egressive pulmonic air. Even the place of articulation, which is one of the three distinctive features for the description of consonant phonemes, is of no relevance here because the place of articulation names the speech organs that obstruct the air-stream, but in the production of vowels the air-stream is not obstructed. The intensity of articulation, on the other hand, does contribute to the distinction between vowel phonemes, as we shall see later, but it is not nearly as important as it is for the description of consonants, and most linguists therefore neglect this feature altogether.

What we are left with, then, and what we solely rely on is the manner in which the English vowels are articulated. In our discussion of the manners of articulation of consonants in the previous lesson, we moved from total closure of the speech organs to a narrowing between them. Since vowels are produced without any obstruction of air, none of the nine categories in that progression applies here. Furthermore, you have learnt that all English sounds, except the three nasal consonants, are usually oral sounds, which are produced with the velum raised and air escaping only through the mouth. It follows that all English vowels are orals, and that this feature can therefore not distinguish different vowel phonemes either. But apart from the raising of the velum, the different manners of vowel articulation also involve slight movements of the tongue and lips, as we shall see below.

Manner of articulation III

Tongue and lip movements result in varying shapes of the mouth, which can be described in terms of (1) closeness/openness, (2) frontness/backness, and (3) the shape of the lips. These are the three criteria for the description of vowel phonemes.

(1) Closeness/openness, or **tongue height** in American terminology, refers to the distance between the tongue and the palate (and at the same time to the position of the lower jaw). If the tongue is high, as in the last sound of the word *bee*, it is close to the palate, and we therefore speak of a **close vowel** [*geschlossener Vokal*]. If the tongue is low, as in the third sound of the word *starling*, the gap between it and the palate is more open, and we speak of an **open vowel** [*offener Vokal*]. Between these extremes, there are three intermediate levels: If the tongue is in a mid-high position, i.e. a bit lower than high, the resultant sound is a **mid-close vowel**, or **half-close vowel** [*halbgeschlossener Vokal*]. If it is mid-low, i.e. a bit higher than low, we hear a **mid-open vowel**, or **half-open vowel** [*halboffener Vokal*]. A vowel that is made with a tongue height somewhere between mid-high and mid-low is simply called a **mid vowel**.

(2) Frontness/backness refers to the part of the tongue that is raised highest. If it is the front of the tongue (in which case the body of the tongue is pushed forward), as in the last sound in *bee*, we speak of a **front vowel** [*Vorderzungenvokal*]. If the back of the tongue is raised highest (in which case the body of the tongue is pulled back), as in the middle sound in *goose*, the resultant sound is a **back vowel** [*Hinterzungenvokal*]. Between these extremes, we recognise one intermediate position: If the centre of the tongue is raised highest, as in the second sound of the word *bird*, we speak of a **central vowel** [*Mittelzungenvokal*].

(3) The shape of the lips can be either spread, neutral, or round. English does not utilise this contrast very much. As in most other languages, the spreading of the lips usually correlates with frontness, and lip-rounding with backness. This means that there are no two vowel phonemes in English that differ only in the shape of the lips. Many linguists therefore do not regard this criterion as relevant, or distinctive, in English. The effect that the shape of the lips has on the vowel quality can be heard when we compare the second sound in *hurt* (which is the same as the one in *bird* above) with the second sound of the German word *hört*: Both sounds are mid central vowels, i.e. they are identical with respect to closeness/openness and frontness/backness. The only difference between them is that the English vowel is produced with the lips in a neutral shape, and the German vowel with rounded lips.

The vowel chart I

Since the spreading or rounding of the lips cannot distinguish vowel phonemes in English, there are only two distinctive features for the description of all English vowels: closeness/openness and frontness/backness. Just as we have arranged the symbols for consonant phonemes in a table, we can also arrange the symbols for vowels schematically on the basis of these two criteria. Depending on the particular language under description, the vowel symbols are superimposed on the space within a triangle or a quadrilateral. Such a **vowel chart**, or **vowel diagram**, was first devised by Daniel Jones. It reflects roughly the space in the centre of the mouth, where the vowels are articulated. You will find a vowel chart containing the symbols for all RP vowel phonemes on the inside back cover of this manual, and it is recommended that you refer to it as you continue reading this lesson.

The closeness or openness of a vowel is shown by the vertical position of the symbol in the vowel chart: The higher the symbol, the closer the tongue is to the palate when articulating the corresponding sound. Conversely, the lower the symbol, the more open the gap between the tongue and the palate. In other words, close vowels occupy the upper part of the vowel chart, and open vowels the lower part. Two horizontal lines mark the mid-close and mid-open positions.

Frontness or backness is indicated by the horizontal position of the symbols: The further left the symbol, the more front the part of the tongue that is raised highest when articulating the corresponding sound. Thus the symbols on the left of the vowel chart represent front vowels. The further right the symbol, the more back the part of the tongue involved. The symbols on the right, then, represent back vowels. It goes without saying that the vowels in the central area of the chart are central vowels.

The vowel systems of most languages of the world can be represented by symbols that are evenly distributed within the vowel chart. This phenomenon is called **vowel dispersion**. Most vowel systems are arranged within a triangle. English belongs to the less than 10 per cent of the languages whose vowel systems have a more or less quadrilateral shape. The vowel chart is then sometimes called a **vowel quadrilateral** [*Vokalviereck*]. More specifically, the English vowel chart has the form of a trapezium, which is reflected in the German term *Vokaltrapez*, but there is no equivalent term used in English.

The cardinal vowels

In order to describe the vowels of any given language, and compare the vowel systems of different languages more precisely than is possible by using only the distinctive features, Daniel Jones invented 18 reference vowels, called **cardinal vowels** [*Kardinalvokale*]. They illustrate the extremes of vowel quality that the vocal tract is able to produce. It is important to understand that the cardinal vowels are not sounds of a particular language. Phoneticians have to learn to recognise and articulate these artificial sounds, so that they can describe all natural vowels in relation to the nearest cardinal vowel. A vowel chart with all cardinal vowels is given in Figure 3.

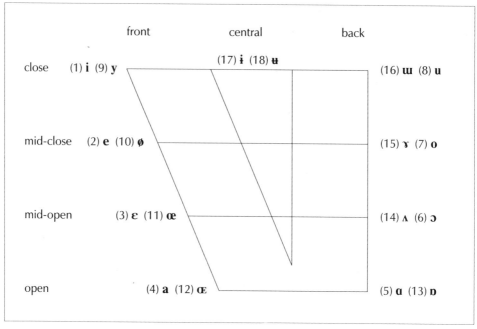

Fig. 3 Cardinal vowel chart

Since the cardinal vowels are extremes, they occupy the very edges of the vowel chart. They are numbered counter-clockwise, beginning in the upper left corner. The vowels 1 to 8 are the **primary cardinal vowels**. They can be described as close front, mid-close front, mid-open front, open front, open back, mid-open back, mid-close back, and close back. We have already mentioned that, in English and most other languages, the spreading of the lips usually correlates with frontness, and lip-rounding with backness. This is also roughly true of the primary cardinal vowels: Vowels 1 to 5 are produced with unrounded, and vowels 6 to 8 with rounded lips. For this reason, the primary cardinal vowels generally sound somewhat familiar to speakers of European languages, and they are, of course, more relevant when describing these languages.

The **secondary cardinal vowels** are the vowels 9 to 16. They occupy the same positions as the primary cardinal vowels in the vowel chart, but they sound less familiar to us because the shape of the lips is reversed: Vowels 9 to 13 are produced with rounded, and vowels 14 to 16 with unrounded lips. The two remaining cardinal vowels 17 and 18 are close central vowels with unrounded and rounded lips, respectively.

All cardinal vowels can be represented by phonetic symbols. Unfortunately, some of these symbols are identical with the symbols that we use to represent English vowels even though the quality of the sounds is quite different. Because the cardinal vowels are not part of a sound system of a language, their symbols are usually enclosed in square brackets, like any other concrete sound. It is therefore important that we gather from the context whether a vowel symbol in square brackets represents a cardinal vowel or a concrete vowel of a particular language.

Vowels

We have seen that the primary and secondary cardinal vowels form pairs whose members occupy the same position in the vowel chart, and can only be distinguished by the shape of the lips. If all the cardinal vowels are arranged in the same chart, it is customary to put the symbol for the unrounded member of a pair on the left, and the one for the rounded counterpart on the right. Thus the two sets of cardinal vowels are mixed, and the distinction between them is not usually reflected in the visual presentation.

The English vowel phonemes

The study of vowels is somewhat complicated by the fact that several different sets of phonetic vowel symbols are used in the linguistic literature even by authors who claim to use IPA symbols. A detailed discussion of the reasons for this would go beyond the scope of an introductory text. Suffice it to say that the specific English pronunciation has made it necessary to modify at least *some* of the IPA symbols, which were, after all, designed to represent the sounds of *all* languages. In this manual, we use the symbols proposed in A. C. Gimson's *Introduction to the Pronunciation of English* (first published in 1962) or its successors. You learnt in Lesson Two, in the section on duration and length, that the difference between two vowels which are commonly described as "long" and "short" lies not only in their relative length, but even more so in their sound quality. One advantage of Gimson's symbols is that they reflect the difference in both length and quality between long and short vowels by using a length mark as well as separate symbols.

Of the 12 vowel phonemes in RP and in most other English accents, 5 are typically long, and 7 typically short. Remember that there is a vowel chart with the symbols for all RP vowel phonemes on the inside back cover of this manual, and a list of all the IPA symbols that we use here on the inside front cover.

Long vowels

The symbols for long vowels are followed by a **length mark** made of two vertical dots. This length mark is not really necessary because every vowel has its own symbol, but it reminds us that some vowels are usually relatively long, and it seems to have established itself as an agreed standard. We now list the 5 long vowel phonemes, describe their manner of articulation, and label them according to the two distinctive features:

(1) The last sound in the word *bee*, represented by the symbol /iː/. The front of the tongue is raised so that it almost touches the palate, and the lips are slightly spread. A **close front vowel**.
(2) The second sound in *bird*, represented by /ɜː/. This sound is also well known as a hesitation sound, usually spelt *er*. The centre of the tongue is raised between mid-close and mid-open position, and the lips are in a neutral shape. A **mid central vowel**.
(3) The third sound in *starling*, represented by /ɑː/. The part of the tongue between the centre and the back is lowered to fully open position, and the lips are in a neutral shape. An **open central-back vowel**.

(4) The second sound in *horse*, represented by /ɔː/. The back of the tongue is raised between mid-close and mid-open position, and the lips are rounded. A **mid back vowel**.
(5) The middle sound in *goose*, represented by /uː/. The back of the tongue is raised so that it almost touches the palate, and the lips are moderately rounded. A **close back vowel**.

Short vowels

We now do the same for the 7 short vowel phonemes:

(1) The middle sound in *fish*, represented by /ɪ/. The part of the tongue between the front and the centre is raised to just above mid-close position, and the lips are slightly spread. A **mid-close front-central vowel**.
(2) The first sound in *egg*, represented by /e/. The front of the tongue is raised between mid-close and mid-open position, and the lips are slightly spread. A **mid front vowel**.
(3) The first sound in *apple*, represented by /æ/. The front of the tongue is raised between mid-open and fully open position, and the lips are slightly spread. A **mid-open-open front vowel**.
(4) The second sound in *butter*, represented by /ʌ/. The centre of the tongue is raised between mid-open and fully open position, and the shape of the lips is neutral. A **mid-open-open central vowel**.
(5) The first sound in *olive*, represented by /ɒ/. The back of the tongue is lowered to almost fully open position, and the lips are slightly rounded. An **open back vowel**.
(6) The second sound in *pudding*, represented by /ʊ/. The part of the tongue between the centre and the back is raised to just above mid-close position, and the lips are rounded. A **mid-close central-back vowel**.
(7) The third sound in *spaghetti*, the first sound in *ago*, or the last sound in *mother*, represented by /ə/. The centre of the tongue is raised between mid-close and mid-open position, and the lips are in a neutral shape. A **mid central vowel**.

This last vowel, /ə/, is called **schwa**. It stands out from all other vowels, and requires some further comment. The term *schwa* comes originally from Hebrew, where it means 'emptiness' and designates a Hebrew vowel of the same quality. You may have noticed that the schwa is articulated in practically the same manner as the long vowel /ɜː/, and therefore the quality of the two sounds is also virtually the same. This is the only exception to the general observation that a difference in length is accompanied by a difference in sound quality. (We should note, however, that there is considerable variation in the way speakers produce the schwa. For example, it is usually more open in word-final position.) But even if the quality of the schwa and /ɜː/ is more or less identical, the function of these two sounds is quite different: Whereas /ɜː/ occurs only in stressed syllables, the schwa occurs solely in unstressed syllables.

The short /ɪ/ and /ʊ/ also often occur in unstressed syllables, but, unlike the schwa, they may occur in stressed syllables as well. Most unstressed syllables contain a schwa, which makes this vowel the most frequently occurring sound in English. One study has shown that almost 11 per cent of the sounds uttered in an English conversation are schwas. The /ɪ/ makes up around 8 per cent, whereas /ʊ/ occurs much less frequently with less than 1 per cent. For comparison, the most frequent consonant is /n/ with around 8 per cent. Such a frequency count shows the important function that the schwa fulfils in unstressed syllables, and underlines the predominance of vowels over consonants. Many languages do not have a sound that occurs in most unstressed syllables. The speakers of these languages may thus find it difficult to pronounce unstressed syllables when they learn English.

It should be added that some linguists analyse the schwa as a pronunciation variant (pertaining to parole or performance) of all English vowel phonemes in unstressed syllables, rather than as a phoneme in its own right. They prove the validity of their approach with word pairs like *compete/competition* or *analysis/analyse*, where /iː/ and /æ/ seem to be neutralised, or reduced, to a schwa. The schwa is therefore sometimes called a **neutral vowel**, or **reduced vowel**.

The vowel chart II

If we now look at the English vowel chart again, we can easily see how certain vowels are similar to each other, and how they differ. We have already noted that /ɜː/ and /ə/ are both mid central vowels. The vowel chart also tells us, for example, that /iː/ and /uː/ are both articulated with the tongue almost touching the palate, i.e. they are both close vowels, but they differ in the part of the tongue that is raised highest (and in the shape of the lips, but since this is not a distinctive feature in English, we do not always need to mention it). Conversely, /ɒ/ and /ɔː/ are both produced with the back of the tongue raised highest, i.e. they are both back vowels, but the significant difference between them is that /ɒ/ is more open. (Incidentally, /ɒ/ is the sound, referred to in Lesson Three, that does not exist in most American English accents. American speakers usually use /ɑː/ or /ɔː/ instead.)

When we compare the English vowel chart with the cardinal vowel chart (in Figure 3), we can also describe the English vowel phonemes in relation to the cardinal vowels. For example, the articulation of English /ɪ/ is more close and more central than cardinal vowel number 2, or [e]. And when articulating English /æ/, the front of the tongue is raised highest, but not as high as in cardinal vowel number 3, or [ɛ].

Intensity of articulation II: Lax and tense

We mentioned at the beginning of this lesson that the intensity of articulation also contributes to the distinction between vowel phonemes. It is not nearly as important here, however, as it is for the description of consonants, where it is one of the distinctive features. In fact, the intensity of vowel articulation has never received much attention in British linguistics. American linguists distinguish between **lax** vowels [*ungespannt*], which are articulated with relatively weak breath force, and **tense** vowels [*gespannt*], which are produced with more energy. These labels correspond to the terms *lenis* and *fortis*, which we use to describe the intensity of consonant articulation.

Since all English vowels are typically voiced, it goes without saying that there cannot be a correlation between the intensity of vowel articulation and voicing, as there is with consonants. There is, however, a correlation between the intensity of vowel articulation and vowel length: All lax vowels are short vowels, and all tense vowels are long. Another interesting regularity is that all five tense, long vowels have lax, short counterparts that are roughly articulated in the same manner. We have already encountered one such pair, namely /ɜː, ə/, where there is practically no difference in the manner of articulation (and sound quality) at all. The difference between these two sounds, in terms of articulatory phonetics, lies merely in their length and, as you now know, in the intensity of their articulation. You also know, however, that a difference in length is normally accompanied by a difference in sound quality. Thus the members within the remaining four pairs are *not* articulated in exactly the same way. In the pair /ɑː, ʌ/, the tense, long member is articulated with a slightly lower tongue position than its lax, short counterpart. This seems to be another exception, since the tense, long members in the last three pairs, /iː, ɪ/, /ɔː, ɒ/, and /uː, ʊ/, are all produced with the tongue slightly higher. In the vowel chart on the inside back cover, the tense-long/lax-short pairs are indicated by ovals.

Diphthongs and triphthongs

The quality of the English long and short vowels remains relatively constant while they are being pronounced, i.e. the speech organs do not usually change their position during articulation. These vowels are therefore called **pure** or **plain vowels**, or **monophthongs** [from Greek *monóphthonggos*, 'single sound']. In addition to these monophthongs (note the correct pronunciation /mɒnəfθɒŋz/), RP and most other English accents have 8 vowel sequences consisting of two sounds. More precisely, they start with a monophthong, and the quality then changes towards, but never quite reaches, another monophthong through a gliding movement of the tongue. These vowel sequences are called **gliding vowels**, **vowel glides**, or **diphthongs** [from Greek *diphthonggos*, 'double sound'; *Doppellaut*, *Zwielaut*]. A vowel chart indicating the starting points and tongue movements of all English diphthongs (note again the correct pronunciation /dɪfθɒŋz/) is given in Figure 4, and the diphthongs are also included in the list of English sounds on the inside front cover.

Diphthongs can be divided into three groups: **(1) Centring diphthongs** move towards schwa. There are 3 centring diphthongs in English, namely /eə/ as in the word *air*, /ɪə/ as in *ear*, and /ʊə/ as in *tour*. The starting points of the last two diphthongs are usually slightly higher than the position of the monophthongs /ɪ/ and /ʊ/, but we nevertheless use the same symbols, just as we use our familiar symbols for the second elements of diphthongs although the corresponding sounds (in this case the schwa) are not actually reached. The last diphthong, /ʊə/, is not used very much in RP. It is often replaced with /ɔː/. **(2) Closing diphthongs** move towards a closer vowel. Of the 5 clos-

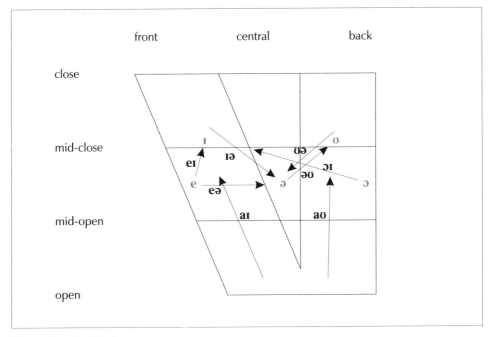

Fig. 4 English diphthongs.

ing diphthongs in English, 3 move towards /ɪ/, namely /eɪ/ as in f*a*ce, /aɪ/ as in m*i*nd, and /ɔɪ/ as in v*oi*ce. The symbols representing the first elements of /aɪ/ and /ɔɪ/ are new to you because the corresponding sounds are not monophthong phonemes of RP. The articulation of [a] is similar to /ʌ/, except that it is more open and more front. And [ɔ] is articulated exactly like /ɔː/, but it is shorter, as the missing length mark indicates. The 2 remaining closing diphthongs move towards /ʊ/, namely /əʊ/ as in n*o*se and /aʊ/ as in m*ou*th. The symbol representing the first element of /aʊ/ may be quite misleading. It looks as though it is identical with the first element of /aɪ/, and this is what we would expect from a consistent phonetic alphabet. Unfortunately, however, even though we use the same symbol, the [a] in /aʊ/ is somewhat different from the [a] in /aɪ/. The first element in /aʊ/ is very similar to /ɑː/, but slightly more close and more front. **(3) Opening diphthongs** move towards a more open vowel. They do not exist in English.

Another categorisation of diphthongs divides them into **diminuendo, descending,** or **falling diphthongs** and **crescendo, ascending,** or **rising diphthongs** [*fallende Doppellaute, steigende Doppellaute*]. In falling diphthongs, the first element is longer and louder than the second. All English diphthongs are usually falling diphthongs. Rising diphthongs, where the second element is more prominent, rarely occur in English. One of the rare examples may be the diphthong /ɪə/ in words like *per*i*od* or *ser*i*ous*, which is sometimes pronounced as rising.

It is important to note that a diphthong is conventionally analysed as one vowel phoneme. We would say, then, that words like *face, voice,* and *mouth* consist of three phonemes. This means that, strictly speaking, RP and most other English accents have

20 vowels, rather than just 12. We should also note, however, that the conventional analysis of a vowel sequence as a single vowel is to a certain extent arbitrary (just like the analysis of a homorganic consonant sequence as an affricate). For example, the words *cue* and *view* are usually transcribed as /kjuː/ and /vjuː/ even though there is no reason why we should not interpret the middle and final sounds of both words as a diphthong (in which case it would be a rising diphthong) represented by /ɪʊ/. For this reason, we hardly ever say that English has 20 vowels. We usually say that it has 12 monophthongs and 8 diphthongs.

English also has typical vowel sequences that consist of three sounds. They are called **triphthongs** [from Greek *tríphthonggos*, 'triple sound']. The 5 English triphthongs (pronounced /trɪfθɒŋz/) are /eɪə/ as in *pla<u>yer</u>*, /aɪə/ as in *f<u>ire</u>*, /ɔɪə/ as in *ro<u>yal</u>*, /əʊə/ as in *l<u>ower</u>*, and /aʊə/ as in *fl<u>our</u>*. Unlike diphthongs, however, triphthongs are not analysed as separate vowel phonemes. They are interpreted as closing diphthongs followed by a schwa. The word *royal*, then, consists of four phonemes: /r/, /ɔɪ/, /ə/, and /l/.

The shortening of vowels, nasals, and the lateral

To round off this lesson on vowels, we should point out briefly that the duration of a vowel, and also that of a nasal and the lateral, is usually shortened when followed by a fortis plosive, affricate, or fricative (except /h/) – in other words, when followed by /p, t, k, tʃ, f, θ, s/ or /ʃ/ – at the end of a syllable. This is most noticeable if the shortened sound is a long vowel or a diphthong. Compare, for example, the different durations of the otherwise identical sounds represented by the underlined letters within the word pairs *b<u>ea</u>d* /biːd/ and *b<u>ea</u>t* /biːt/, and *n<u>o</u>se* /nəʊz/ and *n<u>o</u>te* /nəʊt/, and also within the pairs *bu<u>m</u>ble* /bʌmbl/ and *bu<u>m</u>p* /bʌmp/, and *be<u>ll</u>s* /belz/ and *be<u>l</u>t* /belt/. In the second member of each pair, the duration of the sound in question is shortened through the influence of the following fortis consonant.

This is especially important for the distinction between words like *bead* /biːd/ and *beat* /biːt/, or *cab* /kæb/ and *cap* /kæp/, and *serve* /sɜːv/ and *surf* /sɜːf/, to give two more examples, where the only difference in terms of distinctive features is the intensity of articulation of the final consonants. You know from Lesson Two that some lenis consonants are almost entirely devoiced in word-final position, and this is precisely the case with /d/ in *bead*, /b/ in *cab*, and /v/ in *serve*. You learnt in that lesson that we still recognise these sounds (and we may even wrongly perceive them as voiced) because of their lenis articulation. Now you know that there is a second feature that helps us distinguish between word-final /d/ and /t/, for example, and consequently also between *bead* and *beat*, namely the duration of the preceding vowel.

Exercises

EXERCISES

4.1 Closeness vs. openness

Try saying the sounds [iː, æ, uː, ɑː] represented by the underlined letters in the words below, prolonging the vowel so that you can feel the position of the tongue. Notice how [iː, uː] are both close vowels, that is, the tongue is quite close to the palate. With [æ, ɑː] your tongue is further from the palate and your jaw is lowered.

key, cap, cool, car
sheet, shack, shoot, shark

4.2 Frontness vs. backness

Try saying the sequence of close vowels [iː, uː, iː, uː, iː, uː, iː, uː], and notice how your tongue moves backwards and forwards. You could also repeat the words *he* and *who*. Do the same with the open sounds [æ, ɑː, æ, ɑː, æ, ɑː, æ, ɑː]. This time, you could repeat the words *bad* and *bard*. Again, you should be able to notice the movement of the tongue from the front of your mouth to the back.

4.3 Transcription

Write the IPA symbols for the monophthongs, diphthongs, and triphthongs represented by the underlined letters in the following words:

heel, rib, leg, back, thumb, arm, body, jaw, foot, tooth, girl, finger
hair, ear, cure, eye, face, boy, nose, brow
iron, player, employer, mower, shower

4.4 Transcription

4.4a Write the monophthongs in the following words as IPA symbols and categorise them as close, open, or mid. Then categorise them as either front, back, or central vowels. (In the case of *upper*, which has two monophthongs, transcribe the underlined sound only.)

peak, pork, park, pack, perk, peck, pick, put, spook, pot, upper, puck
bid, bad, bog, bored, bard, bed, boot, bud, wood, about, bird, bead
eat, drink, work, cook, chat, fuss, rest, start, walk, wash, food, sofa

4.4b Write down the diphthongs in the following words as IPA symbols and group them according to whether they are centring, closing to /ɪ/, or closing to /ʊ/.

boat, bay, beer, moor, by, boy, bear, bound
pie, poison, pier, poor, paste, poke, pair, pound
tour, waist, toast, care, fear, write, boil, house

4.5 Reading and writing

Read or write in normal orthography the short text below:

[dʒɒn sæt baɪ ði əʊpən dɔː hɪz brəʊkən fʊt restɪd ɒn ə ʃɔːt piːs ɒv wʊd hɪz brʌðə tʃɑːlz traɪd tʊ kriːp pɑːst wɪðaʊt weɪkɪŋ hɪm bʌt tʃɑːlzɪz ʃuːz hæd verɪ slɪpərɪ səʊlz ænd hɪz leɪsɪz wə ʌndʌn hɪ slɪpt əʊvə nɒkt ðə wʊd ænd wəʊk ʌp pʊə dʒɒn bəʊθ men wə ɒn ðə flɔː wen dʒɪl keɪm ɪn lɑːfɪŋ laʊdlɪ ʃɪ sed ʃɪ θɔːt ðeə həd biːn sʌm kaɪnd əv æksɪdənt naʊ ɪt wəz tʃɑːlz huː wʊd hæv tə spend ðə deɪ restɪŋ ɒn ðə səʊfə]

87 words

LESSON 5
ALLOPHONIC VARIATION

The allo-/-eme relationship

The prefix *allo-* [from Greek *all-*, 'be different from'] is generally used in linguistics to refer to two or more concrete, particular forms of an abstract linguistic unit, which is denoted by the suffix *-eme*. The concrete, particular forms show noticeable variation among themselves – they are different from each other – but they do not affect the underlying linguistic unit's function. This can be illustrated by a simple example: In **graphology**, i.e. the study of the writing system of a language, the abstract linguistic unit is the letter, technically termed **grapheme**. A letter may appear in several different ways, depending on such factors as position within a word or sentence, typeface chosen, and handwriting style. The letter <a>, for instance, may appear as a lower-case 'a', a capital 'A', or an italic '*a*'; it may be badly scribbled, or in the writer's best copybook handwriting. Irrespective of the precise shape, each of these characters is a variant form, or an **allograph,** of the same grapheme <a>. That the function of the grapheme is not affected is illustrated by the fact that the meaning of the word *car* stays the same even if it is written *cAr* or *car* (although the latter two are, of course, not equally acceptable).

The first relationship of this kind was established in the field of phonetics and phonology in the 1930s. The notion was later also introduced into morphology, where it is now an essential element. More allo-/-eme relationships have been postulated in other areas of linguistic analysis (such as graphology), and they have even been extended to the classification of units of dance, song, or taste. Yet the application of the concept to some such areas seems questionable and is not undisputed, to say the least.

Allophone vs. phoneme

In **phonetics** and **phonology**, the abstract linguistic unit is the **phoneme**, which we defined in Lesson Three as the smallest distinctive, or contrastive, unit in the sound system of a language, i.e. a unit that contrasts meaningfully with other speech sounds. In the same lesson, you learnt that a concrete form, or realisation, of a phoneme is called a **phone**. When two or more concrete forms, or realisations, of a phoneme are compared, each of these forms is referred to as an **allophone**, rather than a phone. An allophone can therefore be defined as one realisation of a phoneme among others. Like phones, allophones are enclosed within square brackets, [ ], because they represent a concrete utterance. The terms *phone* and *allophone*, then, pertain to phonetics because they are related to parole or performance, and the term *phoneme* pertains to phonology because it is related to langue or competence.

The relationship between allophone and phoneme can be exemplified by the place of articulation of the English phoneme /n/, which, as you know from Lesson Three, is normally articulated at the alveolar ridge (behind the upper teeth), as in te*n*. Its place of articulation shifts forward to the upper teeth, however, if the sound occurs before the dental /θ/, as in te*n*th. We thus speak of the alveolar and dental allophones of the alveolar phoneme /n/.

It should be pointed out, here, that the concept of allophone is not entirely new to you: We have already encountered allophones in previous lessons, but have so far simply referred to them as "pronunciation variants" or "realisations" of a phoneme. In Lesson Two, for example, we briefly touched on the fact that lenis sounds, which are usually voiced, may also occur as voiceless variants; and in Lesson Three, we had the glottal stop, [ʔ], as a variant of the /t/ phoneme, and you learnt that the /r/ phoneme can be realised in different ways. All these variants and realisations are allophones, and we shall look at them more systematically later in this lesson and in Lesson Eleven.

The two allophone criteria

We now turn to the question of how allophones can be identified. As a starting point, it is useful to recapitulate briefly the criterion used for identifying phonemes, which we discussed in Lesson Three: A phoneme of a language is identified through a minimal pair, i.e. a pair of words that differ in meaning and in only one sound, such as ca*b*/ca*p* and ser*v*e/sur*f*. A minimal pair shows us that each of the two contrasting sounds can differentiate words, and is therefore a phoneme. More precisely, we should say that each of the two contrasting phones can differentiate words, and is therefore a realisation of a separate phoneme. Through minimal pairs, we established in Lesson Three that /b, p, v, f, uː, ʊ, z, s, t/ and /m/ are phonemes of English.

Conversely, we can deduce from the foregoing that, if *no* minimal pair can be found for two particular phones, these phones cannot differentiate words, and are therefore allophones of the same underlying phoneme. The single most important criterion for identifying allophones, then, is the **absence of a minimal pair**. Through the presence or absence of minimal pairs, we can determine, for example, that /s/ and /θ/ are two separate phonemes in English, because they can differentiate words like *s*ink and *th*ink, but allophones of the same phoneme in German, because there are no two German words that are differentiated by them. Furthermore, a lisped pronunciation of German words like *Post* and *Kasper*, where [s] is replaced by [θ], does not endanger intelligibility, which shows that the function of the underlying phoneme /s/ is not – at least not seriously – affected.

There are two phones in English, however, for which no minimal pair can be found, and which consequently should be regarded as allophones, although it would be clearly wrong to do so: No minimal pair can be found for [h] and [ŋ] because the former occurs only before a vowel (as in be*h*ave) while the latter never occurs before a vowel (as in si*ng*). Yet they cannot be considered allophones of the same phoneme because they are too dissimilar with respect to the intensity, place, and manner of their articulation, and the resultant sound quality. Replacing one with the other *does* endanger intelligibility, which shows that the function of the underlying phoneme *is* affected. Because of this one case, phoneticians have introduced a second necessary criterion for identifying allophones, namely that they must exhibit **articulatory similarity**, or **phonetic similarity**.

Allophones in free variation

If two or more allophones can replace one another, i.e. if they can occur in the same position, these allophones are said to be **free variants** [*freie Varianten, fakultative Varianten*] or in **free variation**. Some of the allophones we have already encountered in previous lessons can be used to illustrate this phenomenon. In Lesson Two, for example, in the section on the intensity of articulation, we saw that the phoneme /z/ in *z*eal can be realised as a voiceless, or devoiced, allophone when whispered, or as a voiced allophone when pronounced "normally". And in Lesson Three, in the section on the place of articulation, we saw that the phoneme /t/ in bu*tt*er can be realised as a glottal stop, [ʔ], by speakers of some non-standard British accents, but the same speakers may realise the phoneme as [t] when they aim at a more standard pronunciation. The examples show that the choice of one allophone rather than another may depend on such factors as communicative situation, language variety, and social class, and the example of the lisped [θ] in German shows that the choice can even be determined by a language handicap. Yet when we consider the wide range of possible realisations of any given phoneme (even by a single speaker), it becomes clear that we owe the vast majority of allophones in free variation to idiolects or simply to chance, and that the number of such allophones is virtually infinite.

The expressions *free variants* and *free variation* are also, but probably less commonly, used in the few exceptional cases where two phonemes can replace each other *without* causing any change of meaning. You know that phonemes usually *do* cause a change of meaning – in fact, they distinguish meaning by definition – but in some words, two normally contrasting phonemes are both acceptable. Examples of phonemes in free variation include /iː/ and /e/ as the initial sound in the words *economics* and *evolution*, and /iː/ and /aɪ/ as the initial sound in *either*.

Allophones in complementary distribution

If two or more allophones can*not* replace one another, i.e. if they do not occur in the same position, because their occurrence is determined by the surrounding sounds, these allophones are said to be **contextual variants** [*kombinatorische Varianten*] or in **complementary distribution** [*komplementäre Verteilung*]. In other words, complementary distribution is a systematic relationship between two or more allophones, whereby one allophone can only occur in a phonetic environment in which none of the others can: They are mutually exclusive. Again, some of the allophones we have already encountered so far can be used to illustrate this phenomenon. In Lesson Two, for example, you learnt that some lenis phonemes (which are usually voiced) can be realised as largely voiceless allophones not only when whispered, but also word-finally, as in the word ca<u>b</u>, a position in which the corresponding voiced allophones do not occur. And earlier in the present lesson, you saw that the alveolar phoneme /n/ can be realised either as an alveolar allophone, as in te<u>n</u>, or as a dental allophone, as in te<u>n</u>th, depending on the following sound, or the lack of a following sound.

If allophones in complementary distribution did replace one another for some reason (most likely because of a slip of the tongue), the resultant pronunciation would merely sound odd, or the articulation would feel awkward, but this would not cause a change of meaning. Both free variation and complementary distribution are thus relationships of **non-contrastive distribution**. (The only relationship of **contrastive distribution** in phonetics and phonology is the one between phonemes.) The next two sections and several more sections in Lessons Ten and Eleven will introduce the major types of allophonic variants, both free and contextual.

TIP Before you continue with the next section, it is advisable to reread the sections "Voicedness and voicelessness: The state of the glottis" and "Intensity of articulation I: Lenis and fortis" in Lesson Two.

Devoicing

If an intrinsically voiced, or underlyingly voiced, sound is articulated with less voice than usual or with no voice at all, i.e. without vibration of the vocal folds during part or all of its duration, that sound is said to be partly or fully **devoiced** [*verhärtet, verschärft*]. Since devoicing is usually conditioned by the phonetic environment, a devoiced allophone and its corresponding voiced allophone are usually in **complementary distribution**. You already know from Lesson Two that some lenis consonants are partly devoiced in word-initial position. The reason is that the vocal folds do not usually begin to vibrate at the onset of speaking. The time that elapses between the onset of speaking and the point at which the vocal folds begin to vibrate is called **voice onset time**, or **VOT**. The lenis consonants referred to in Lesson Two are the lenis plosives, /b, d, g/, the lenis affricate, /dʒ/, and the lenis fricatives, /v, ð, z, ʒ/. Because of the voice onset time, they are partly devoiced in words like <u>b</u>ill, <u>j</u>oy, and <u>v</u>an. There are numerous other cases of partial devoicing, but we want to confine ourselves here to giving an overview of the three main processes whereby lenis consonants are being fully, or almost fully, devoiced. Full devoicing, or almost full devoicing, can be indicated in the IPA by a small circle, [̥], under the relevant symbol, as in the transcription [kæb̥] for the word ca<u>b</u>.

(1) /b, d, g, dʒ, v, ð, z, ʒ/. The vibration of the vocal folds generally diminishes at the end of speaking, so that all lenis plosives, the lenis affricate, and all lenis fricatives can be fully devoiced in word-final position, as in *ca*b̥ [kæb̥], *li*d̥ [lɪd̥], *ba*g̥ [bæg̥], *ju*d̥ʒ̊ [dʒʌd̥ʒ̊], *lea*v̥ [liːv̥], *breat*ð̥ [briːð̥], *free*z̥ [friːz̥], and *rou*ʒ̊ [ruːʒ̊].

(2) /l, r, w/. The lenis lateral and these two lenis approximants can be fully devoiced when they follow any one of the fortis plosives, /p, t, k/, in stressed syllables, as in *p*l̥*ease* [pl̥iːz], *t*r̥*y* [tr̥aɪ], and *qu*w̥*ick* [kw̥ɪk].

(3) /j/. This lenis approximant can be fully devoiced when it follows any one of the fortis plosives, /p, t, k/, or the fortis glottal fricative, /h/, in stressed syllables. While the first two devoicing processes do not significantly affect the intensity of the articulation (i.e. lenis consonants remain lenis), full devoicing here produces a sound that is not only voiceless, but also fortis, namely a fortis palatal fricative. We have already encountered this sound in Lesson Three, in the High German pronunciation of the word *ic*h. It is transcribed as [ç], as in [pçuː] for *p*ew, [tçuːn] for *tu*ne, [kçuːb] for *cu*be, and [hçuː] for *hu*e. Since the symbol [ç] already indicates voicelessness, we do not attach the usual small circle to it.

The opposite process, the **voicing** of an intrinsically voiceless sound, does not occur very often. If it occurs, it can be indicated by the diacritic [ˬ] under the relevant symbol. The fortis glottal fricative, /h/, to give only one example, may be somewhat voiced between voiced sounds, as in the word *any*h*ow*, which can then be transcribed as [enihˬaʊ].

Fronting and retraction

If a sound is articulated further forward in the mouth than the underlying phoneme, usually under the influence of the surrounding sounds, that sound is said to be **fronted**, or **advanced**. Conversely, if a sound is articulated further back in the mouth than the underlying phoneme, again usually under the influence of the surrounding sounds, that sound is said to be **retracted**, or, less commonly, **backed**. Since fronting and retraction are usually conditioned by the phonetic environment, a fronted or retracted allophone and its corresponding "normal" allophone are usually in **complementary distribution**. We saw earlier in this lesson, for example, that the alveolar phoneme /n/ can be realised as an alveolar allophone, as in *te*n, or as a dental allophone before the dental /θ/, as in *ten*th. When fronting results in a dental sound, articulated with the tongue tip and rims touching the teeth, we speak of **dentalisation**. This process is subsumed under the first of the two main types of fronting and retraction outlined below. Dental articulation can be indicated in the IPA by the diacritic [̪] under the relevant symbol, as in the transcription [ten̪θ] for the word *ten*th; other fronting processes can be indicated by a small cross, [˖], as in [k̟iː] for *k*ey; and retraction can be indicated by an underbar, [ˍ], as in [kɔːd] for *c*ord.

(1) /t, d, n/. The alveolar plosives and the alveolar nasal may be fronted, or, more specifically here, dentalised, through the influence of the place of articulation of a following consonant, particularly the dental fricatives, /θ, ð/. The dentalisation process can be exemplified by the word pairs *eigh*t [eɪt] / *eigh*th [eɪt̪θ], *wi*de [waɪd] / *wi*dth

[wɪd̪θ], and *ten* [ten] / *tenth* [ten̪θ]. Similarly, /t, d, n/ may be retracted through the influence of the place of articulation of a following consonant, namely the post-alveolar approximant, /r/. The retraction process can be exemplified by adding the words *try* [t̠raɪ], *dry* [d̠raɪ], and *unrest* [ʌn̠rest] to the word pairs above. Each of the three alveolar phonemes, then, has one "normal", alveolar allophone (e.g. [t] in [eɪt]), one fronted, dental allophone (e.g. [t̪] in [eɪt̪θ]), and one retracted, post-alveolar allophone (e.g. [t̠] in [t̠raɪ]). When contrasting the three allophones by pronouncing their respective example words (e.g. *eight*, *eighth*, *try*), we can actually feel how our tongue moves forwards and backwards. For the sake of simplicity, we mainly use examples here that illustrate how fronting and retraction, and other phonetic processes discussed earlier and later in this manual, take place within single words. It should be noted, however, that these processes also operate across word boundaries, in connected speech. For example, /t, d, n/ may be dentalised in such sequences as *not thin* [nɒt̪ θɪn], *had then* [hæd̪ ðen], and *when they* [wen̪ ðeɪ] if spoken without a pause.

(2) **/k, g/.** The velar plosives are often fronted through the influence of a following front vowel, and retracted through the influence of a following back vowel. (It should be remembered, here, that *front* and *back*, in connection with vowels, are strictly speaking not associated with a place of articulation, as is the case with consonants, but refer to the part of the tongue that is raised highest, and to the direction in which the body of the tongue is pushed or pulled.) Thus each of the velar plosives has three allophones: A "normal", or "central", [k] or [g] as in *curb* [kɜːb] and *gun* [gʌn], a fronted [k̟] or [g̟] as in *key* [k̟iː] and *get* [g̟et], and a retracted [k̠] or [g̠] as in *cord* [k̠ɔːd] and *goose* [g̠uːs].

Yet fronting and retraction are sometimes also conditioned by social factors, such as the dialect spoken or the age and sex of the speaker, in which case the resultant allophones are in **free variation**. In Irish English (also referred to as Hiberno-English), for example, the alveolar plosives, /t, d/, are usually dentalised. In some varieties of Scottish English, the close back vowel, /uː/, is fronted, so that words like *moon* and *use* are heard with [y] (as in the final sound in the French word *tu*), and are written in such dialect spellings as *muin* and *yuise*. (The written representation of dialectal speech in this way is called **eye dialect**.) In New Zealand English, the mid-close front-central vowel, /ɪ/, is retracted, so that it sounds like a schwa. And in Canadian English, one study suggests that, especially among younger female speakers, the first element of the diphthong /aʊ/ in words like *out* is not just articulated in a more central position than in RP, so that *out* sounds more like *oat* (which is referred to as "Canadian raising", and is one of the main identifying features of that variety), but that it is now often fronted. These examples show that the choice between two allophones is, of course, not always as "free" as the term *free variation* suggests. Theoretically, however, one and the same speaker can, consciously or unconsciously, realise a particular phoneme as a dialectal variant in one situation, and as a more standard variant in another.

Finally, we should point out that the term *fronting* is also used to refer to a type of sound change in historical linguistics, and in the description of children's language,

Allophonic Variation

which may contain sounds that are articulated further forward in the mouth than is required by adult speakers' norms. It is also a term in syntax, where it refers to the unusual placing of a sentence element in initial position.

Two (or three) types of phonetic transcription

In the section "Phonetic transcription" in Lesson One, you learnt that we use phonetic symbols in order to write down speech sounds as accurately as possible, and that both the process of writing down spoken language in this way and the resultant written text are referred to as phonetic transcription. Later on, however, in the section "The phoneme" in Lesson Three, you learnt that the term *phonetic symbol* is sometimes used in a broader sense, covering not only phonetic symbols (i.e. IPA symbols representing phones or allophones), but also phonemic symbols (i.e. IPA symbols representing phonemes). In general, we can say that the terminological distinction between the adjectives *phonetic* and *phonemic*, or *phonological*, is not always strictly observed, and that *phonetic* is sometimes used generically. This is also true of the terms *phonetic transcription* and *phonemic transcription* although there *is*, of course, a distinction between the two that is worth observing, as we shall see below.

Phonetic transcription proper

A phonetic transcription in the narrower sense aims to represent actual speech sounds, i.e. concrete utterances of an individual speaker on a particular occasion. It does so with a high degree of accuracy, showing a lot of articulatory details. This type of transcription is also called **narrow transcription** [*enge Umschrift*]. It is occasionally also referred to as **impressionistic transcription**, or said to be "objective", because the transcriber simply writes down what he hears (even if he does not know what the utterance means). It is a **phonetic transcription proper** because it represents spoken language at the level of phonetics, through a wide range of phonetic symbols for phones or allophones. The transcribed text is therefore enclosed in square brackets, [ ]. As we saw earlier in this lesson, slight alterations to the usual value of a phonetic symbol can be indicated by diacritics, showing such processes as devoicing, voicing, fronting, and retraction. The diacritics used in this manual are listed together with the list of phonetic symbols on the inside front cover. Examples of phonetic transcriptions of words with a considerable degree of accuracy are [kçu:b̥] for *cube* and [kɔ:d̪] for *cord*.

Phonemic transcription

A phonetic transcription in the broadest sense, on the other hand, aims to represent abstract speech sounds, i.e. idealised utterances conforming to a speech community's shared knowledge of the sound system of a language. It does so with a moderate degree of accuracy, showing only those articulatory details that can distinguish meaning, i.e. only the distinctive features. This type of transcription is also called **broad transcription** [*weite Umschrift*]. Here, the transcriber does not write down what he hears, but what he expects he would hear. It is best referred to as a **phonological transcription** [*phonologische Umschrift*] or **phonemic transcription** [*phonematische Umschrift*] because it represents spoken language at the level of phonology, through "phonetic" symbols that are taken to represent phonemes, and are thus better regarded as phonemic symbols. The transcribed text is therefore enclosed in slashes, //. Allophonic variation is ignored entirely, and the only mark attached to phonemic symbols is the length mark (which is not regarded as a diacritic in IPA terminology) after the symbols for the five long vowel phonemes.

The difference between a narrow, phonetic transcription and a broad, phonemic transcription can be illustrated by our tried and trusted example *cube*. As we saw above, the phonetic transcription proper, [kçuːb̥], contains the symbol for the fortis palatal fricative [ç] and a diacritic indicating a devoiced lenis bilabial plosive, [b̥]. You know from Lesson Three, however, that there is no palatal fricative phoneme in English, and that the lenis bilabial plosive is intrinsically voiced. The two sounds represented, then, are devoiced allophones of the phonemes /j/ and /b/, respectively, and it is these latter symbols, therefore, that are used in the phonemic transcription, /kjuːb/. A phonemic transcription, possibly with minor modifications, is the type of transcription used in most British dictionaries, probably because it is simpler than a phonetic transcription. The disadvantage is, however, that it requires a fair knowledge of, or intuition for, the allophonic variation of the language if it is to be read aloud with a high degree of accuracy.

Broad phonetic transcription: An intermediate type

For the learning and teaching of English pronunciation, the phonetic transcription proper certainly shows too many fine details whereas a phonemic transcription often does not seem detailed enough. For that reason, it has become customary, for pedagogic purposes, to use an intermediate type of transcription, which is largely phonemic, but shows several more articulatory details. It shows, for example, linking *r*-sounds, syllabic consonants, and stress, all of which will be discussed in later lessons. It does *not* usually show allophonic variation, caused by such processes as devoicing, voicing, fronting, and retraction. This type of transcription is best regarded as a **broad phonetic transcription**. Although it is largely phonemic, we cannot use the word *phonemic* in the label because two of the symbols that are commonly used are not phonemes of English, as we shall see in the next section. Consequently, the transcribed text should be enclosed in square brackets, [ ]. A broad phonetic transcription is used in most university courses in phonetics and phonology, and in the transcription course integrated with this manual.

Unstressed *i*- and *u*-sounds

A good example to illustrate the intermediate status of a broad phonetic transcription is the representation of *i*- and *u*-sounds in some unstressed syllables. In stressed syllables, it is relatively easy to distinguish the long /iː/ (as in b*ee*) from the short /ɪ/ (as in f*i*sh), and the long /uː/ (as in g*oo*se) from the short /ʊ/ (as in p*u*dding). In some unstressed syllables, however, the distinction is not so clear. In words like *easy*, r*e*act, eval*u*ate, and *actual*, the *i*- and *u*-sounds in the unstressed syllables seem to be intermediate between the respective long and short vowels. What symbols, then, do we use to transcribe these sounds? Neither /iː/ nor /ɪ/, and neither /uː/ nor /ʊ/, seem to be wholly satisfactory here. In a broad phonetic transcription, therefore, the sounds in question are often represented by [i] or [u], using the basic symbols for the long vowels, but without a length mark. This compromise suggests that the two sounds have the quality of the respective long vowels, and the length of the respective short vowels. You may have noticed that we have already used the symbol [i] in the transcription of the word *anyhow*, [enihaʊ], in the section on devoicing earlier in this lesson. As indicated above, a transcription using [i] and [u] cannot be regarded as phonemic because the symbols represent sounds that are not phonemes of English.

We said that the distinction between the long and the short *i*- and *u*-sounds is not so clear in "some" unstressed syllables. More specifically, the intermediate [i] usually occurs in unstressed syllables in the following phonetic environments:

- in word-final position (if the final *i*-sound is not the second element of one of the three closing diphthongs moving towards /ɪ/), as in *easy* [iːzi] or *hurry* [hʌri], even when followed by suffixes beginning with a vowel, as in *easiest* [iːziəst] or *hurrying* [hʌriɪŋ];
- in prefixes like *re-*, *pre-*, and *de-* when followed by a vowel, as in *react* [riækt] or *preoccupied* [prɪɒkjʊpaɪd];
- in suffixes like *-ial*, *-iate*, and *-ious* when they are pronounced as two syllables, as in *appreciate* [əpriːʃieɪt] or *hilarious* [hɪleəriəs];
- in the words *he*, *she*, *we*, *me*, *be*, and *the* when followed by a vowel, as in *the enemy* [ði enəmi].

In most other phonetic environments, an *i*-sound in an unstressed syllable can be interpreted as a short [ɪ], as in *resist* [rɪzɪst] or *orchestra* [ɔːkɪstrə].

The intermediate [u] is much less common, but if it occurs, it usually occurs in unstressed syllables in these phonetic environments:

- in the words *you*, *to*, *into*, and *do* when followed by a vowel or pause, as in particle-infinitive sequences like *to eat* [tu iːt];
- in the words *through* and *who* in all positions;
- before a vowel within a word, as in *evaluate* [ɪvæljueɪt] or *actual* [æktʃuəl].

A brief excursion into morphophonology

We have already encountered the notion of **morphology** twice in this manual: You know from Lesson One that morphology is concerned with the structure of words, and you learnt at the beginning of the present lesson that it also employs the allo-/-eme relationship. In morphology, the abstract linguistic unit is the **morpheme**, which can be defined as the smallest unit of meaning within the words of a language. Examples of morphemes are prefixes meaning 'not' or 'the opposite of' (so-called negative prefixes), suffixes denoting participles, and roots like *cat*, *dog*, and *fox*. When a morpheme has only one concrete form, or realisation, that form is called a **morph**. The present participle morpheme, for example, is always realised by the morph *-ing*. When a morpheme has two or more realisations, however, each of these forms is called an **allomorph**. For example, one type of negative prefix can be realised by *il-*, *im-*, *in-*, or *ir-* (as in *illogical*, *immoral*, *infinite*, and *irrelevant*). Irrespective of the exact forms, all of these concrete prefixes are allomorphs of the same morpheme.

Although you learnt in Lesson One that morphology is a separate level of language description, it overlaps with phonetics and phonology when the choice of one allomorph rather than another is determined by the surrounding sounds (as is the case with the allomorphs of the negative prefix above). The overlap between the two core areas of linguistics is referred to as **morphophonology, morphonology**, or, in American terminology, **morphophonemics**. If the choice between allomorphs is determined by the surrounding sounds, i.e. if the choice is rule-governed, the allomorphs can be said to be in **complementary distribution** (the term being used here analogously to its use in conjunction with allophones). There are several cases of allomorphs in complementary distribution that are important to know when making a phonetic or phonemic transcription. The rules governing the choices will be briefly discussed in the next two sections.

The regular plural, the possessive case, and the third-person singular morphemes

The morpheme for the regular plural, the morpheme for the possessive case, and the morpheme for the third-person singular in the simple present tense are all conventionally symbolised by {S}. We also speak of the "plural *-s*", the "possessive *'s*", and the "third-person singular *-s*". These morphemes are realised by three allomorphs, transcribed as /s, z, ɪz/. The allomorphs are distributed according to the following rules:

- /s/ after fortis (voiceless) consonants, except after the fortis sibilants, /s, ʃ, tʃ/;
- /z/ after vowels and lenis (voiced) consonants, except after the lenis sibilants, /z, ʒ, dʒ/;
- /ɪz/ after the sibilants, /s, z, ʃ, ʒ, tʃ, dʒ/.

These rules, and the different allomorphs, can be illustrated by the following words: *cats* /kæts/, *dogs* /dɒgz/, and *foxes* /fɒksɪz/ illustrate the allomorphs of the regular plural morpheme; *dentist's* /dentɪsts/, *children's* /tʃɪldrənz/, and *waitress's* /weɪtrəsɪz/ illustrate the allomorphs of the possessive case morpheme; and *writes* /raɪts/, *goes* /gəʊz/, and *reaches* /riːtʃɪz/ illustrate the allomorphs of the third-person singular morpheme.

The regular past tense and past participle morphemes

The morpheme for the regular past tense and the morpheme for the regular past participle are conventionally symbolised by {D}, and are usually – but not always – written as *-ed*. These morphemes, too, are realised by three allomorphs, transcribed as /t, d, ɪd/. Here are the rules according to which the allomorphs are distributed:

- /t/ after fortis (voiceless) consonants, except after /t/;
- /d/ after vowels and lenis (voiced) consonants, except after /d/;
- /ɪd/ after /t, d/.

These rules, and the different allomorphs, can be illustrated by the words *looked* /lʊkt/, *turned* /tɜːnd/, and *pointed* /pɔɪntɪd/.

The pronunciation of the letter sequence <ng>

Another morphophonological phenomenon, though *not* another case of allomorphs in complementary distribution, is the pronunciation of the letter sequence <ng>. The pronunciation of <ng> always involves the velar nasal, /ŋ/, but the question here is whether or not that /ŋ/ is followed by a /g/. Neither the letter sequence <ng> nor the phoneme /ŋ/ can occur at the beginning of an English word, and <ng> is simply pronounced /ŋ/, without a following /g/, when it occurs at the end, as in *sing* /sɪŋ/ or *long* /lɒŋ/. But how is <ng> pronounced when it occurs word-internally, as in *singer* or *finger*?

The rules governing the pronunciation of word-internal <ng> in RP are as follows: When <ng> occurs at the end of a morpheme, i.e. at the end of a minimal unit of meaning, it is simply pronounced /ŋ/. For example, the words *singer* and *longish* consist of the morphemes *sing* (root) + *er* (suffix meaning 'person concerned with') and *long* (root) + *ish* (suffix meaning 'fairly'), and are therefore pronounced /sɪŋə/ and /lɒŋɪʃ/. When, however, <ng> occurs in the middle of a morpheme, i.e. in the middle of a minimal unit of meaning, it is pronounced /ŋg/. The words *finger* and *anger*, for example, consist of one morpheme each (because *fing* and *ang* have no meaning), and are therefore pronounced /fɪŋgə/ and /æŋgə/.

An exception to these rules is the pronunciation of <ng> in comparative and superlative forms of adjectives and adverbs: Even when <ng> occurs at the end of a morpheme, it is pronounced /ŋg/ when it is followed by the comparative suffix *-er* or the superlative suffix *-est*. This means that, although *long* /lɒŋ/ and *longish* /lɒŋɪʃ/ are pronounced without a /g/, the comparative and superlative forms are pronounced *longer* /lɒŋgə/ and *longest* /lɒŋgəst/.

Exercises

In this manual, we use a broad phonetic transcription. This type of transcription has already been explained, but it is worth repeating a few key points here.

As was highlighted in this lesson, the exact quality of unstressed *i-* and *u*-sounds in English is phonologically determined. That means we can tell whether [i] will be pronounced depending on its position in a word, and the sounds around it. It will be pronounced, for example, in word-final position often represented by the spelling <y>, as in *city* [sɪti] or *quality* [kwɒlɪti], or in pronouns before a vowel, such as *she is* [ʃi ɪz]. The same holds true for [u], an example being *you ought to ask* [ju ɔːt tu ɑːsk].

Since we include the phonetic forms [i] and [u], the transcriptions as a whole should be considered phonetic, and so are given in square brackets. As the lessons progress, we will include some more phonetic features of English which are important for natural and correct pronunciation. Nonetheless, our transcription remains broad, since we will not include every phonetic detail. For example, you are not expected to include the phenomena of devoicing, fronting, and retraction, all of which you have learnt about in this lesson.

Thus the exercises in this manual require a little more than purely phonemic transcription since you should show certain features of English that are relevant to how it actually sounds. To get a better representation of English, then, we ask you to include some "narrow" features, such as the intermediate [i] and [u] along with other particular phenomena, such as the linking *r*-sound and syllabic consonants (details you will learn about in Lessons Six and Seven). We enclose the transcriptions in square brackets to indicate that they are phonetic.

Another point to note is that you should always think of the written texts as representing speech. Thus, from the start, there are some natural features of spoken English which appear in the solutions at the end of this manual before they are covered in the lessons. For example, the word *the* is rarely pronounced as [ðiː]. Rather it is pronounced in one of its weak forms, for example as [ðə]. Similarly, *and*, *for*, *had*, *of*, *that*, and *to*, which all appear in the texts below, normally occur as weak forms, for example as [ənd, fə, həd, əv, ðət, tə]. You will learn more about weak forms in Lesson Eight. For now, you should at least be aware that many so-called grammatical words in English have such weak forms, and you should try to use them from the start in your transcriptions.

You do not punctuate your transcriptions with normal orthographic marks. Thus you should not include full stops, commas, semicolons, exclamation marks, question marks, etc. As was mentioned above, you only need to use square brackets.

The transcription of written texts in this manual conforms to standard RP English, as does the pronunciation of most of the spoken texts appearing from Lesson Seven on. However, there may also be some variation from the norm on the part of individual speakers. Where this is perceptually relevant, it is indicated in the annotations to the model solutions.

The model solutions, which you will find at the end of this manual, have been carefully prepared and annotated to give you the best guidance in completing and correcting your own transcriptions. Even so, it is quite possible that you may arrive at a different transcription, especially of the spoken texts. There are a number of factors to consider here:

❖ Your own pronunciation of a sound, a word, or a sequence of words will affect how you perceive the way others pronounce those sounds or words. In this case, you should be aware of the differences in varieties of English, and remember that in this manual we use standard RP as the model pronunciation.
❖ When you listen closely for transcription, you may concentrate on some features that you would not normally pay attention to in normal conversation with native speakers. Although we ask you to attend to some particular traits of English, as was mentioned above, the exercises train you in broad phonetic transcription, and the focus of the exercises is on transcribing the overall phonemic patterns correctly with some additional phonetic details.
❖ It may be that you yourself incorrectly pronounce a word or words, or have difficulty in correctly articulating a particular phoneme of English. In this case, the model transcriptions should be taken as a standard which your pronunciation too should approach, for example in the case of the phonemes /ð, θ/ or /v, w/.

As a reminder, in this lesson you have covered the following features which you should include in your transcriptions:

feature	IPA symbols
intermediate *i*-sound	[i]
intermediate *u*-sound	[u]
regular plural morpheme	[s, z, ɪz]
possessive case morpheme	[s, z, ɪz]
third-person singular morpheme	[s, z, ɪz]
regular past-tense morpheme	[t, d, ɪd]
regular past participle morpheme	[t, d, ɪd]
letter sequence <ng>	[ŋ, ŋg]

5.1 Reading and writing

Read or write in normal orthography the short text below:

[ʃærən wɔːkt əkrɒs ðə lɪvɪŋ ruːm wʌndərɪŋ wɒt ʃi ʃʊd du əbaʊt ðə njuːz ʃi həd dʒʌst rɪsiːvd ʃi traɪd tu əpɪə kɑːm ənd rɪzɪst getɪŋ æŋgri ʃærənz jʌŋgə brʌðə həd faʊnd tu əreɪndʒ hɪz steɪ wɪð hɜː nekst wiːk ðə prɒbləm wɒz ðət ʃi wɒntɪd tu ɪskeɪp ðə hɒt sɪti fə ðə wiːkend ənd ðæt wʊd miːn liːvɪŋ dʒɔːdʒ ɔːl ələʊn wɪðaʊt eni kʌmpəni

hi nəʊz səʊ fjuː frendz əv maɪn hi dʌzənt laɪk fɪlmz ɔː kɒnsəts ənd hi heɪts pleɪsɪz wen ðeɪ ɑː empti θɔːt ʃærən ðeə ɪz nʌθɪŋ aɪ kən du əbaut ɪt ɪksept steɪ hɪə ðɪs wiːkend ɔː pərhæps ɪf hi juːzɪz keɪts bɔɪfrendz flæt ɪnsted aɪm ʃɔː tʃɑːlzɪz pleɪs ɪz bɪg ɪnʌf fə tuː ʃi əʃɔːd hɜːself

jes əv kɔːs tʃɑːlz wʊdənt maɪnd pʊtɪŋ hɪm ʌp ɪn ðə gest ruːm wɪð ðə sɪŋgəl bed

raɪt aɪm gəʊɪŋ tə rɪŋ hɪm streɪt əweɪ]

147 words

5.2 Transcribe the following text into IPA symbols

Joyce had cooked supper, but Hamish wanted nothing to eat. He needed time to think. He wondered what had happened to all the pictures and books he had placed so carefully around the flat.

"Joyce always tidies things away," he said to himself.

"I stacked all the new bits and pieces you had scattered everywhere in the hall," she answered his thoughts.

"Those works of art, journals, and diaries are precious to me even if Joyce thinks they're out of fashion now and not worth much," he muttered quietly to himself.

All manner of objects from Hamish's famous brother's huge output in his short time as a fine artist now turned pop singer clogged up every inch of space in the cramped flat. Now he had stopped and lingered in front of his favourite picture: He adored it. His finger traced a faint line across the image. For too long he had waited for something to occur in his life.

"David gets on with things and manages to enjoy life. So does Joyce," he enviously thought.

She opted to leave him alone and hoped he would return to the table later. For hours she had been mobbed by unrelenting crowds of admiring fans egged on by a crazed media. Her latest novel "wept, no sobbed with emotion," read one review. Hamish was sick with envy; Joyce was over the moon.

230 words

LESSON 6
CONNECTED SPEECH

As was pointed out in the previous lesson, the phenomena discussed in this manual so far have been illustrated, for the sake of simplicity, mainly by single-word examples, rather than by words in connected speech. However, although speakers and listeners are able to distinguish the separate words of an utterance, much spoken language actually consists of a continuous sequence of words, i.e. words run together with only a few pauses between them (despite what the written language, with its spaces between the words, might suggest). This running together of words often results in pronunciations that are markedly different from the way the words are pronounced in isolation, i.e. in their **citation form**. While the pronunciation of individual sounds and words was the subject matter of Lessons Two to Five, we now turn our attention to the changes sounds and words undergo when they are used in connected speech. The various aspects of connected speech can be grouped together under five headings: linking, strong and weak forms, rhythm, assimilation, and elision. Linking will be discussed in this lesson, and we shall return to the other aspects in Lessons Eight and Nine.

Linking

Liaison

Different authors use the term **liaison** [French, 'link'] in different ways, but all agree that it refers to a transition or link between sounds or words. A rather broad and somewhat vague definition, then, sees liaison merely as a transition between words in connected speech, particularly when this involves an unusual phonetic feature. A frequently cited example is the carrying over of a word-final consonant to a word beginning with a vowel in a stressed syllable. This type of liaison is sometimes heard between *at* and *all* in the sequence *not at all*, which could be transcribed in broad phonetic transcription as [nɒt ət‿ɔːl] or [nɒt ə tɔːl].

More narrowly, liaison has been defined as a link between words through the articulation of a normally unarticulated word-final consonant, which is articulated only when preceded by a vowel in the same word, and followed by an initial vowel in the next word. In other words, liaison here refers to a process whereby a word that ends in a vowel when pronounced in isolation acquires a final consonant when followed by a word beginning with a vowel. This type of liaison is a notable feature of French, and, in fact, the term is sometimes restricted to the description of that language. The final consonants in the French words *les* and *est*, for example, are articulated only when followed by a vowel, as in the sequences *les amis* and *c'est une maison*. A sound that is absent in a word when that word is pronounced in isolation, but present in the same word in certain phonetic environments in connected speech – usually for ease of pronunciation – is called a **linking sound**. The final consonants in *les* and *est*, then, are linking sounds. In English, the most prominent example is the so-called linking *r*, which will be discussed in the next section.

According to another definition, liaison is a link between sounds or words through the insertion of an additional sound, again usually for ease of pronunciation. This type of liaison often links two consecutive vowels belonging to different syllables or words (i.e. *not* two elements of a diphthong), in which case the articulatory break, or gap, at the syllable or word boundary is referred to as a **hiatus** [Latin, 'gap'], and the consecutive vowels are said to be "in hiatus". A hiatus, then, can be heard in words like *playoff*, *reassure*, *skiing*, and *cooperate*, and in sequences like *he is silly and stupid* and *to England*. Of course a hiatus does not necessarily have to be removed, i.e. the vowels in question do not necessarily have to be linked. On the contrary, the hiatus in *playoff*, *reassure*, and *skiing* is likely to be present whereas the hiatus in *cooperate*, *he is silly and stupid*, and *to England* may be removed, i.e. the vowels in question may be linked, through the insertion of a glottal stop, as in [kəʊˀɒpəreɪt], or a semi-vowel, or glide, as in [hiʲ ɪz sɪliʲ ən stjuːpɪd] and [tuʷ ɪŋglənd]. As these transcriptions show, a symbol representing a linking sound usually appears as a small superscript and, if the sound links words, is attached to the preceding word (but transcription practice here may vary). The most prominent example of a linking sound removing a hiatus is the so-called intrusive *r*, which will be discussed together with the linking *r* in the next section.

Linking *r* and intrusive *r*: Two cases of liaison

As has already been mentioned, in English, or at least in some accents of it, the most prominent example of the second type of liaison described above is the **linking *r***. The term refers to a link between words through the articulation of a normally unarticulated word-final /r/, which is articulated only when preceded by a vowel in the same word, and followed by an initial vowel in the next word. In the words *far*, *four*, and *tsar*, for example, the *r*-sounds suggested by the spelling are not normally pronounced, so that the words usually end in vowels: [fɑː], [fɔː], [zɑː]. The *r*-sounds are pronounced only when followed by words beginning with a vowel, as in the sequences *far away* [fɑːr əweɪ], *four eggs* [fɔːr egz], and *tsar of Russia* [zɑːr əv rʌʃə]. As the transcriptions show, a symbol representing a linking *r* usually appears in normal size and position, contrary to the common transcription practice for other linking sounds.

We speak of a linking *r* only when the *r*-sound in question occurs in the spelling in the form of the letter <r>. In Lesson One, you learnt that, in the history of the English language, many sound changes were not accompanied by changes in the spelling, and that the orthography in general became less variable after William Caxton had brought the art of printing to England in 1476. Consequently, we said that the spelling of many words in present-day English reflects the pronunciation used in the time from Chaucer to Shakespeare. This is precisely the case with words containing a normally unarticulated final /r/, like *far, four*, and *tsar*: In the past, these words were pronounced with a final /r/ in all phonetic environments, they then lost their final /r/ in the course of the centuries, and the final /r/ now reappears as a linking *r* only when followed by a word-initial vowel. As was indicated at the beginning of this section, however, this is only true of some accents of English, namely of the non-rhotic accents, which will be discussed in the next section.

Yet many English speakers use an *r*-sound in a similar way even when that sound does *not* occur in the spelling in the form of the letter <r>. Such an *r*-sound is called an **intrusive *r***. More specifically, the term refers to a link between two consecutive vowels belonging to different words or, less commonly, to different syllables within the same word through the insertion of an /r/ that has no historical justification. As has already been mentioned, the intrusive *r* is the most prominent example of the third type of liaison described in the previous section, the type removing a hiatus. The hiatus in the sequences *media event, visa application*, and *shah of Persia* and in the word *drawing*, for example, may be removed through the insertion of an intrusive *r*, as in [miːdiəʳ ɪvent], [viːzəʳ æplɪkeɪʃn], [ʃɑːʳ əv pɜːʃə], and [drɔːʳɪŋ]. Transcription practice varies here, but we suggest that the symbol representing an intrusive *r* appears as a small superscript and, if the intrusive *r* links words, is attached to the preceding word (as is the common transcription practice for all linking sounds except the linking *r*).

The intrusive *r* – especially the word-internal one – is widely stigmatised by language purists, who regard it as a non-standard pronunciation, or simply as incorrect. It is quite commonly heard, however, ironically also in the speech of those who criticise it. Many (overly) careful speakers nevertheless try to avoid it, and, in fact, some try so hard to avoid an intrusive *r* that they even seem to be afraid to use a linking *r*. Instead, they use a glottal stop or a semi-vowel as a linking sound, or no linking sound at all, producing such pronunciations as [mɔːʔ ən mɔː] and [mɔː ən mɔː] for the sequence *more and more*, rather than the more natural [mɔːr ən mɔː]. Such an over-correction, resulting from an attempt to adjust one's speech to a prestige norm, is called **hypercorrection**, or **hyperurbanism** [*Hyperkorrektur, Hyperurbanismus*]. On the other hand, the intrusive *r* is sometimes used purposefully to achieve a humorous effect, as when the phrase *law and order* [lɔːʳ ən ɔːdə] is personified as Laura Norder [lɔːrə nɔːdə], a friend of the police.

Whereas the linking sounds in the examples in the previous section (such as the glottal stop in [kəʊʔɒpəreɪt] and the /w/ in [tuʷ ɪŋglənd]) are usually recorded only in a phonetic transcription proper, the linking *r* and the intrusive *r* are also recorded in a broad phonetic transcription (the linking *r* is recorded even in a phonemic transcription), and they are therefore relevant to the transcription course integrated with this manual.

Non-rhotic and rhotic accents

We said in the previous section that, in some accents of English, the linking *r* is the most prominent example of the second type of liaison described earlier, namely of liaison through a normally unarticulated consonant. These are accents that have lost the /r/

phoneme almost entirely over the centuries (although it still occurs in the spelling), except when followed by a vowel, either in the same or in the next word, but only if that vowel follows immediately, without a pause in between. In other words, the /r/ phoneme in these accents is articulated only before a vowel, not before a consonant or pause. Such an accent is called a **non-rhotic accent** [from Greek *rhô*, name of the Greek letter corresponding to <r>, and *-ic*, 'connected with'], an **r-less accent**, or a **non-r-pronouncing accent**. We have already encountered examples of non-rhotic pronunciations in connection with the linking *r* above: *far* [fɑː], *four* [fɔː], and *tsar* [zɑː] do not have a final *r*-sound when pronounced in isolation, because the unarticulated /r/ is not followed by a vowel, but they do have a final *r*-sound in the sequences *far away* [fɑːr əweɪ], *four eggs* [fɔːr egz], and *tsar of Russia* [zɑːr əv rʌʃə], because here the normally unarticulated /r/ *is* followed by a vowel. For the same reason, *bird* [bɜːd], *farther* [fɑːðə], and *hard* [hɑːd] do not have a word-internal *r*-sound in non-rhotic accents whereas *barrel* [bærəl], *pressure* [preʃə], and *worry* [wʌri] do. In non-rhotic accents, then, *farther* is pronounced the same as *father*, and *far* rhymes with *shah*.

Conversely, a **rhotic accent**, an **r-ful accent**, or an **r-pronouncing accent** is one that has *not* lost the /r/ phoneme over the centuries (not even when followed by a consonant or pause). To put it simply, the /r/ phoneme in rhotic accents is articulated wherever it occurs in the spelling. (It becomes clear now that, in rhotic accents, the linking *r* cannot be a prominent example of liaison through a normally unarticulated consonant because the /r/ in these accents is not normally unarticulated, and the linking *r* therefore, strictly speaking, does not exist.) The same words that were used above to exemplify non-rhotic pronunciations can be used again here to exemplify rhotic pronunciations: *far* [fɑːr], *four* [fɔːr], and *tsar* [zɑːr] have a final *r*-sound in rhotic accents even when pronounced in isolation, and *bird* [bɜːrd], *farther* [fɑːrðər], and *hard* [hɑːrd] have a word-internal *r*-sound although it is followed by a consonant.

The distinction between non-rhotic accents and rhotic accents forms the basis for one of the fundamental categorisations of varieties of English. Non-rhotic accents are typical of varieties spoken in the larger part of England, in Wales, on the east coast and in the south of the United States, in parts of the Caribbean (e.g. Trinidad and Tobago), in Australia, New Zealand, and most parts of sub-Saharan Africa. Rhotic accents, on the other hand, are typical of varieties spoken in the south-west of England and parts of the north, in Scotland, Ireland, Canada and most of the United States, in much of the Caribbean (e.g. Barbados and Jamaica), and in India. RP is a non-rhotic accent. Since we use RP, or near RP, as our model in this manual, you should pay especial attention in your transcriptions to where *r*-sounds are appropriate, and where they are not.

Juncture

We pointed out at the beginning of this lesson that speakers and listeners are able to distinguish the separate words of an utterance despite the fact that much spoken language actually consists of a continuous sequence of words, with only a few pauses between them. But how is that possible? If, for the purpose of demonstration, we transcribed an utterance without the conventional spaces between the words, i.e. if we depicted connected speech the way it really is, namely as an uninterrupted string of sounds, then how could we identify where one word ends, and the next word begins? It is certainly relatively easy to see, for example, that /əhaʊs/ consists of the words *a* and *house*, but what about /əneɪm/? Does it consist of *a* and *name*, or of *an* and *aim*? To give another example, /naɪtʃɪft/ is easily recognisable as *night* and *shift*, but what about /naɪtreɪt/? Is it *night rate* or just one word, *nitrate*? These examples show that a phonemic, or phonological, transcription cannot always disambiguate potentially ambiguous utterances. There are, nevertheless, phonological and, in actual speech, also phonetic features that mark the beginning and the end of linguistic units, i.e. they signal the boundary between syllables, words, and clauses, thus enabling us to distinguish between *a name* and *an aim*, and between *night rate* and *nitrate*. Such boundary signals are collectively termed **junctures** [from Latin *iunctura*, 'joint'; *Junktur, Grenzsignal*] or **juncture** (used as a mass noun).

There are principally four different ways of realising juncture. Firstly, the most obvious junctural features, or boundary signals, are of course pauses, including pauses filled with hesitation noises such as *er* and *um*. But pauses, as has already been indicated above, are far less common than is widely assumed. Secondly, at the phonological level, linguistic boundaries are marked by restrictions on the possible positions and combinations of phonemes. Certain phonemes and phoneme combinations never occur at the beginning or at the end of a syllable or word, for example, and certain phoneme combinations do not occur in a word at all. The part of phonology that deals with the rules governing the possible positions and combinations of phonemes is called "phonotactics", and will be discussed in more detail in the next lesson. Thirdly, back at the phonetic level, linguistic boundaries are signalled by the suprasegmental features of loudness, pitch, and duration, which are components of stress, and thus shape the intonation of connected speech. And fourthly, what may be the most reliable boundary signals are the rule-governed phonetic processes that take place when phonemes occur at the beginning or end of linguistic units, such as the partial devoicing of some lenis consonants in word-initial position, and the full devoicing of these consonants in word-final position. In other words, maybe the most reliable clues as to how to distinguish the separate words of an utterance come from allophones in complementary distribution.

Juncture through allophones can be exemplified by the sequence /ðætstʌf/. (Remember that we leave out the space between the words here only for demonstration purposes. Common transcription practice requires spaces between words even though they might be mistaken as signalling pauses.) It is the allophonic realisation of the phonemes preceding and following the word boundary which makes that word boundary perceptible, and helps us recognise the sequence as either *that stuff* or *that's tough*. In *that stuff*, the word-final /t/ is unaspirated, i.e. not accompanied by an audible release of air, and the word-initial /s/ is articulated with its usual fortis intensity. In *that's tough*, on the other hand, the word-final /s/ is articulated with less intensity (although it is still a fortis sound), and the word-initial /t/ is aspirated, i.e. accompanied by an audible release of air. Further examples of unaspirated or aspirated plosives signalling word boundaries are *keep sticking* vs. *keeps ticking*, *all that I'm after today* vs. *all the time after today*, and *I scream* vs. *ice cream*. We shall return to aspiration and discuss it in greater detail in Lesson Ten.

There have been several attempts to establish a typology of junctures. The most common one is based on the notions of "open" and "close". Junctural features at a word boundary are referred to as **open juncture**, or **plus juncture** (because, in a phonetic transcription proper, it may be represented by a plus sign). If that word boundary is not preceded or followed by a pause, i.e. if the words on both sides of the boundary are run together, we speak of **internal open juncture**. The sequence *night rate*, for example, has internal open juncture between /t/ and /r/, and it is the location of the internal open juncture that distinguishes *a name* from *an aim*. If the word boundary *is* preceded or followed by a pause, i.e. if the word boundary occurs at the beginning or at the end of an utterance, we speak of **external open juncture**. The "normal" transitions between sounds within a word, on the other hand, are referred to as **close juncture**. (The use of the term *juncture* here is justified only by the fact that there is a kind of "boundary" even between sounds.) The word *nitrate*, then, has close juncture between /t/ and /r/.

It should be noted that the concept of juncture is not undisputed. It is often argued, for example, that the different types of juncture are blurred in rapid speech, so that sequences like *a name* and *an aim*, or *that stuff* and *that's tough*, seem to have the same close juncture between all their sounds. In that case, of course, it is not the boundary signals, but the context that helps us distinguish the separate words. Also, juncture does not *always* demarcate linguistic units, as it has in the examples given in this section so far. In *beetroot* and *bedroom*, for example, (which are regarded here as sequences consisting of two words, despite the fact that they are written without a space) there is internal open juncture before /t/ and /d/, respectively, and the sequence *at all*, as we already know from the section on liaison, sometimes has the same internal open juncture as *a tall*.

Finally, it should also be noted that juncture is sometimes defined not only as boundary signals between syllables, words, or clauses, but also more broadly as a transition between them. Such a broad concept of juncture overlaps considerably with the concept of liaison, and, in fact, some linguists include liaison as a part of juncture. It seems more appropriate, however, to use the narrower definition of juncture, and to regard juncture and liaison as related concepts, without much overlap.

EXERCISES

The exercises in this lesson focus on liaison in connected speech, and continue to practise the intermediate [i] and [u], various endings, and the letter sequence <ng>, which you learnt about in Lesson Five. Remember that there are two types of *r*-sound used to link words in connected speech: the linking *r* and the intrusive *r*.

The linking *r* occurs between two words. The final sound in the first word is a schwa or any of the back vowels, the following word begins with a vowel, and the spelling at the end of the first word must contain the letter <r>. The intrusive *r* occurs in exactly the same phonetic context, but there is no historical justification for the sequence to be pronounced with /r/, i.e. there is no letter <r> in the spelling.

linking *r*		intrusive *r*	
orthography	IPA	orthography	IPA
The chair in the corner	ðə tʃeər ɪn ðə kɔːnə	*The sofa in the corner*	ðə səʊfəʳ ɪn ðə kɔːnə
She works on the fourth	ʃɪ wɜːks ɒn ðə fɔːθ	*It's a flaw in the design*	ɪts ə flɔːʳ ɪn ðə dɪzaɪn
floor in design	flɔːr ɪn dɪzaɪn		

In this manual, we use RP as our model, and you should use the following guidelines for transcribing linking *r* and intrusive *r*:

❖ In written texts, you should *always* transcribe a linking *r* and an intrusive *r*. Although many speakers of RP, in careful speech, consciously try to avoid both linking and more so intrusive liaison in many contexts, most will produce these forms in natural speech nevertheless.

❖ In spoken texts, you should transcribe a linking *r* and an intrusive *r* only if you hear them. Some speakers do avoid liaison in the recorded exercises that follow. All cases of linking and intrusive *r* are both transcribed and annotated in the model solutions at the end of the manual. Linking *r* is transcribed as [r] attached to the preceding word, intrusive *r* as a small superscript [ʳ], also attached to the preceding word. This practice is shown in the table above.

6.1 Reading and writing

Read or write in normal orthography the short text below:

[meəriz luːs tʃeɪndʒ dʒæŋɡld ɪn hə pɒkɪts ə strɒŋɪʃ kʌp əv kɒfi wəz wɒt ʃi niːdɪd naʊ evri θɜːzdeɪ mɔːnɪŋ ʃi ɡəʊz tə ðə dʒɪm ənd præktɪsɪz hər eərəʊbɪk tekniːk ənd streŋkθənz hə tendənz sɪns ʃi ɪz treɪnɪŋ fər ə lɒŋ dɪstəns reɪs mɔːr ɒftən ðən nɒt ʃi miːts ʌp wɪð hər eks bɒs dʒeɪn huː bɪlɒŋz tə ðə seɪm spɔːts klʌb

ðə kæfiːn stɑːtɪd tə wɜːk ənd meəri felt mʌtʃ betər ɑːftə ðə strenjuəs wɜːkaʊt dʒeɪn həd əraɪvd faɪv mɪnɪts bɪfɔː meəri ənd wəz ɔːlredi sɪtɪŋ ɒn ə səʊfəʳ ənd stʌdiɪŋ ðə menjuː waɪl sɪpɪŋ ɒn hə mæŋɡəʊ dʒuːs kɒkteɪl wen meəri həd wɔːkt ɪn ənd plɒŋkt həself daʊn nekst tə hə aɪ fiːl betə fə ðæt meəri sed braɪtli pʊʃɪŋ ðə taɪni kʌp meɪd əv tʃaɪnəʳ əkrɒs ðə treɪ ənd steərɪŋ aʊt əv ðə kæfeɪ wɪndəʊ ət ðə stɔːr ɒpəzɪt

ʃi nʌdʒd dʒeɪn

aɪ dʒʌst sɔːʳ ændʒələʳ əpɪərɪŋ frəm dʒəʊnsɪz ʃuːz əkrɒs ðə rəʊd aɪ θɔːt ʃi wəz ɪn dʒəniːvəʳ ɔː sʌmweəʳ ɪn swɪtsələnd ʃi wɪspəd tʊ hə frend]

170 words

6.2 Transcribe the following text into IPA symbols

Deborah opened her eyes and then blinked again.

"There must be something wrong or I'm dreaming," she murmured to herself.

She seemed to be hungry, thirsty and tired all together at once. On the ceiling she could make out a small triangle directly above her of a darker orange against the rest of the rusty coloured paint.

"How are you feeling today?" echoed a voice from the sofa in the corner of the room.

"Well there's a tingling in my toes, my fingers are stinging and my head's buzzing like crazy; my jaw and neck still ache, but overall I'm better than yesterday," she replied unconvincingly.

Deborah's doctor often visited just after evening mealtime and asked a number of questions before assessing whether or not to prescribe any new pills or tablets. He took his time, he lingered: He liked to draw out the agony.

"Alright! Two extra injections of morphine," he decided. "But for no longer than three days."

Despite her hunger and thirst, Deborah was relieved when the odd shape above her receded into the rest of the ceiling and she drifted into another deep sleep.

188 words

LESSON 7
THE SYLLABLE

One notion that we have used freely in previous lessons without giving any explanation is the notion of the syllable [from Latin *syllaba*, Greek *sullabé*, 'taken, brought, or put together'; *Silbe*]. The reason why we have been able to do so is that most people have an intuitive sense of what a syllable is, and they can probably define a syllable vaguely as the smallest rhythmic unit of spoken language, for example, or a unit that is typically larger than a single sound and smaller than a word. Even without being able to give an exact definition, most people feel they can count syllables, and say how many syllables there are in a given word or sequence of words. On the other hand, studies have shown that, when English speakers are asked to count the syllables of a concrete utterance, there is bound to be considerable disagreement among them. It becomes clear, then, that the notion of the syllable is more elusive than is widely thought. In this lesson, we shall therefore discuss the syllable in some detail.

A phonetic approach to the syllable

You learnt in Lesson Three that consonants and vowels can be described both from a phonetic point of view, i.e. in terms of how they are produced, and from a phonological point of view, i.e. in terms of where they occur. The same is true of the syllable. Phonetically, a syllable can be described as having a **centre**, also called **peak** or **nucleus** [*Silbenkern, Silbengipfel, Nukleus*], which is produced with little or no obstruction of air, and is therefore usually formed by a vowel (either a monophthong or a diphthong). The minimal syllable, then, is typically a single, isolated vowel, as in the words *are* /ɑː/, *err* /ɜː/, and *I* /aɪ/. The few consonants that can occur in isolation, such as the interjections *mm* /m/ (used to express agreement) and *sh* /ʃ/ (used to ask for silence), are not regarded as minimal syllables by all linguists.

In many syllables, the centre is preceded by an **onset** [*Kopf*], which is produced with greater obstruction of air, and is therefore always formed by one or more consonants. Such syllables are exemplified by words like *ba<u>r</u>* /bɑː/, *<u>st</u>ir* /stɜː/, and *<u>m</u>y* /maɪ/. A syllable that ends in a vowel, i.e. one that ends with the centre, is commonly referred to as an **open syllable** [*offene Silbe*]. In many other syllables, there is no onset, but the centre is followed by a **coda** [*Koda*], which is also produced with greater obstruction of air, and is therefore also formed by one or more consonants. Such syllables are exemplified by words like *ar<u>t</u>* /ɑːt/, *urg<u>e</u>* /ɜːdʒ/, and *ic<u>e</u>* /aɪs/. Most syllables, however, have both an onset and a coda, like *<u>bath</u>* /bɑːθ/, *<u>perk</u>* /pɜːk/, and *<u>m</u>ine* /maɪn/. (If they do not, we also speak of a **zero onset** and a **zero coda**.) A syllable that ends in a consonant, i.e. one that ends with a coda – irrespective of whether it has an onset or not – is commonly referred to as a **closed syllable** [*geschlossene Silbe*]. It is sometimes also termed a **checked syllable**, and the vowel forming the centre is then a **checked vowel**. The centre and the coda (if there is one) together account for the rhyming potential of a syllable, as can be illustrated by word pairs like *mine*/*fine* and *err*/*stir*, and they have therefore collectively been referred to as the **rhyme**.

From the point of view of auditory phonetics, which was defined in Lesson One as investigating the perception of speech sounds by the listener, the centre of a syllable is perceived to be more prominent than the margins, i.e. onset and coda. The **prominence** of a syllable centre (and the prominence of a particular sound in relation to its surrounding sounds in general) can be attributed mainly to a combination of greater loudness, higher (or sometimes lower) pitch, and greater duration, but also to sound quality: Each phoneme has, besides the absolute loudness of its phonetic realisation, an intrinsic, relative loudness (or "carrying-power"), referred to as its **sonority**, and, according to a common sonority hierarchy, vowels are more sonorous (i.e. they "carry further") than consonants.

On the basis of what you have just learnt, we can say that the word *knowing* consists of two syllables: the open syllable /nəʊ/, ending in a diphthong, and the closed syllable /ɪŋ/, without an onset. Here, syllable boundary and morpheme boundary clearly coincide (in other words, syllables and morphemes in this example are identical), but this is not usually the case. The word *standing*, for example, is commonly divided into the syllables /stæn/ and /dɪŋ/ (although its morphemes are *stand* and *-ing*). This analysis is probably guided by the desire to have two evenly balanced syllables, namely two closed syllables with an onset, but the word could theoretically also be divided into the syllables /stænd/ and /ɪŋ/ if that were "felt" to be more appropriate. (Incidentally, syllable boundaries and morpheme boundaries are the two competing criteria for hyphenating a word at the end of a line, with American English favouring the former, and British English favouring the latter.) The example shows, then, that the division of words into syllables, referred to as **syllabification** or **syllabication**, is based to a considerable extent on intuition – certainly to a greater extent than is desirable for a science that aims to be exact and objective.

The difficulty of determining the exact boundaries between consecutive syllables can be further exemplified by words like *master* and *extra*. Most English speakers feel that *master* consists of two syllables, but should the word be divided as /mɑː-stə/ (with two evenly balanced open syllables in non-rhotic accents), /mɑːs-tər/ (with two evenly balanced closed syllables in rhotic accents), or maybe even /mɑːst-ə(r)/ (because the word *mast* consists of one syllable when it occurs alone)? The word *extra* is also felt to have two syllables, but should it be divided as /ek-strə/, /eks-trə/, /ekst-rə/, or /ekstr-ə/? While it is simply not possible to say which of these syllabifications is "correct", /ek-strə/ and /eks-trə/ are certainly the most common.

The answer to such questions is influenced by factors like accent, rapidity of speech, level of formality, and communicative situation. The examples nevertheless suggest

The Syllable

that a description of the syllable merely in terms of how its segments are produced (or perceived) is less than sufficient. In order to give a more satisfactory description, we also have to investigate the possible positions and combinations of particular phonemes within a syllable. In other words, the syllable must be described not only from a phonetic, but also from a phonological point of view.

Phonotactics

As was briefly mentioned in the previous lesson, the part of phonology that deals with the rules governing the possible positions and combinations of phonemes is called **phonotactics** [*Phonotaktik*]. The range of environments in which a linguistic unit can occur is referred to as its **distribution** [*Distribution, Verteilung*], a term we are already somewhat familiar with from the concept of complementary distribution, discussed in Lesson Five. Every language has restrictions on the distribution of phonemes within a syllable, morpheme, or word. In English, for example, /ŋ/ occurs only after some short vowels, more specifically after /ɪ, æ, ʌ, ɒ/, and no word ends with the sequence /æh/.

Especially important, here, are the rules governing the possible sequences of consonants, i.e. consonants pronounced consecutively without an intervening vowel or pause, such as the initial /st/ in *stir*. Such a consonant sequence is technically termed **consonant cluster**, or simply **cluster**. (It goes without saying that the term cannot be applied to a mere sequence of letters. The word *scythe* /saɪð/, for instance, does not contain a cluster, despite its spelling, and *perk* contains the cluster /rk/ only in rhotic accents.) Languages differ considerably in their tolerance for clusters: Hawaiian, for example, permits no clusters at all, and Japanese allows only very few clusters word-internally. English, on the other hand, has numerous clusters, and many of them are quite complex. Some phonotactic rules governing the distribution of consonants and vowels will be explored in the next section.

A phonological approach to the syllable

Concerning the possible positions of phonemes within a syllable, you already know that one or more consonants can occur at each margin, and that either a monophthong or a diphthong usually occurs at the centre, which could mean in the middle, but also at the beginning (if there is no onset), at the end (if there is no coda), or alone (if there is neither onset nor coda). As far as the possible positions of *particular* phonemes and their combinations are concerned, there are many more restrictions than can be outlined here. In this section, we shall therefore look at the particular phonemes and phoneme combinations that can occur at the beginning of a word, or more precisely of a word-initial syllable, in some detail, and shall touch on those that can occur at the end only briefly.

A word begins either with the centre or with the onset of its first syllable. If it begins with the centre (as in *art* /ɑːt/), that centre can be formed by any vowel (although /ʊ/ occurs rarely in word-initial position). If it begins with the onset, that onset can be formed either by one consonant or by a cluster consisting of two or three consonants. If the onset is formed by one consonant (as in *bar* /bɑː/), that consonant can be any consonant except /ŋ/ (although /ʒ/ is also rare word-initially). If the onset is formed by two consonants (as in *stir* /stɜː/), the two-consonant cluster must be one of the following: /pl, pr, pj, bl, br, bj, tr, tj, tw, dr, dj, dw, kl, kr, kj, kw, gl, gr, mj, nj, fl, fr, fj, vj, θr, θw, sp, st, sk, sm, sn, sf, sl, sj, sw, ʃr, hj, lj/, plus a few unusual clusters in some proper names, in some archaic or otherwise rare words (such as /vr/ in *vroom*), and in certain pronunciation variants of words (such as /sr/ in *syringe* when that word is pronounced /srɪndʒ/ instead of /sɪrɪndʒ/). We note that, with the exception of clusters beginning with /s/, the second (or last) element of a word-initial two-consonant cluster is always one of the four frictionless continuants, /l, r, j, w/. If the onset is formed by three consonants (as in *street* /striːt/), the three-consonant cluster must be one of the following: /spl, spr, spj, str, stj, skl, skr, skj, skw/. Here, we note that the first element is always /s/, the second element is always one of the three fortis plosives, /p, t, k/, and the third (or last) element is again always one of the four frictionless continuants, /l, r, j, w/. No English word, and no English syllable, for that matter, begins with more than three consonants, and many consonant combinations, such as /tl/, /fs/, and /spm/, are not possible in word-initial position.

A word ends either with the centre or with the coda of its last syllable. If it ends with the centre (as in *my* /maɪ/), that centre can be formed by any vowel except /e, æ, ʌ, ɒ/, or it can be formed by a syllabic consonant, which will be explained in the next section. If it ends with the coda, that coda can be formed either by one consonant or by a cluster consisting of up to four consonants. If the coda is formed by one consonant (as in *mine* /maɪn/), that consonant can be any consonant except /h/, the semi-vowels, /j, w/, and in non-rhotic accents /r/. If the coda is formed by two, three, or four consonants (as in *help* /help/, *next* /nekst/, and *glimpsed* /glɪmpst/), there are numerous restrictions similar to those applying to clusters at the beginning of a word-initial syllable. No English word, and, again, no English syllable, ends with more than four consonants, and, as before, many consonant combinations are not possible in word-final position.

Phonologically, the English syllable can thus be described (with a capital 'C' representing a consonant, and a capital 'V' representing a vowel) as having the maximal structure CCCVCCCC (as in *strengths* /streŋkθs/, although the /k/ is prone to deletion), the minimal structure V (as in *are* /ɑː/), or any structure in between, such as CCVC (as in *stop* /stɒp/), CVCC (as in *cats* /kæts/), and CCCVCC (as in *streets* /striːts/).

Syllabic consonants

In the previous sections, we said that the centre of a syllable is "usually" formed by a vowel. This is true, without exception, in words consisting of only one syllable, like *art* /ɑːt/, *my* /maɪ/, *help* /help/, and most of the other example words given in this lesson so far. As the tentative wording suggests, however, there are syllables whose centre is *not* formed by a vowel, but by a consonant instead. Such syllables contain no vowel at all, and the consonant forming the centre is termed **syllabic consonant**. This is the case in some words consisting of two or more syllables, as we shall see shortly.

Before we proceed, however, a brief note on terminology: A word that consists of a single syllable is referred to as a **monosyllabic word**, or simply as a **monosyllable**. One that consists of two syllables, like *clever* /klev-ə/ and *delay* /dɪ-leɪ/, is referred to as a **disyllabic** or **bisyllabic word**, or as a **disyllable** or **bisyllable**, and one that consists of three syllables, like *compulsive* /kəm-pʌl-sɪv/ and *delicious* /dɪ-lɪʃ-əs/, is referred to as a **trisyllabic word**, or as a **trisyllable**. Less specifically, a word that consists of two or more syllables is also called a **polysyllabic word**, or a **polysyllable**.

The word *student* /stjuːdnt/, then, could theoretically be analysed as a monosyllable with a vowel as its centre, a three-consonant cluster as its onset, and another three-consonant cluster as its coda. Most English speakers feel that *student* consists of two syllables, however, and the word is therefore commonly analysed as a disyllable with /stjuːd/ as the first syllable, and /nt/ as the second, and with /uː/ and /n/ as the syllable centres. One justification for such an analysis might be that *student* is pronounced /stjuːdənt/, with a schwa, when it is pronounced very slowly, in which case it is the schwa that forms the centre of the second syllable. In "normal" speech, when the schwa is omitted, the centre simply shifts to the following sound.

In more general terms, we could say that a syllabic consonant can occur in certain phonetic environments where, in very slow speech, there would be a schwa, or where we imagine there *could* be a schwa, as a syllable centre. The time needed to pronounce the (real or imaginary) schwa is then added to the duration of the following consonant, thus transforming that consonant into a syllabic consonant. As a syllabic consonant always forms the centre of a syllable, it has the phonological characteristics of a vowel, but, of course, it retains the phonetic characteristics of a consonant.

A syllabic consonant and a corresponding non-syllabic consonant cannot usually distinguish meaning, or differentiate words, which means that they must be regarded as allophones of the same phoneme. You learnt in Lesson Five that allophones are not recorded in a phonemic transcription, and the transcription /stjuːdnt/ is therefore correct and sufficient for that degree of accuracy. In a phonetic transcription proper, on the other hand, and, to a very limited extent, in a broad phonetic transcription, allophones *are* recorded. In those types of transcription, a syllabic consonant is indicated by a small vertical line, [ˌ], under the relevant symbol, as in [stjuːdn̩t]. There are five consonants that can be transformed into syllabic consonants. They are, roughly in order of frequency: /l, n, m, ŋ, r/. The specific environments in which they occur as syllabic consonants will be described below.

(1) [l̩]. The syllabic [l̩] is probably the most frequent of the five. It is most noticeable when it is represented in the spelling by the letter sequence <le> at the end of a word, and is preceded by a consonant, as in *table* [teɪbl̩], *double* [dʌbl̩], and *coddle* [kɒdl̩]. Each of these words, or roots, consists of two syllables, with a syllabic [l̩] as the centre of the second: *table* [teɪ-bl̩], *double* [dʌb-l̩], and *coddle* [kɒd-l̩]. The [l̩] remains syllabic even when a suffix is added, as in *tables* [teɪbl̩z], *doubled* [dʌbl̩d], and *coddling* [kɒdl̩ɪŋ]. Whereas *tables* and *doubled* still consist of two syllables, [teɪ-bl̩z] and [dʌb-l̩d], *coddling* now consists of three, [kɒd-l̩-ɪŋ], because the vowel in the suffix *-ing* must form the centre of a syllable too. Alternatively, and less frequently, the /l/ in *coddling* could be pronounced, or perceived, as having lost its syllabic quality, and as forming the onset of a syllable, rather than the centre, and the word would then consist of two syllables as well: [kɒd-lɪŋ].

It should be pointed out that, although spelling is regarded as largely irrelevant in linguistics, it is certainly helpful to resort to it here because phonetically similar words whose roots do *not* end with the letter sequence <le> do *not* have a syllabic [l̩]. For example, the word *codling* [kɒdlɪŋ], 'small cod', is derived by adding the diminutive suffix *-ling* to the root *cod*, and its pronunciation differs from that of *coddling* only in that the /l/ is always, necessarily, pronounced as a "normal", non-syllabic [l]. Thus *codling* always consists of the two syllables [kɒd-lɪŋ].

The syllabic [l̩] also occurs when it is represented in the spelling by the letter sequences <al> or <el> at the end of a word, and is preceded by a consonant, as in *propo<u>s</u>al* [prəpəʊzl̩], *pe<u>d</u>al* [pedl̩], and *sho<u>v</u>el* [ʃʌvl̩]. As before, it forms the centre of the syllable in which it occurs, and it usually remains syllabic even when a suffix is added, as in *proposal<u>s</u>* [prə-pəʊ-zl̩z], *pedall<u>ed</u>* [ped-l̩d], and *shovell<u>ing</u>* [ʃʌv-l̩-ɪŋ].

In most cases, the syllabic [l̩] is obligatory. In other words, pronouncing the word *table* as [teɪbəl], with a schwa, would be plain wrong, except perhaps in very slow speech. It is optional mainly in those cases where it is followed by a suffix with a vowel, as was seen above, and in some less common or more technical words, such as *acquittal* [əkwɪtl̩/əkwɪtəl], *missal* [mɪsl̩/mɪsəl], and *shrapnel* [ʃræpnl̩/ʃræpnəl].

(2) [n̩]. The syllabic [n̩] often occurs when /n/ is preceded by a plosive or fricative (not by an affricate) in unstressed syllables, but not usually in word-initial position. It is especially frequent when preceded by an alveolar plosive or fricative, as in *bu<u>tt</u>on* [bʌtn̩] and *hori<u>z</u>on* [həraɪzn̩], and in contracted negations like *ha<u>dn</u>'t* [hædn̩t] and *i<u>sn</u>'t* [ɪzn̩t]. It is also frequent when preceded by a labiodental fricative, but here the /n/ can also be pronounced as [ən]. The words *hy<u>ph</u>en* and *se<u>v</u>en*, for example, are usually pronounced [haɪfn̩] and [sevn̩], but less commonly also [haɪfən] and [sevən]. Otherwise, however, the syllabic [n̩] is largely obligatory in this environment. Pronouncing a schwa here would usually sound odd or, at best, overcareful.

In other environments, the syllabic [n̩] is relatively rare. After bilabial and velar consonants, [n̩] and [ən] seem to be virtually interchangeable, or in free variation, as in *ha<u>pp</u>en* [hæpn̩ / hæpən], *ri<u>bb</u>on* [rɪbn̩ / rɪbən], and *thi<u>ck</u>en* [θɪkn̩ / θɪkən]. After velar consonants, when it is represented in the spelling by the letter sequences <an> or <on>, as in *wagon*, and after the phoneme sequence nasal or /s/ or /l/ plus plosive, as in *Lon<u>d</u>on*, the syllabic [n̩] may be acceptable, resulting in such pronunciations as [wægn̩] and [lʌndn̩], but pronunciations with [ən], as in [wægən] and [lʌndən], are certainly much more common.

(3, 4) [m̩, ŋ̩]. Although the syllabic [m̩] and [ŋ̩] are not uncommon, they can occur only as a result of phonetic processes such as assimilation and elision, which will be discussed in detail in Lesson Nine. When they occur in words like *happen* and *thicken*, for example, these words are pronounced [hæpm̩] and [θɪkŋ̩], but, as we saw above, the pronunciations [hæpn̩/hæpən] and [θɪkn̩/θɪkən] are also possible.

(5) [r̩]. While the syllabic [r̩] is very common in many rhotic accents, it is rare in non-rhotic accents, where the /r/ phoneme has disappeared almost entirely (except before a vowel). The words *particular* and *perhaps*, for example, are often pronounced [pr̩tɪkjəlr̩] and [pr̩hæps] in General American English whereas in RP they are usually pronounced [pətɪkjələ] and [pəhæps]. There are only two environments in which the syllabic [r̩] can occur in RP, and even in those environments it is usually optional. Firstly, it can occur when /r/ is preceded by one consonant (and followed by a vowel) in unstressed syllables, as in *flattery* [flætr̩i] and *watering* [wɔːtr̩ɪŋ]. Here, the syllabic [r̩] is usually interchangeable with [ər], and the example words would then be pronounced [flætəri] and [wɔːtərɪŋ]. Secondly, the syllabic [r̩] can occur when /r/ is preceded by two or more consonants (and followed by a vowel) in unstressed syllables, as in *history* [hɪstr̩i] and *wanderer* [wɒndr̩ə]. Here, the syllabic [r̩] is usually interchangeable with a non-syllabic [r], without a schwa. The example words would then be pronounced [hɪstri] and [wɒndrə], the only difference being that a syllabic consonant always has a greater duration than its non-syllabic counterpart.

As was mentioned earlier in this section, a syllabic consonant and a corresponding non-syllabic consonant cannot usually distinguish meaning, i.e. there are few minimal pairs in which they appear to be contrasting sounds. One such minimal pair seemed to be *coddling* [kɒdl̩ɪŋ] / *codling* [kɒdlɪŋ], but we said that *coddling* is occasionally also pronounced [kɒdlɪŋ], in which case the two words have the same pronunciation (and are then termed **homophones**). All in all, there is not enough reason to regard a syllabic consonant and its non-syllabic counterpart as two separate phonemes. They are, as mentioned before, allophones of the same phoneme.

Finally, it should be noted that neither the choice between the various pronunciation variants discussed here nor their exact pronunciations are usually as clear-cut as the description of the environments and a neat transcription might suggest. The word *veteran*, for example, can be pronounced [vetərən] with [ər], [vetrən] with a syllabic [r̩], less commonly also [vetrən] with a non-syllabic [r], [vetərn̩] with a syllabic [n̩], possibly even [vetr̩n̩] with two consecutive syllabic consonants, or some way in between. When we transcribe spoken language, the choice is therefore often arbitrary, and the representation through IPA symbols is often only approximate.

Stressed and unstressed syllables vs. strong and weak syllables

You learnt earlier in this lesson that, at the level of auditory phonetics, the **prominence** of a sound can be attributed mainly to a combination of loudness, pitch, duration, and sound quality. Just as there are more prominent and less prominent sounds within a syllable (the most prominent being the syllable centre), there are more prominent and less prominent syllables within a (polysyllabic) word. Furthermore, you learnt in Lesson Two that, at the level of articulatory phonetics, the same four features mentioned above – loudness, pitch, duration, and sound quality – are also the main components of **stress**. Prominence in the perception of speech, then, results from stress in its production, and we therefore speak of a **stressed syllable** and an **unstressed syllable**. These terms seem to be largely self-explanatory (which is the reason why we have been able to use them from Lesson Four onwards), but when we look at stressed and unstressed syllables more closely, we see that they need more explanation than their simple labels might suggest. One aspect in particular that must be explained is the sound quality of the vowels in stressed and unstressed syllables. An important role is played, here, by the schwa, and it is therefore advisable to reread the relevant passage in the section "Short vowels" in Lesson Four, which describes this phoneme in some detail.

While stressed syllables can contain any vowel (monophthong or diphthong) except /ə/, unstressed syllables contain

- mainly /ə/, /ɪ/, and /ʊ/ (in order of frequency), as in *agree* /əgriː/, *regard* /rɪgɑːd/, and *neighbourhood* /neɪbəhʊd/ (including, at the phonetic level, the intermediate [i] and [u], described in the section "Unstressed *i*- and *u*-sounds" in Lesson Five);
- less commonly, other vowels such as /ʌ/ in *unsafe* /ʌnseɪf/ and /əʊ/ in *obese* /əʊbiːs/;
- and, in a sense, also the syllabic consonants, [l̩, n̩, m̩, ŋ̩, r̩], because, as we said earlier in this lesson, they are vowels from a phonological point of view.

And while the vowels in stressed syllables always have their "full", original sound quality, it can be demonstrated that most /ə/ and /ɪ/ phonemes in unstressed syllables result from a **reduction**, or **weakening**, of such full vowels owing to a shift in stress. For example, the /æ/ in *land* /lænd/ remains an /æ/ in *landing* /lændɪŋ/ because it occurs in a stressed syllable, but it is reduced to /ə/ in *England* /ɪŋglənd/ because here it occurs in an unstressed syllable. Similarly, the /e/ in the noun *present* /preznt/ is reduced to /ɪ/ in the verb *present* /prɪznt/ because the shift in word class is accompanied, or rather brought about, by a shift in stress, from the first syllable to the second. (Sometimes the reduced vowels in unstressed syllables cannot be clearly identified as either /ə/ or /ɪ/, and the choice between the two symbols is then largely arbitrary.) But there are, of course, also cases where the vowels in unstressed syllables retain their original sound quality. The /ɑː/ in *art* /ɑːt/, for example, remains an /ɑː/ in *artistic* /ɑːtɪstɪk/ although in the latter word it occurs in an unstressed syllable, and the /uː/ in *stupid* /stjuːpɪd/ remains an /uː/ in *stupidity* /stjuːpɪdətɪ/.

Any vowel that has its full, original sound quality, except /ə/, is referred to as a **strong vowel**, and the syllable of which it forms the centre, irrespective of whether it is stressed or unstressed, is called a **strong syllable**. The first syllable in *unsafe* /ʌnseɪf/, for example, is strong and unstressed, and the second syllable is strong and stressed. A vowel that results from a reduction (as is often the case with /ə/ and /ɪ/) or one that occurs solely in unstressed syllables (i.e. again /ə/, but also [i], [u], and the syllabic consonants) is referred to as a **weak vowel**, and the syllable of which it forms the centre is called a **weak syllable**. The first syllable in the verb *present* /prɪznt/, for example, is weak because the /ɪ/ is reduced from /e/, and the second syllable in *England* /ɪŋglənd/ is weak not only because the /ə/ is reduced from /æ/, but also because /ə/ generally occurs only in unstressed syllables.

It is important to note, then, that there is no one-to-one correspondence between stressed syllable and strong syllable (and, by extension, strong vowel), or between unstressed syllable and weak syllable (and weak vowel): While all stressed syllables are also strong (as in <u>lan</u>ding /ˈlændɪŋ/), strong syllables can be either stressed (again, as in <u>lan</u>ding) or unstressed (as in <u>ar</u>tistic /ɑːˈtɪstɪk/). And while unstressed syllables can be either strong (again, as in <u>ar</u>tistic) or weak (as in E<u>ng</u>land /ˈɪŋglənd/), weak syllables are always unstressed (again, as in E<u>ng</u>land).

 REMEMBER Weak syllables – i.e. syllables containing /ə/, /ɪ/ when that vowel results from a reduction, [i], [u], or a syllabic consonant – are always unstressed in English.

We pointed out in the section on short vowels in Lesson Four that many languages do not have a sound, like the English schwa, that occurs in most unstressed syllables. This, together with the reduction of vowels in unstressed syllables, is one of the most important distinguishing features of English, and is particularly important for foreign learners. Especial attention must therefore be paid to it in the teaching of English as a foreign language.

Stress patterns in polysyllabic words

The stress carried by a syllable within a word is referred to as **word stress**, or **lexical stress**. It must be distinguished from the stress carried by a word within an utterance, which is (strictly speaking, not quite appropriately) referred to as **sentence stress**. This section, and, in fact, much of this lesson, is concerned with word stress. Sentence stress determines the occurrence of strong and weak forms, which will be discussed in the next lesson, and is closely related to intonation, which will be the topic of Lesson Twelve.

Word stress in many languages is fairly predictable, i.e. it is governed by rules that apply to almost the entire vocabulary, or lexicon. These languages are said to have **fixed stress**, or to be fixed-stress languages. In French, for example, the stress usually falls on the last syllable, in Polish and Welsh on the last but one, and in Czech on the first. In other languages, word stress is more difficult to predict, i.e. it is rule-governed only to a very limited extent. These languages are said to have **free stress**, less commonly also called **movable stress**, or to be free-stress languages. English is a free-stress language. Although some linguists propose numerous rules which English word stress supposedly follows, these rules seem to have even more numerous exceptions, and thus give the impression that they do not do justice to the complexity of the phenomenon. English word stress is therefore best considered a feature of the individual word, and foreign learners must learn it as such. Nevertheless, there are some very broad tendencies that can be observed, relating to word origin, word class, and the presence of suffixes, as we shall see shortly. Before we look at these tendencies, however, we shall look at how word stress can be indicated in a phonetic transcription.

Stress in polysyllabic words can be indicated by a small, raised vertical line, [ˈ], just before the stressed syllable, as in the transcription [ˈlændɪŋ] for the word <u>lan</u>ding, and [ɑːˈtɪstɪk] for <u>ar</u>tistic. (In many older publications, however, the line is placed *after* the stressed syllable, as in [lænˈdɪŋ] or [ɑːtɪsˈtɪk].) If a word has two or more stressed syllables, the strongest stress is referred to as **primary stress** [*Hauptton*], and can be indicated in the way just described. The second-strongest stress is referred to as **secondary stress** [*Nebenton*], and can be indicated by a small, *lowered* vertical line, [ˌ], just before (or, in many older publications, after) the stressed syllable. Examples of transcriptions showing primary and secondary stress are [ˌfəʊtəˈɡræfɪk] for *photographic*, and [ˌvæksɪˈneɪʃn̩] for *vaccination*. The line used to indicate stress, irrespective of whether it is raised or lowered, is called a **stress mark** [*Betonungszeichen*]. A transcription that includes stress marks cannot, strictly speaking, be a purely phonemic transcription any more, and the transcribed text should therefore be enclosed in square brackets, [ ]. Some linguists also recognise a third-strongest stress, referred to as **tertiary stress**, but this need not concern us here. We recommend that, from now on, you indicate in your transcriptions only one stress per word (in words that have two or more stressed syllables, that would be the primary stress), but only if that stress is not predictable. For example, while the stress in *agree* [əɡriː] and *react* [riækt] is predictable (because the schwa and the intermediate *i*-sound cannot occur in stressed syllables), and therefore does not have to be indicated, the stress in *regard* [rɪˈɡɑːd] is *not* predictable (because both /ɪ/ and /ɑː/ can occur in stressed syllables), and therefore should be shown in the transcription.

As we have already said above, factors that influence stress are word origin, word class, and the presence of suffixes, but they influence stress only in non-compound words (not in words like *bookcase* and *home-made*, which are compounds). **Word origin** influences stress in that words of Germanic origin (mainly from Old English and Old Norse, the language of the early Scandinavians) tend to have first-syllable stress, as in *answer* [ɑːnsə] and *brotherhood* [ˈbrʌðəhʊd], while words of Romance origin (mainly from French and Latin) tend to have their stress on later syllables, as in *respond* [rɪˈspɒnd] and *fraternity* [frəˈtɜːnəti]. **Word class** influences stress in that nouns tend to have first-syllable stress, as in *present* [preznt] and *record* [ˈrekɔːd], while verbs tend to have second-syllable stress, as in *present* [prɪˈzent] and *record* [rɪˈkɔːd]. And the **presence of suffixes** influences stress in that some suffixes usually attract stress, other suffixes usually determine which of the syllables of a word carries (or carry) stress, and still other suffixes usually effect a shift in stress. For example, syllables containing the suffixes *-ee*, *-eer*, *-ese*, *-esque*, and *-ette* usually carry the (primary) stress regardless of which syllable was stressed before the suffix was added, as in *mountaineer* [maʊntəˈnɪə], derived from *mountain* [maʊntən], and *kitchenette* [kɪtʃɪˈnet], derived from *kitchen* [ˈkɪtʃɪn]. Syllables containing the suffix *-ate* also usually carry the stress (although in American English they usually don't) when they occur in disyllabic verbs, as in *dictate* [dɪkˈteɪt] and *frustrate* [frʌsˈtreɪt] (in American English [ˈdɪkteɪt] and [ˈfrʌstreɪt]); but in longer verbs, they carry secondary stress at most: In trisyllabic verbs, the (primary) stress is usually on the first syllable, as in *dominate* [ˈdɒmɪneɪt] and *fluctuate* [ˈflʌktʃueɪt]; and in four-syllable verbs, the (primary) stress is usually on the second syllable, as in *deliberate* [dɪˈlɪbəreɪt] and *facilitate* [fəˈsɪlɪteɪt]. And the suffixes *-ial*, *-(i)an*, *-ic*, and *-ity* usually shift the stress from the syllable that carried the stress before the suffix was added to the syllable immediately preceding the suffix, as in *tutorial* [tjuːˈtɔːriəl], derived from *tutor* [tjuːtə], and *climatic* [klaɪˈmætɪk], derived from *climate* [klaɪmət]. (Note that suffixes may extend over two syllables: This is the case in *tuto<u>ri</u>al* [tjuː-ˈtɔːr-i-əl], but not, for example, in *off<u>ici</u>al* [ə-fɪʃ-l̩].) There are also suffixes, however, that do *not* usually influence stress at all. Among such stress-neutral suffixes are *-ish*, *-ism*, *-ite*, *-less*, *-ment*, *-ness*, *-ous*, and *-y*. They usually keep the stress on the same syllable that carried the stress before the suffix was added, as in *in<u>volve</u>ment* [ɪnˈvɒlvmənt], derived from *in<u>volve</u>* [ɪnˈvɒlv], and *<u>moun</u>tainous* [maʊntənəs], derived from *<u>moun</u>tain* [maʊntən].

As we have already seen above, the noun *<u>pre</u>sent* [preznt̩] and the verb *pre<u>sent</u>* [prɪˈzent], and the noun *<u>re</u>cord* [ˈrekɔːd] and the verb *re<u>cord</u>* [rɪˈkɔːd], are related disyllabic words with identical spelling, which are differentiated most obviously by their stress patterns, i.e. they have **contrastive stress**. Words that have the same spelling, but differ in meaning (and sometimes also in pronunciation), are termed **homographs**. English has several dozen pairs of related disyllabic homographs of this type, where the word with first-syllable stress is either a noun or an adjective (or both), and the word with second-syllable stress is a verb. Other examples are *abstract, conduct, contest, contract, contrast, decrease, desert, escort, export, import, increase, insult, perfect, rebel*, and *transfer*. Pairs of *un*related disyllabic homographs with contrastive stress, like the noun *<u>con</u>tent* [ˈkɒntent], 'subject matter of a book, speech, programme, etc.', and the adjective *con<u>tent</u>* [kənˈtent], 'satisfied with what one has', are rare, and so are pairs of unrelated disyllabic words whose pronunciation differs solely in their stress patterns, like *<u>bil</u>low* [ˈbɪləʊ] and *be<u>low</u>* [bɪˈləʊ].

EXERCISES

In this lesson, we discussed the role of syllabic consonants in the normal pronunciation of English: A syllabic consonant can occur in certain phonetic environments where, in very slow speech, there would be a schwa, or where we imagine there *could* be a schwa, as a syllable centre. The time needed to pronounce the (real or imaginary) schwa is then added to the duration of the following consonant, transforming that consonant into a syllabic consonant. As a syllabic consonant always forms the centre of a syllable, it has the phonological characteristics of a vowel, but, of course, retains the phonetic characteristics of a consonant. The syllabic consonants you will need to transcribe here are the syllabic [l] and the syllabic [n]. The other syllabic consonants occur much less frequently, and you do not need to consider them in your transcriptions. The occasional occurrence of syllabic [r] is noted in the model solutions at the end of the manual.

In the exercises up to this lesson, no stress marks were placed in the transcriptions. In fact, there have been few words where stress needed to be marked since nearly all the disyllabic words which have appeared up to now have schwa as one of their syllable centres, and schwa is always unstressed. Stress will fall on the other syllable in such cases. From now on, however, you should mark the stress of two-or-more-syllable words where the stress cannot be determined from the rules discussed in the lesson.

There are now two types of exercises for each lesson: transcription from a written text, and transcription from a spoken monologue or dialogue on the CD. Each spoken exercise is presented as a continuous text and then as a text with tracks to make it easier to break your listening down into shorter lengths. We recommend that you first listen to the whole recording for that lesson, then work on transcribing the shorter tracks.

From now on, we no longer annotate the following forms in the solutions unless there is a special reason for doing so: intermediate [i] and [u], regular plural, possessive case, third-person singular, regular past-tense, and regular past participle morphemes, and the letter sequence <ng>.

7.1 Transcribe the following text into IPA symbols

Joseph was seated on his balcony in the feeble illumination of the nearly extinguished sun. The day was no longer hot and exotic birds mingled with the dying rays, swooping after clouds of hovering midges. He looked out over the river raging in the valley filled with huge rocks below. The roar of gushing water deafened his ears and a fine spray permeated the cool air. Normally he mixes a drink, sits unperturbed and wishes away the hours. But this evening happened to be unlike any other evening.

"I've finished chapter seven," he thought "and written the beginning of section two."

He was supremely pleased, since his daily efforts for a good few months had often ended in disappointment and frustration. For some reason, the raw ideas he was toying with had formed themselves into a concrete and convincing whole that really worked.

"All I have to do is keep on going like this, in this perfect situation and I'll be finished by June next year."

166 words

Exercises

7.2 Transcribe the spoken monologue on the CD into IPA symbols
Track 1 and tracks 2-6

121 words

Lesson 8
Strong and Weak Forms

What are strong and weak forms?

Just as there are more prominent and less prominent sounds within a syllable, and more prominent and less prominent syllables within a word, there are also more prominent and less prominent words within an utterance or a sentence. You already know from the previous lesson that the prominence, or the stress, of some words in relation to others shapes the **sentence stress**. In the sentence *John had ordered a pint of beer*, for example, the words *John, ordered, pint*, and *beer* are normally stressed whereas *had, a*, and *of* are normally unstressed. The latter group of words would typically be pronounced /əd/, /ə/, and /əv/ although, when they occur in isolation, as citation forms, they are pronounced /hæd/, /eɪ/, and /ɒv/. There are a number of monosyllabic words in the English language, like *had, a*, and *of*, that can undergo a **reduction**, or **weakening**, of the vowel to /ə/ or /ɪ/, or an **omission**, technically termed **elision**, of one or more sounds, or both, when they occur in non-prominent positions. These changes are not normally represented in the spelling.

A **strong form**, then, is that pronunciation variant of a given word which contains a strong vowel, and from which no sounds have been omitted (or elided), like /hæd/, /eɪ/, and /ɒv/. Strong forms, like strong syllables, can occur in both prominent and non-prominent positions, i.e. they can be either stressed or unstressed. A **weak form**, on the other hand, is a pronunciation variant which contains a weak vowel, or from which one or more sounds have been omitted, or both, like /əd/, /ə/, and /əv/. Some words have more than one weak form: The word *had*, for example, has /həd/, /əd/, and /d/, and *of* has /əv/, /ə/, and /v/. The degree to which a word is weakened, or, in other words, the choice between two or more weak forms, depends on such factors as communicative situation and social class. Weak forms, like weak syllables, can occur only in non-prominent positions, i.e. they are always unstressed.

In the previous lesson, we encountered the reduction of vowels in isolated words, owing to a shift in stress. In this lesson, we shall see that reduction is also an aspect of **connected speech**, which we began to discuss in Lesson Six, and shall continue to discuss in Lesson Nine. In fact, you may have noticed that, in Lesson Six, we transcribed monosyllables such as *at* and *and* as /ət/ and /ən/, instead of /æt/ and /ænd/, in sequences like *not at all* [nɒt ə tɔːl] and *silly and stupid* [sɪliʲ ən stjuːpɪd].

Grammatical words

We said above that there are a number of monosyllabic words that have strong and weak forms. More specifically, these are words that primarily fulfil a grammatical function, but have little or no lexical content. (We might also say they have little or no "meaning" although this is not entirely correct because the term *meaning* includes both lexical and grammatical meaning.) Such a word is called a **grammatical word**, or **function word** [*Funktionswort*], less commonly also **form word**, **structural word**, **structure word**, **empty word**, or **functor**. In terms of word classes, grammatical words comprise determiners (including articles), pronouns, prepositions (including particles), conjunctions, auxiliary verbs, and a few adverbs, such as *not* and *there*. With the exception of adverbs, these word classes are **closed**, i.e. the number of words they contain is limited and largely fixed, and new words are rarely or never added. (Numerals and interjections are closed word classes as well, but they are not counted among the grammatical words.)

By contrast, a word that does have lexical content (or "meaning") is called a **lexical word**, or **content word** [*Inhaltswort*]. Lexical words comprise nouns, full (or lexical) verbs, adjectives, and the vast majority of adverbs. These word classes are **open**, i.e. the number of words they contain is, in principle, unlimited because new words are continually added.

All determiners, pronouns, prepositions, conjunctions, and auxiliary verbs are grammatical words, but not all of them have strong and weak forms. The words *it* and *mine*, for example, are both pronouns, but each has only one form: /ɪt/ and /maɪn/. Furthermore, many grammatical words are polysyllabic, like the preposition *above* /əbʌv/ and the conjunction *whereas* /weəræz/, and therefore (theoretically) cannot have strong and weak forms although there is the occasional exception, like the conjunction *because*, which has the strong form /bɪkɒz/ and the weak forms /bɪkəz/ and /kəz/. The number of grammatical words that do have strong and weak forms is usually put at around fifty.

The distribution of strong and weak forms

You already know that strong forms can occur in both prominent and non-prominent positions, i.e. they can be either stressed or unstressed, and that weak forms can occur only in non-prominent positions, i.e. they are always unstressed. This means that prominent positions are always occupied by strong forms while non-prominent positions can be occupied by either strong or weak forms. As grammatical words usually do not express most of the message of an utterance, they are not often made prominent through stress. On the contrary, they usually (but not always) occur in non-prominent positions, and are therefore usually unstressed. Although we have just noted that non-prominent positions can be occupied by either strong or weak forms, weak forms are much more common – so common, in fact, that they can be regarded as the "usual" pronunciation variants. When discussing the distribution of strong and weak forms, it is therefore sufficient to describe the relatively few environments in which strong forms usually occur. In all other environments, weak forms predominate.

Strong and weak forms

The rules governing the occurrence of strong (and weak) forms are not hard and fast, but they may serve as a general guideline for foreign learners, and for your transcriptions. Strong forms usually occur in the following environments:

- in isolation, as in *Who?* /huː/ (as opposed to *I wonder who did it* /hʊ/);
- when being quoted, as in *I said "of", not "off"* /ɒv/ (as opposed to *He is a friend of mine* /əv/);
- at the end of a phrase or sentence, as in *What are you looking at?* /æt/ (as opposed to *I am looking at the wall* /ət/);
- as the first of two consecutive auxiliary verbs without a full verb, as in *I would have* /wʊd/ (as opposed to *I would have liked it* /wəd/);
- in coordinations, as in *He travels to and from London a lot* /tuː, frɒm/ (as opposed to *He travels to London* /tə/ and *He travels from London* /frəm/);
- in contrasts, as in *I have a message from Ike, not for Ike* /frɒm, fɔːr/ (as opposed to *I have a message from Ike* /frəm/ and *I have a message for Ike* /fər/);
- and when used to emphasise a particular aspect of the message for whatever reason, as in *London is the place to be* /ðiː/ (as opposed to *London is the place where I met my wife* /ðə/).

The forms

This section lists frequently used grammatical words that have strong and weak forms, and it lists the transcriptions of these forms as they are pronounced in RP. Several of the transcriptions of the weak forms are enclosed in square brackets because these transcriptions indicate the intermediate [i] and [u]. The annotations following the list include more detailed information on the specific distribution of some of the forms than was given in the previous section, which was restricted to fairly general rules. It is important to note that words which belong to more than one word class only have weak forms when they are indeed used as grammatical words. The word *can*, for example, has no weak form when it is used as a noun, as in *a can of fish* /kæn/, or as a full verb, as in *The factories along the coast can fish* /kæn/, but it does have a weak form when it is used as an auxiliary verb, as in *I can see* /kən/.

	strong form	weak form(s)
a [1]	/eɪ/	/ə/
am [2] [3]	/æm/	/(ə)m/
an [1] [3]	/æn/	/(ə)n/
and [3]	/ænd/	/(ə)n(d)/
are [1] [2] [3]	/ɑː(r)/	/ər, ə, r/
as	/æz/	/əz/
at	/æt/	/ət/
be [2]	/biː/	/bɪ/, [bi]
because	/bɪkɒz/	/(bɪ)kəz/

	strong form	weak form(s)
been [2]	/biːn/	/bɪn/
but	/bʌt/	/bət/
can [2][3]	/kæn/	/k(ə)n/
could [2][3]	/kʊd/	/k(ə)d/
do [2][3][4]	/duː/	/də, dʊ, d/, [du]
does [2][3][5]	/dʌz/	/dəz, z, s/
for [1][3]	/fɔː(r)/	/fə(r), fr/
from [3]	/frɒm/	/fr(ə)m/
had [2][3][6]	/hæd/	/(h)əd, d/
has [2][3][5][6]	/hæz/	/(h)əz, z, s/
have [2][3][6]	/hæv/	/(h)əv, ə, v/
he [6][7]	/hiː/	/(h)ɪ, iː/, [(h)i]
her [1][6][7]	/hɜː(r)/	/(h)ə(r), ɜː(r)/
him [6][7]	/hɪm/	/ɪm/
his [6]	/hɪz/	/ɪz/
is [2][3][5]	/ɪz/	/z, s/
me	/miː/	/mɪ/, [mi]
must [1][2]	/mʌs(t)/	/məs(t)/
not [3]	/nɒt/	/n(t)/
of [3]	/ɒv/	/əv, ə, v/
shall [2][3]	/ʃæl/	/ʃ(ə)l/
she [7]	/ʃiː/	/ʃɪ/, [ʃi]
should [2][3]	/ʃʊd/	/ʃ(ə)d/
so	/səʊ/	/sə/
some [3][8]	/sʌm/	/s(ə)m/
such	/sʌtʃ/	/sətʃ/
than [3]	/ðæn/	/ð(ə)n/
that [9]	/ðæt/	/ðət/
the [4]	/ðiː/	/ðə, ðɪ/, [ði]
them [3][7]	/ðem/	/(ð)əm, m/
there [1][7][10]	/ðeə(r)/	/ðə(r)/
they	/ðeɪ/	/ðə/
to [4][7]	/tuː/	/tə, tʊ/, [tu]
us [3][7]	/ʌs/	/(ə)s/
was [2]	/wɒz/	/wəz/
we [7]	/wiː/	/wɪ/, [wi]
were [1][2]	/wɜː(r)/	/wə(r)/
who [6]	/huː/	/(h)ʊ, uː/, [(h)u]
will [2][3]	/wɪl/	/(ə)l/
would [2][3]	/wʊd/	/(w)əd, d/
you [7]	/juː/	/jʊ/, [ju]
your [1]	/jɔː(r)/	/jə(r)/

Strong and weak forms

Annotations:

(1) The strong and weak forms of several grammatical words end in a linking sound, i.e. a sound that is absent when the word is pronounced in isolation, but present in certain phonetic environments in connected speech. A case in point is the indefinite article *a* and its variant *an*: The former occurs only before consonants, the latter only before vowels. It is probably the most prominent example because here the absence or presence of the linking sound, /n/, is represented in the spelling through separate word forms (which is the reason why they appear as separate entries in the above list). In most cases, however, the linking sound is a linking *r* (which was discussed in detail in Lesson Six), as in *are, for, her, there, were,* and *your*. A related case is that of *must*: The final /t/ is a kind of linking sound because it is usually absent before consonants, and present before vowels, as in *He must go* /məs/ and *He must eat* /məst/. But it differs from other linking sounds in that it is always present when *must* is pronounced in isolation.

(2) The auxiliary verbs *am, are, be, been, can, could, do, does, had, has, have, is, must, shall, should, was, were, will,* and *would* are usually used in their strong forms when they occur in negations with *not*, as in *are not* /ɑː nɒt/, *cannot* /kænɒt/, and *have not* /hæv nɒt/. The same is true of these auxiliary verbs when they occur in contracted negations with *-n't*, as in *aren't* /ɑːnt/ and *haven't* [hævn̩t] (remember that the syllabic [n̩] typically occurs after plosives and fricatives). But *can, do, shall,* and *will* have separate strong forms specifically for this construction, which combine with *-n't* /nt/ to form *can't* /kɑːnt/, *don't* /dəʊnt/, *shan't* /ʃɑːnt/, and *won't* /wəʊnt/. The auxiliary verbs are of course *not* used in their strong forms – irrespective of whether they occur in negations or not – when they themselves are contracted, as in *I've* /aɪv/ (for *I have*) and *he's* /hiːz/ (for *he is*). Here they are used in their weak forms, and, as an exception to the rule, these weak forms are, or rather can be, represented in the spelling.

(3) The words *am, an, and, are, can, could, do, does, for, from, had, has, have, is, not, of, shall, should, some, than, them, us, will,* and *would* can be weakened to a degree where there is no vowel left. The remaining consonant or one of the remaining consonants may be non-syllabic (e.g. the /v/ of the word *have* in *I've* /aɪv/), or, in the case of /l, n, m, r/, it may be syllabic (e.g. the /n/ of the word *not* in *haven't* [hævn̩t]), depending on the phonetic environment and the individual pronunciation. The weak forms of *an* and *are*, then, may consist merely of a linking sound, and that of *for* may consist of the initial consonant plus a linking sound, but of course only when followed by a vowel, as in *they're excellent* /ðər eksələnt/. In a transcription, as we have seen here and under (2) above, a weak form without a vowel is normally attached to the preceding word.

(4) The words *do, the,* and *to* each have a weak form that ends in a schwa, and one that ends in an *i-* or *u-*sound (either /ɪ/ or /ʊ/, or [i] or [u], depending on the actual pronunciation and the type of transcription). The weak form ending in a schwa occurs before consonants, as in *the door* /ðə dɔː/ and *to go* /tə ɡəʊ/, and that ending in an *i-* or *u-*sound occurs before vowels, as in *the end* [ði end] and *to eat* [tu iːt].

(5) The words *does*, *has*, and *is* each have two weak forms that consist of a single sound: /z/, as in *there's* /ðəz/, and /s/, as in *it's* /ɪts/. While the former is an unaltered remnant of the strong forms (/dʌz/, /hæz/, and /ɪz/), the latter is a result of the process of assimilation, which will be discussed in the next lesson.

(6) The weak forms of *had*, *has*, *have*, *he*, and *her* usually drop their initial /h/ except when they occur at the beginning of a sentence. In principle, this is also true of the weak form(s) of *who*, but the dropping of the /h/ here is not quite so common. The weak forms of *him* and *his* do not have an initial /h/ at all. When these words occur at the beginning of a sentence, they are therefore always used in their strong forms, with an /h/. In the case of *his*, the occurrence of the weak form is further restricted by word class: The weak form is used only as a determiner, i.e. when followed by a noun, as in *I like his car* /ɪz/, but never as a pronoun, i.e. when replacing a noun, as in *This car is his* /hɪz/.

(7) Although we said in the previous section that strong forms usually occur (among other positions) at the end of a phrase or sentence (and, by extension, weak forms usually don't), the weak forms of *he*, *her*, *him*, *she*, *them*, *there*, *to*, *us*, *we*, and *you* also commonly occur in that environment, as in *I've met her* /ə/ and *We saw all of them* /ðəm/, typically also in question tags, such as *wasn't he?* /ɪ/ and *aren't we?* /wɪ/.

(8) The word *some* is always used in its strong form when it is a pronoun, as in *Some like it hot* /sʌm/, or a determiner referring to certain members of a group or certain types of a thing, but not all of them, as in *Some people like it hot* /sʌm/. It can only be used in its weak form when it is a determiner referring to an unspecified quantity, as in *There are some people waiting outside* /səm/.

(9) The word *that* is always used in its strong form when it is a determiner, as in *Look at that car!* /ðæt/, or a demonstrative pronoun, as in *Look at that!* /ðæt/. It can only be used in its weak form when it is a relative pronoun, as in *This is the car that was looked at* /ðət/, or a conjunction, as in *She said that she had looked at the car* /ðət/.

(10) The word *there* is always used in its strong form when it is an adverb of place, as in *Look over there!* /ðeə/. It is always used in its weak form when it is an existential *there* (i.e. a dummy subject plus a form of *be*), as in *There's no place like home* /ðə/.

We said earlier in this lesson that words which have strong and weak forms are primarily grammatical words. Two examples of lexical words with strong and weak forms are the nouns *saint* /seɪnt, s(ə)n(t)/ and *sir* /sɜː(r), sə(r)/. The former is used in its weak form(s) mainly in British English when it is part of proper names, as in *St. Andrews* /sənt ændruːz/. In American English, the strong (but unstressed) form is more typical in proper names, as in *St. Louis* /seɪnt luːɪs/.

Finally, it is important to emphasise that weak forms are *not* per se a feature of careless or perhaps even sloppy speech. Although they may be slightly more common in informal situations, they are a typical feature of any kind of spoken English.

Exercises

EXERCISES

In this lesson, we have discussed strong and weak forms, and considered their distribution. Remember that strong and weak forms have been included in our transcriptions from the start, but now you can transcribe them with more certainty. The following exercises focus on strong and weak forms while continuing to practise features that you are now familiar with from the previous lessons. Remember always to mark linking *r* and intrusive *r*, the syllabic consonants [l̩] and [n̩], and stress in polysyllabic words when it cannot be determined from the rules you have learnt.

8.1 Transcribe the following dialogue into IPA symbols

A: "There is little time to lose. Come on, we must hurry. The train leaves in half an hour."

B: "Don't panic, we'll easily get there by taxi. I've just rung for one now."

A: "I had told Jeffrey we'd be there on time for once. Judging from the traffic this morning we should be leaving more or less now. You never know what can happen on the way to the station."

B: "You know what Jeffrey says though; he decided that he would do exactly what he always wanted on this holiday. So no rush; no hassle; no pressurizing."

A: "Yes, but if we're not there by ten, that's precisely how he'll be feeling. And unpredictability of the traffic is the flaw in your plans."

B: "Do stop meddling with Jeffrey's affairs; I'm sure he can manage perfectly well on his own."

137 words

8.2 Transcribe the spoken monologue on the CD into IPA symbols

Track 7 and tracks 8–12

111 words

LESSON 9
CONNECTED SPEECH, CONTD.

The aspects of connected speech discussed so far are **linking**, in Lesson Six, and **strong and weak forms**, in Lesson Eight. It was seen that the latter is closely interrelated with the **reduction** of vowels, or the **elision** of sounds, or both. (We also encountered the reduction of vowels, albeit in isolated words, in Lesson Seven.) In this lesson, then, we shall discuss further aspects of connected speech, namely **rhythm** and **assimilation**, and we shall look at **elision** more systematically.

Rhythm

What is rhythm?

The **rhythm** of a language is the recurrence of prominent elements of speech at what are perceived to be regular intervals of time. Depending on the particular language, the prominent elements are usually either stresses or syllables, but they can also be high pitches, for example, as is the case in many oriental languages. Yet whatever the prominent elements are, the time that passes from one prominent element to the next is always of approximately equal duration. The type of rhythm is a characteristic suprasegmental feature, or prosodic feature, of the pronunciation of any given language, and therefore forms the basis for one of the fundamental categorisations of the languages of the world.

Two types of rhythm

If the prominent elements that determine the rhythm of a language are stresses, as is the case in English, Russian, and Modern Greek, we speak of a **stress-timed language**, or of an **isochronous rhythm**, or simply of **stress-timing**, or **isochrony** or **isochronism** (pronounced [aɪˈsɒkrəni, -nɪzəm, -nəs]) [from Greek *ísos*, 'equal', and *khrónos*, 'time'; *Isochronie*]. In stress-timed languages, then, strong stresses tend to occur at relatively equal intervals of time, irrespective of the number of the lesser-stressed syllables or words between them. In other words, the amount of time between strong stresses is always roughly the same, and the more intervening lesser-stressed syllables or words there are, the faster they are pronounced in order to fit them into the time span available.

The distance beginning with (and including) a strong stress and ending right before (and excluding) the next strong stress is called a **foot** (a term more commonly used in the study of poetry). That all feet are of approximately equal duration in English can be illustrated by sentences (1), (2), and (3) below, where word-internal syllable boundaries are indicated by hyphens, foot boundaries by vertical lines, and strong stresses appear in italics:

(1) *What* are the | *plans* for to- | -*morr*-ow, | *John*?
(2) *All* of these are | *old* | *phot*-o-graphs.
(3) The | *con*-se-quen-ces of his | *ac*-tion are | *ob*-vi-ous.

(The first foot of a sentence sometimes begins with a pause, as in (3). *The*, here, is comparable to an upbeat in a piece of music.) If these sentences are read aloud, we see that *What are the* in (1), for example, occupies approximately the same amount of time as *John*. Likewise, *All of these are* in (2) is of more or less equal duration as *old*, and *consequences of his* in (3) sounds roughly as long as *obvious*. It follows that the tempo of pronunciation of the three syllables of *What are the* is greater than that of the monosyllable *John*, the tempo of pronunciation of the four syllables of *All of these are* is greater than that of the monosyllable *old*, and the tempo of pronunciation of the six syllables of *consequences of his* is greater than that of the three syllables of *obvious*. The fact that one foot can contain two, three, or four times as many syllables as another foot in the same sentence can be achieved through **compression**, i.e. through the reduction of vowels and the elision of sounds in unstressed syllables, and consequently also through the use of weak forms of grammatical words, like *are*, *the*, *for*, *of*, and *his*. Without reduction and weak forms, an isochronous rhythm would be impossible to maintain.

If, on the other hand, the prominent elements that determine the rhythm of a language are syllables (both stressed and unstressed), as is the case in French, Spanish, and Japanese, we speak of a **syllable-timed language**, or of an **isosyllabic rhythm**, or simply of **syllable-timing**, or **isosyllabicity** or **isosyllabism** (pronounced [aɪsəsɪləˈbɪsɪti, -ˈsɪləbɪzəm, -sɪˈlæbɪk]) [from Greek *ísos*, 'equal', and *sullabé*, 'taken, brought, or put together'; *Isosyllabismus*]. In syllable-timed languages, then, all syllables tend to occur at relatively equal intervals of time, irrespective of whether they are stressed or unstressed (thus creating a *rat-a-tat-a-tat* impression that has also been described as a "'machine-gun' effect"). In other words, the amount of time taken to pronounce a syllable is always roughly the same, and since generally no syllables or words are pronounced faster than others, there is *no* necessity for compression. This type of rhythm is also characteristic of the pronunciation of some second-language varieties of English, for example those spoken in sub-Saharan Africa and India, owing to the influence of local mother tongues. The resultant lack of reduction, elision, and weak forms in such varieties might, at first sight, seem to make the pronunciation clearer. Yet by distorting the natural, isochronous rhythm of English, second-language varieties (largely) sacrifice those parts of the message of an utterance that are (mainly) expressed by strong stresses, and thereby reduce intelligibility (at least for native speakers).

We said above that the prominent elements that determine the rhythm of a language are "perceived" to recur, or "tend" to recur, at "relatively" equal intervals of time. As the tentative wording suggests, stress-timing and syllable-timing (and other, rarer types of rhythm not discussed here) are more an ideal than a reality. We often speak arhythmically, i.e. with a very low degree of rhythmicality or without any rhythm at all, for example when we are hesitant or excited. Given the many variations heard in speech, the types of rhythm can only indicate very general tendencies, not absolute distinctions. Nevertheless, the subjective impression of characteristic rhythmic patterns remains.

Assimilation

What is assimilation?

The fact that, in stress-timed languages like English, several syllables may have to be fitted into a relatively short time span requires various means of making the pronunciation easier (and thus faster). Among them are not only the processes of reduction and elision, but also a process whereby one sound, usually a consonant, becomes more like, or identical with, a neighbouring sound regarding one or more of the distinctive features (which were discussed in detail in Lessons Two, Three, and Four). More specifically, the articulation of one sound is influenced by the articulation of a neighbouring sound in that a speech organ either prolongs a distinctive feature of a preceding sound or anticipates a distinctive feature of a following sound. This process is called **assimilation** [from Latin *assimilatio*, 'making one thing like another'].

For example, you know that /n/ is an alveolar sound, i.e. its place of articulation is the bony ridge behind the upper teeth, and /p/ is a bilabial sound, i.e. its place of articulation is the lips. When producing the /n/ in a sequence like *ten pigs*, however, the lips, which are not primarily involved in the production of /n/, often anticipate the place of articulation of the following /p/, thus changing the /n/ into a bilabial sound. The new place of articulation is identical with the place of articulation of /m/ (/m/ is also a bilabial), and since the intensity and manner of articulation of /n/ and /m/ are also identical (both are lenis nasals), the /n/ now sounds like /m/, or we could say that the /n/ has been substituted with /m/. The sequence *ten pigs*, then, is often pronounced [tem pɪgz] instead of /ten pɪgz/. (Note that the former transcription is enclosed in square brackets because, even though it only contains symbols representing phonemes, the assimilation suggests actual, concrete speech, rather than an idealised utterance.)

Like reduction and elision, assimilation is not per se a feature of careless or perhaps even sloppy speech, but a typical feature of any kind of spoken English. Its degree and frequency, however, usually depend to a greater extent than is the case with reduction and elision on such factors as tempo of pronunciation, communicative situation, and social class. In other words, assimilation goes much further and is much more common in rapid speech, in informal situations, and in working-class accents than in slow speech, formal situations, and upper-class accents.

Assimilation frequently occurs across word boundaries, as when *ten pigs* is pronounced [tem pɪgz], but it can also occur within a word, as when the plural *-s* in *pigs* is pronounced /z/, thus prolonging the intensity of articulation, or the voicing, of the preceding lenis consonant, /g/. If assimilation occurs within a word, the resultant pronunciation is often the only possible standard, as in *pigs* /pɪgz/. It is sometimes difficult to say, however, whether assimilation within a word can be considered an aspect of connected speech, especially when, as in *pigs* /pɪgz/, it occurs even if the word is spoken in isolation. The position taken in this manual is that, because assimilation is an important means of making the pronunciation easier, and consequently of maintaining the natural, isochronous rhythm of English, it should be considered an aspect of connected speech not only when it occurs across word boundaries, but also usually when it occurs within a word.

Various types of assimilation

Assimilation can be described in terms of four (hierarchically unrelated) categorisations, based on the distance between the two sounds involved, the direction of the influence exerted, the particular distinctive feature affected, and the degree to which one sound assimilates to another.

The first categorisation (although there is of course no logical order) distinguishes (a) assimilation between two consecutive sounds, called **contiguous assimilation**, or **contact assimilation** [*Kontaktassimilation*], from (b) assimilation between two sounds further apart, known as **non-contiguous assimilation**, or **distance assimilation**, or **distant assimilation** [*Fernassimilation*].

(a) The former type, illustrated by our two examples *ten pigs* [tem pɪgz] and *pigs* /pɪgz/, is so much more common in English that we were able to say in the preceding section that assimilation makes one sound more like "a neighbouring sound", implying that assimilation is *always* contiguous. This is, strictly speaking, not quite correct, but (b) non-contiguous assimilation is so rare in English that it can safely be neglected. One example that is cited in some linguistic textbooks is the idiom *turn up trumps*, in which the /n/ in *turn* is supposedly sometimes articulated bilabially, as /m/, under the influence of the later bilabial sounds /p/ and /m/. The example could probably also be taken to show, however, that non-contiguous assimilation, if indeed it occurs, is barely distinguishable from a simple slip of the tongue.

The second categorisation distinguishes between (a) assimilation brought about by the influence of a preceding sound, called **progressive assimilation** [*vorauswirkende Assimilation*], or **perseverative assimilation**, (b) assimilation brought about by the influence of a following sound, known as **regressive assimilation** [*rückwirkende Assimilation*], or **anticipatory assimilation**, and (c) assimilation brought about by the influence of two sounds upon each other, termed **coalescent assimilation**, or **reciprocal assimilation** [*reziproke Assimilation*], or **mutual assimilation**.

(a) Progressive assimilation within a word largely determines the choice between the various endings for the regular plural, the possessive case, the third-person singular, the regular past tense, and the regular past participle (which were all described in detail in Lesson Five). This can be illustrated by our familiar example *pigs* /pɪgz/, but also by words like *dentist's* /dentɪsts/, *goes* /gəʊz/, *looked* /lʊkt/, and *turned* /tɜːnd/, where the choice between /s/ and /z/, or /t/ and /d/, is influenced by the intensity of articulation, or by the voicing, of the respective preceding sounds.

Progressive assimilation across word boundaries can be illustrated by sequences like *shut your mouth* and *Church Street*. In the former, the /j/ in *your* can become identical with the preceding /t/ in *shut* regarding its intensity of articulation, and it can become more like the /t/ regarding its place and manner of articulation: The /j/ can be articulated with more force, slightly further forward, and with a narrower gap between the speech organs, thus changing from a lenis palatal approximant to a fortis palatoalveolar fricative. In other words, the /j/ can be substituted with /ʃ/, and the whole sequence would then be pronounced [ʃʌt ʃə mauθ]. In the latter, the /s/ in *Street* can become identical with the preceding /tʃ/ in *Church* regarding its place of articulation, while its intensity and manner of articulation remain unchanged: The /s/ can be articulated slightly further back, thus changing from a fortis alveolar fricative to a fortis palatoalveolar fricative. In other words, the /s/ can again be substituted with /ʃ/, and the whole sequence would then be pronounced [tʃɜːtʃ ʃtriːt]. As these examples suggest, progressive assimilation across word boundaries is not very common.

(b) Regressive assimilation across word boundaries occurs much more often. In the most typical case, the place of articulation of a word-final alveolar consonant is influenced by that of a following, word-initial consonant. This can be illustrated by our original example *ten pigs* [tem pɪgz], but also by sequences like *that case*, when it is pronounced [ðæk‿keɪs], where the /t/ in *that* is articulated further back, thus changing to /k/, and *good boy*, when it is pronounced [gʊb‿bɔɪ], where the /d/ in *good* is articulated further forward, thus changing to /b/. If an assimilation process results in two identical sounds, as in the last two examples, the two sounds are usually pronounced as one, but with greater duration, and are then transcribed with a lowered, swung horizontal line, [‿], connecting them. In another typical case, it is the intensity of articulation, or the voicing, that is influenced. This can be illustrated by the sequences *have to*, when it is pronounced [hæf tə], and *I've seen*, when it is pronounced [aɪf siːn], where the /v/ in *have* and *I've* is articulated with more force, or less voicing, as /f/, under the influence of the following fortis /t/ and /s/, respectively.

Regressive assimilation within a word can be illustrated by words like *statement*, when it is pronounced [steɪpmənt], where the second /t/ changes to /p/ under the influence of the place of articulation of the following /m/, and *width*, when it is pronounced [wɪt̪θ], where the /d/ changes to /t/ under the influence of the intensity of articulation, or the voicing, of the following /θ/.

(c) Coalescent assimilation always merges two sounds to form a single, new sound, or rather phoneme. The new phoneme is often an affricate, and it is therefore important to remember, here, that an affricate, although it consists of two elements, is conventionally analysed as one unit. If coalescent assimilation occurs across word boundaries, the two words involved are usually transcribed without a space between them. All this can be illustrated by the sequences *don't you* /dəʊnt jʊ/, where the /t/ and the /j/ can merge into /tʃ/, resulting in the pronunciation [dəʊntʃu], *could you* /kʊd jʊ/, where the /d/ and the /j/ can merge into /dʒ/, resulting in the pronunciation [kʊdʒu], and *What d'you want?* /wɒt djʊ wɒnt/, where the /d/ and the /j/ can merge into /ʃ/, resulting in the pronunciation [wɒt ʃʊ wɒnt]. The sequence *shut your mouth*, used to illustrate progressive assimilation above, might also be added here, which shows that the distinction between progressive assimilation and coalescent assimilation is sometimes unclear and possibly arbitrary.

Coalescent assimilation within a word can be illustrated by the words *intuition* /ɪntjuːɪʃn/, where the /t/ and the /j/ can merge into /tʃ/, resulting in the pronunciation [ɪntʃuːˈɪʃn̩], and *duel* /djuːəl/, where the /d/ and the /j/ can merge into /dʒ/, resulting in the pronunciation [dʒuːəl]. Coalescent assimilation is often regarded as *very* colloquial or even non-standard except when it constitutes a historical sound change that took place within a word, and is now firmly established. This can be illustrated by the words *picture*, which used to be pronounced with internal /tj/ before the two sounds merged into the single phoneme /tʃ/, *soldier*, which used to be pronounced with internal /dj/ before the two sounds merged into /dʒ/, and *sugar*, which used to be pronounced with initial /sj/ before the two sounds merged into /ʃ/. When /t, d, s/ or /z/ merges with /j/ – either across word boundaries or within a word – to form /tʃ, dʒ, ʃ/ or /ʒ/, respectively, we speak of **yod coalescence**.

The third categorisation distinguishes between (a) assimilation regarding the intensity of articulation, in short **assimilation of intensity**, (b) assimilation regarding the place of articulation, in short **assimilation of place**, and (c) assimilation regarding the manner of articulation, in short **assimilation of manner**. All three types have already been illustrated by examples given earlier in this section.

(a) Assimilation of intensity across word boundaries usually results in a fortis, or voiceless, sound, and is typically regressive, as we saw in *have to*, where the lenis /v/ can change to fortis /f/ under the influence of the following fortis /t/, and *I've seen*, where the lenis /v/ can change to fortis /f/ under the influence of the following fortis /s/. But it can also be progressive, as we saw in *shut your mouth*, where the lenis /j/ can change to fortis /ʃ/ under the influence of the preceding fortis /t/. This kind of assimilation is often not very noticeable because, as you know from Lessons Two and Five, some lenis (voiced) sounds are at least partly devoiced in word-initial and word-final positions anyway. The word *have*, for example, is often fully devoiced at the end even when it is pronounced in isolation.

Assimilation of intensity within a word, as was seen earlier in this section, determines the choice between /s/ and /z/, or /t/ and /d/, as endings for the regular plural, the possessive case, the third-person singular, the regular past tense, and the regular past participle. We encountered a similar phenomenon within certain contractions (which can legitimately be regarded as single words) in the previous lesson, when we said that the grammatical words *does*, *has*, and *is* each have two weak forms that consist merely of /s/, as in *it's* /ɪts/, and /z/, as in *there's* /ðəz/. The choice, here, between /s/ and /z/ is again determined by the intensity of articulation, or the voicing, of the preceding sound.

It is difficult to say whether assimilation of intensity affects only voicing, or whether it affects also the force with which the air-stream is pushed up. Voicing, as you know from Lessons Two and Four, is closely connected with the lenis/fortis contrast of consonants, but not with the lax/tense contrast of vowels (which are usually voiced). It might be seen as one aspect of intensity, but it is strictly speaking not a distinctive feature in its own right. If assimilation of intensity affects only voicing, the sequence *have to*, for example, is best transcribed as [hæv̥ tə], with a small circle indicating a devoiced /v/. If it affects also the force of the air-stream, we can postulate a complete substitution of phonemes, and transcribe *have to* as [hæf tə]. But this subtle distinction need not concern us here.

(b) Assimilation of place typically occurs across word boundaries, is regressive, and affects alveolar consonants, as we saw in *ten pigs*, where the alveolar /n/ can be articulated further forward under the influence of the following bilabial /p/, thus changing to bilabial /m/, *good boy*, where the alveolar /d/ can be articulated further forward under the influence of the following bilabial /b/, thus becoming identical with /b/, and *that case*, where the alveolar /t/ can be articulated further back under the influence of the following velar /k/, thus becoming identical with /k/. There are of course also other, less typical cases of assimilation of place, as we saw in *shut your mouth*, where the palatal /j/ can be articulated slightly further forward (and undergo other alterations) under the influence of the preceding alveolar /t/, thus changing to palatoalveolar /ʃ/, *Church Street*, where the alveolar /s/ can be articulated slightly further back under the influence of the preceding palatoalveolar /tʃ/, thus changing to palatoalveolar /ʃ/, and *statement*, where the second alveolar /t/ can be articulated further forward under the influence of the following bilabial /m/, thus changing to bilabial /p/.

(c) Assimilation of manner is usually heard only in very rapid speech, or very informal situations. The only example we have encountered so far was in *shut your mouth*, where the approximant /j/ can be articulated with a narrower gap between the speech organs (and undergo other alterations) under the influence of the preceding plosive /t/, thus changing to fricative /ʃ/. Another case of progressive assimilation of manner affects a word-initial fricative /ð/ when it is preceded by a word-final plosive or nasal. In that environment, the /ð/ can again be articulated with a narrower gap between the speech organs, and become identical with the preceding sound, but both sounds together are then usually fronted, or, more specifically, dentalised (a process that was described in detail in the section "Fronting and retraction" in Lesson Five). This can be illustrated by the sequences *get them* /get ðəm/, when it is pronounced [get̪ t̪əm], and *in the* /ɪn ðə/, when it is pronounced [ɪn̪ n̪ə]. In general, however, assimilation of manner tends to be regressive, and to result in a sound that is articulated with a *wider* gap between the speech organs, i.e. with less obstruction of air. This can be illustrated by the sequences *that side*, when it is pronounced [ðæs saɪd], where the plosive /t/ becomes fricative /s/, and *good night*, when it is pronounced [gʊn naɪt], where the plosive /d/ becomes nasal /n/.

The fourth categorisation distinguishes between (a) **partial assimilation**, where the two sounds involved remain distinguishable through at least one of the distinctive features, and (b) **total assimilation**, where the two sounds involved become wholly identical. These two types, too, have already been illustrated by examples given earlier in this section.

(a) We saw partial assimilation in *ten pigs* [tem pɪgz], for example, where the original /n/ has become identical with the following /p/ regarding the place of articulation, but still differs from it in the intensity and manner of articulation, *shut your mouth* [ʃʌt ʃə maʊθ], where the original /j/ has become identical with the preceding /t/ regarding the intensity of articulation, has become more like it regarding the place and manner of articulation, but still differs from it in those two respects, and *I've seen* [aɪf siːn], where the original /v/ has become identical with the following /s/ regarding the intensity of articulation, has always been identical with it regarding the manner of articulation, but still differs from it in the place of articulation.

(b) We saw total assimilation only in *that case* [ðæk‿keɪs] and *good boy* [gʊb‿bɔɪ], where the original /t/ and /d/ have become identical with the following /k/ and /b/ regarding the place of articulation, and have always been identical with them regarding the intensity and manner of articulation. In both cases, the two sounds involved are now wholly identical.

Admittedly, it could be seen as naive to regard changes like the one from /n/ to /m/ in the sequence *ten pigs*, for example, as substitutions of phonemes, as we have throughout this and the previous section. Many linguists would regard the [n] and [m] here as radically different allophones of the same /n/ phoneme. In that approach, then, all the examples given above illustrate not only assimilation, but also allophonic variation.

The opposite of assimilation: Dissimilation

A process whereby, conversely, one sound becomes *less* like a neighbouring sound or a sound in close proximity is called **dissimilation** [from Latin *dissimilatio,* 'making something unrecognisable']. The purpose of making two similar or identical sounds different from each other is, as before, to achieve greater ease of pronunciation, but also greater clarity. (Just think of the difficulty of pronouncing the accumulation of similar or identical consonants in tongue-twisters, like *truly rural* or *She sells seashells on the seashore*.) Dissimilation has played an important part in the historical development of English pronunciation, but is largely irrelevant in present-day English.

Elision

What is elision?

You already know from the previous lesson that the omission of one or more sounds in spoken language is technically termed **elision** [from Latin *elisio,* 'pushing out']. You also know from that lesson that sounds are frequently omitted from certain grammatical words when they occur as weak forms in non-prominent positions, and that the process of omitting, or eliding, sounds is not normally represented in the spelling. (But we saw that elision *can* be represented in the spelling of contractions, like *I've* and *he's*.) In the present lesson, you have learnt so far that elision (together with reduction and assimilation) is an important means of making the pronunciation easier, and consequently of maintaining the natural, isochronous rhythm of English. You have also learnt in this lesson that (as with reduction and assimilation) elision is not necessarily a feature of careless or sloppy speech (although it is certainly more common in rapid speech, informal situations, and working-class accents). In the next section, then, we shall describe elision in some more detail.

Connected speech, contd.

As was the case with assimilation, however, it is sometimes difficult to say whether elision influenced by a sound or sounds belonging to the same word can be considered an aspect of connected speech, especially when it occurs even if the word is spoken in isolation. As before, the position taken here is that, because elision is instrumental in maintaining an isochronous rhythm, it should be considered an aspect of connected speech not only when it is influenced by a sound or sounds belonging to a *neighbouring* word, but also usually when it is influenced by a sound or sounds belonging to the *same* word.

Various types of elision

Elision can be described in terms of two (hierarchically unrelated) categorisations, based on the kind and the position of the sound(s) omitted. Elision in grammatical words, resulting in weak forms (and often in contractions), should be seen as a separate type, which is left out of the discussion here because all the relevant weak forms were listed as transcriptions in the previous lesson.

The categorisation based on the kind of sound(s) omitted distinguishes between (a) elision of consonants, (b) elision of vowels, and (c) elision of whole syllables.

(a) Elision of consonants often occurs in order to simplify consonant clusters (which may or may not stretch across word boundaries). The consonants elided are most typically plosives and fricatives, as in *old man* /əʊld mæn/, when it is pronounced [əʊl mæn], *acts* /ækts/, when it is pronounced [æks], *clothes* /kləʊðz/, when it is pronounced [kləʊz], and *months* /mʌnθs/, when it is pronounced [mʌns]. (Note, here, that the elision of /t/ and /d/ can result in the neutralisation of the distinction between past tense and present tense, as in *looked back* /lʊkt bæk/, when it is pronounced [lʊk bæk].) Often affected are ordinal numbers, like *twelfth* /twelfθ/, when it is pronounced [twelθ], and the possessive case of ordinal numbers, like *sixth's* /sɪksθs/, when it is pronounced [sɪks]. Elision is particularly common in a larger accumulation of consonants, as in the cluster /kstpl/ in *next, please*, which is usually pronounced [neks pliːz]. (Pronouncing the cluster /ksθsθr/ in *Henry the Sixth's three advisers* borders on the impossible.)

In the historical development of the English language, some words have omitted consonants from clusters permanently in speech although the corresponding letters still occur in the spelling. In the following words, for example, pronouncing the consonants represented by the underlined letters was correct in earlier times, but would be incorrect today: *knife, knight, lamb, listen, whistle,* and *wrong*. A letter in the written form of a word that is not sounded in speech is called a **silent letter**.

(b) Elision of vowels can occur in unstressed syllables of polysyllabic words, most typically just before or after a stressed syllable, and after one of the fortis plosives, /p, t, k/. In the following words, for example, we often do not hear the vowels represented by the underlined letters: *perhaps, potato, today,* and *tomato*. Here, the gap left by the elided vowels is filled by a puff of breath, or a brief *h*-sound, stemming from the sudden release of air in the articulation of the preceding plosive. Such a puff of breath is referred to as **aspiration**, and it can be indicated by a small, raised *h*-like symbol, [ʰ]. (Note that we have already encountered aspiration in Lesson Six, in the section on juncture.) The words *potato* and *today*, then, if they are pronounced without their respective first vowels, can be transcribed in a phonetic transcription proper as [ˈpʰteɪtəʊ] and [tʰdeɪ]. When elision is compensated for with aspiration, it always results in a reduction in the number of syllables. The word *potato*, for example, can be pronounced with a schwa as trisyllabic /pə-teɪt-əʊ/ or without a schwa, but with aspiration, as disyllabic [ˈpʰteɪt-əʊ]. If an elided vowel is followed by /n, l/ or /r/, however, the gap is sometimes filled, or the elision compensated for, by transforming that consonant into a syllabic consonant (which has a greater duration than a non-syllabic one). Thus the number of syllables remains the same, but the syllable boundary usually moves. This can be illustrated by the words t*o*night /tə-naɪt/, when it is pronounced [tn̩-aɪt], p*o*lice /pə-liːs/, when it is pronounced [pl̩-iːs], and c*o*rrect /kə-rekt/, when it is pronounced [kr̩-ekt].

As before, some words have omitted vowels permanently in the course of time although the corresponding letters still occur in the spelling. The vowels represented by the underlined letters in ev*e*ning, diction*a*ry, and secret*a*ry, for example, are not pronounced in present-day English, or rather in present-day *British* English. In American English, which, contrary to popular belief, is in many respects more old-fashioned, *dictionary* and *secretary* have retained the vowels.

(c) Elision of whole syllables can occur when the syllables are unstressed, most typically just before or after a stressed syllable, especially when the elided syllable contains a consonant that is repeated in the following syllable. This can be illustrated by the words lib*ra*ry /laɪb-rə-rɪ/, when it is pronounced without the middle syllable as [laɪbri], and particu*la*rly /pə-tɪk-jə-lə-lɪ/, when it is pronounced without the penultimate syllable as [pətɪkjəli] (although here the stressed syllable is further away). Pronunciations resulting from this type of elision are, again, often firmly established today. This is the case with the disyllabic pronunciation of *library*, for example, which could therefore equally well be transcribed in phonemic transcription, as /laɪbrɪ/.

The categorisation based on the position of the sound(s) omitted distinguishes between (a) elision at the beginning of a word, (b) elision in the middle of a word, and (c) elision at the end of a word. All three types have already been illustrated by examples given above.

(a) Elision at the beginning of a word is technically termed **aph(a)eresis** (pronounced [æˈfɪərəsɪs], and spelt in American English without the second *a*) [from Latin *aphaeresis*, Greek *aphaíresis*, 'a taking away'; *Aphärese, Deglutination*]. We saw aphaeresis in the historical omission of the initial consonant in *k*nife, *k*night, and *w*rong. If the omitted initial sound is a vowel (in which case it has to occur, as you know, in an unstressed syllable of a polysyllabic word), aphaeresis is sometimes termed, more specifically, **aphesis** (pronounced [ˈæfəsɪs]) [from Greek *áphesis*, 'letting go']. Aphesis can be illustrated by the omission of the initial vowel in *a*pprentice, resulting in *prentice*, and *o*possum, resulting in *possum*. Sometimes aphesis results in a word with a new meaning and use, as when *a*lone becomes *lone* ('without a husband, wife, or partner to share the care of children', as in *a lone mother*), or when *E*squire becomes *squire* (used informally or humorously by a man as a friendly way of addressing another man). When whole syllables or entire parts of words are omitted, we also speak of **clipping** (a term more associated with morphology), here more precisely of **fore-clipping** because a syllable or part is taken from the beginning of a word. Fore-clipping can be illustrated by the change from *alligator* to *gator*, from *omnibus* to *bus*, and from *telephone* to *phone*.

(b) Elision in the middle of a word is technically termed **syncope**, or **syncopation** (pronounced [sɪŋkəpi, sɪŋkəˈpeɪʃn̩]) [from Greek *sunkopḗ*, 'a cutting off'; *Synkope*]. The term most commonly refers to the elision of vowels (which, again, can only occur in unstressed syllables of polysyllabic words), as we saw, for example, in *today*, *tonight*, *evening*, *dictionary*, and *secretary*. But the term can also refer to the elision of consonants, as we saw, for example, in *clothes* and *twelfth*, and, historically, in *listen* and *whistle*, and it can refer to the elision of whole syllables, as we saw in *library* and *particularly*. Syncope is sometimes represented in the spelling by an apostrophe, as in *t'day* and *t'night*, in an attempt to reflect spoken language as closely as possible, especially in poetry.

(c) Elision at the end of a word is technically termed **apocope**, or **apocopation** (pronounced [əpɒkəpi, əpɒkəˈpeɪʃn̩]) [from Greek *apokopḗ*, 'a cutting off'; *Apokope*]. We saw apocope in *old man*, *looked back*, *next, please*, and, historically, in *lamb*. When whole syllables or entire parts of words are omitted, we can again speak of clipping, here more precisely of **back-clipping** because a syllable or part is taken from the end of a word. Back-clipping can be illustrated by the change from *advertisement* to *ad*, from *hippopotamus* to *hippo*, from *laboratory* to *lab*, and from *margarine* to *marge*. It also frequently results in nicknames, as when *David* becomes *Dave*, and *William* becomes *Will*. Aphaeresis and apocope often occur together, and when whole syllables or entire parts of words are omitted, we can speak of **fore-and-aft clipping**, as when *influenza* becomes *flu*, and *Elizabeth* becomes *Liz*.

There are many words in English that have undergone several of the processes described in this lesson and earlier in this manual. Two of the most prominent examples are the informal words *gonna* [gɒnə], from *going to*, and *wanna* [wɒnə], from *want to* or *want a*, which seem to be the result of reduction, assimilation, and elision all at once.

The opposite of elision: Intrusion

A process whereby, conversely, a sound that is not represented in the spelling and has no historical justification is added to a word or sequence in spoken language is called **intrusion**. By far the most common example is the intrusive *r*, discussed in Lesson Six in connection with linking, and illustrated there by examples like *media event* [miːdiəʳ ɪvent], *visa application* [viːzəʳ æplɪˈkeɪʃn̩], and *drawing* [drɔːˈrɪŋ], but we also saw other examples in that lesson, namely the intrusion of a glottal stop in *cooperate* [kəʊˀɒpəreɪt], and the intrusion of semi-vowels in *he is silly and stupid* [hiʲ ɪz sɪliʲ ən stjuːpɪd] and *to England* [tuʷ ɪŋglənd]. Linking sounds, then, are one type of intrusion. We said in Lesson Six that symbols representing linking sounds usually appear as small superscripts, and the same is true of symbols representing other types of intrusion, such as the intrusion of a schwa between two consonants, as in *athletics*, when it is pronounced [æθᵊletɪks], and *please*, when it is pronounced [pᵊliːz].

In traditional rhetoric, an intrusion in word-initial position, which does not usually occur in English, is termed **prothesis**, or, less commonly, **prosthesis** (pronounced [ˈprɒθəsɪs, ˈprɒsθəsɪs]) [from Greek *prothesis*, 'a placing before', *prosthesis*, 'addition'; *Prothese, Prosthese*]. An intrusion in word-internal position, as in *drawing* [drɔːˈrɪŋ] and *please* [pˤliːz], is termed **epenthesis** (pronounced [eˈpenθəsɪs]) [from Greek *epénthesis*, 'putting in'; *Epenthese*]. Linguists therefore sometimes refer to an inserted vowel like the schwa in *please* as an "epenthetic vowel" although there is an even more specific term available that can be used when a vowel is inserted between two consonants, namely **anaptyxis** (pronounced [ænəpˈtɪksɪs]) [from Greek *anaptyxis*, 'unfolding'; *Anaptyxe*]. An intrusion in word-final position, as in *media event* [miːdiəʳ ɪvent] and *to England* [tuʷ ɪŋglənd], is termed **paragoge** (pronounced [pærəˈɡəʊdʒi]) [from Greek *paragōgē*, 'addition'; *Epithese*].

Intrusive sounds are usually recorded only in a phonetic transcription proper. Only the intrusive *r* is also recorded in a broad phonetic transcription. Therefore, of all the intrusive sounds described in this section, only the intrusive *r* is relevant to the transcription course integrated with this manual.

Exercises

EXERCISES

In this lesson, assimilation was introduced as a feature of connected speech, and you should try to include this feature in your transcriptions. Remember that, if an assimilation process results in two identical sounds, the two sounds are usually pronounced as one, and are then transcribed with a lowered horizontal swung line, [‿], connecting them. You should use this swung line accordingly in your transcriptions.

Elision was also introduced in this lesson. From now on, elision will be marked in the model solutions by enclosing the elided sounds in parentheses. The only exception is where schwa is elided, and this is compensated for by a syllabic consonant.

In the solutions, we continue to annotate linking *r* and intrusive *r*, but no longer annotate syllabic consonants unless there is a special reason for doing so. These features should, of course, still be included in your transcriptions.

9.1 Transcribe the following text into IPA symbols

Early on Thursday morning just before eight o'clock, the first ten groups arrived, ready to start their new training regime. Within four hours few of the participants were able to resist the temptation of sitting, even though the only space left uncluttered with equipment was the freezing cold stone floor.

They were all completely surprised to find that their months of preparation had been useless. Mental stamina and physical agility were required for this kind of exercise, but no one expected such gruelling tasks to be assigned from the start. Now the length of the hall was littered with young students, puzzled, exhausted, and depressed.

"Frankly, the whole thing is a total shambles; today's been a complete write-off," said their trainer.

"Tomorrow I anticipate more, and I'll get them working non-stop," was her only idea of how to improve their awful performance.

143 words

9.2 Transcribe the spoken monologue on the CD into IPA symbols

Track 13 and tracks 14–20

124 words

LESSON 10
ALLOPHONIC VARIATION, CONTD.

We have now discussed all the phonetic and phonological phenomena relevant to the type of transcription you are asked to perform in the transcription course integrated with this manual. For example, you should now be able to transcribe unstressed *i*- and *u*-sounds, endings for the regular plural, the possessive case, the third-person singular, the regular past tense, and the regular past participle, the letter sequence <ng>, linking *r*- and intrusive *r*-sounds, syllabic consonants, unpredictable stress in polysyllabic words, strong and weak forms of grammatical words, assimilation, and elision. These are the elements of a broad phonetic transcription. Everything we shall discuss in this and in the next lesson is relevant only to a phonetic transcription in the narrower sense, i.e. a phonetic transcription proper.

To recapitulate briefly, you learnt in Lesson Five that an allophone is one of two or more pronunciation variants of a phoneme, and that the two criteria for identifying allophones are the absence of a minimal pair and articulatory similarity. Furthermore, we distinguished between allophones in free variation, which can occur in the same environment, and allophones in complementary distribution, which can*not* occur in the same environment. The allophones we have encountered so far include various *t*- and *r*-sounds (in Lessons Three, Five, and Seven), devoiced, fronted, and retracted sounds (in Lesson Five), aspirated and unaspirated plosives (in Lessons Six and Nine), and syllabic consonants (in Lesson Seven). As this list shows, allophonic variation can be described in terms of the particular *phonemes* that appear in different variants (such as *t*-sounds and *r*-sounds), and in terms of the *processes* that result in these variants (such as devoicing and fronting). The next lesson will be concerned with the former. More specifically, it will describe the allophones of the /t/ and /r/ phonemes (more systematically and comprehensively than was done in the earlier lessons) as well as those of the /l/ phoneme. The present lesson, on the other hand, will shed more light on the latter. In other words, it will continue with the description of the major processes resulting in allophones begun in Lesson Five.

Aspiration

You know from Lessons Six and Nine that **aspiration** [from Latin *aspirare*, 'breathe out'; *Behauchung*] is the audible puff of breath, or the brief *h*-sound, stemming from the sudden release of air in the articulation of a plosive. You also know that aspiration can be indicated in a phonetic transcription proper by the diacritic [ʰ] after the symbol for the plosive in question. We have seen that aspiration can make the word boundary in a sequence like /ðætstʌf/ perceptible, helping us recognise it as either *that stuff* [ðæt stʌf] or *that's tough* [ðæts tʰʌf]. And we have seen that aspiration can fill the gap left by an elided vowel, as in *potato* [ˈpʰteɪtəʊ] and *today* [tʰdeɪ].

What needs to be added, here, is that it is mainly the *fortis* plosives, /p, t, k/, that are aspirated. The lenis plosives are usually unaspirated, or, at most, scarcely aspirated. The fortis plosives, then, are aspirated most typically in the following environments:

- when they are pronounced in isolation;
- when they occur at the onset of a stressed syllable immediately before a vowel, as in *p̲in* [pʰɪn], *t̲ough* [tʰʌf], and *k̲ey* [kʰiː], except when preceded by /s/, as in *sp̲in* [spɪn], *st̲uff* [stʌf], and *sk̲i* [skiː] (note that phonologically, or phonotactically, no consonant other than /s/ can precede a fortis plosive in a syllable-initial cluster);
- when they occur at the onset of a stressed syllable immediately before one of the four frictionless continuants, /l, r, j, w/, in which case the aspiration usually results in the devoicing of these continuants (because they are articulated while the vocal folds are still apart), as in *p̲lease* [pʰl̥iːz], *t̲ry* [tʰr̥aɪ], *t̲une* [tʰjuːn], and *q̲uick* [kʰw̥ɪk], except, again, when preceded by /s/, as in *sp̲leen* [spliːn] and *sq̲uiggle* [skwɪɡl̩] (remember that we have already encountered the devoicing of the frictionless continuants in Lesson Five, and that it is explained there why, in a phonetic transcription proper, *tune* is better transcribed as [tçuːn]).

In most other environments, the fortis plosives are usually *un*aspirated, or scarcely aspirated, and the aspiration in *potato* [ˈpʰteɪtəʊ] and *today* [tʰdeɪ] must therefore be regarded as not quite typical. Note also, in this connection, that there exists a diacritic indicating the absence of aspiration, namely a raised equals sign placed after the relevant symbol, as in [t⁼], but it is hardly ever used.

As you know from Lesson Five, the lenis plosives, /b, d, g/, the lenis affricate, /dʒ/, and the lenis fricatives, /v, ð, z, ʒ/, are partly devoiced in word-initial position because of the voice onset time. The difference, therefore, between the /b/ in *b̲in* [bɪn] and the /p/ in *sp̲in* [spɪn], for example, is barely noticeable: Besides the fact that both sounds are bilabial plosives, both have little or no voicing, and both are unaspirated. Experiments have shown that most people actually hear [sbɪn] for *spin* because our perception of plosives (which is the realm of auditory phonetics) seems to be influenced to a high degree by the presence or absence of aspiration. The difference that remains is, of course, that the /p/ is produced with more force, i.e. with fortis articulation, and the correct transcription of *spin* is therefore still [spɪn]. The difference between the /b/ in *b̲in* [bɪn] and the /p/ in *p̲in* [pʰɪn], on the other hand, is very noticeable even though, again, both sounds are bilabial plosives and have little or no voicing. However, it is not just the fortis articulation, here, that enables us to recognise the initial sound in *pin* as /p/, it is first and foremost the aspiration. We can say, then, that the most significant difference between an initial lenis plosive and an initial fortis plosive is the aspiration of the latter.

But, if aspiration is so vital for distinguishing meaning, and consequently for differentiating words, as was clearly illustrated by *bin* and *pin*, how can we avoid the conclusion that an aspirated fortis plosive and an unaspirated fortis plosive are two separate phonemes in English, rather than two allophones of the same phoneme? After all, even the sequences *that stuff* and *that's tough* could be seen as a kind of minimal pair (because they differ mainly in the presence or absence of aspiration of the second /t/), and the presence of minimal pairs is, as you learnt in Lesson Three, the sole criterion for identifying phonemes. The answer is that the realisation of a fortis plosive as either aspirated or unaspirated is determined by the phonetic environment, i.e. it is rule-governed. Aspirated fortis plosives and unaspirated fortis plosives are therefore allophones in complementary distribution.

Secondary articulation

If a sound is produced by obstructing an air-stream simultaneously in two different places (i.e. with different speech organs), the two overlapping articulations in these places are referred to as **coarticulation** [from Latin *coarticulare*, 'articulate together'], or **double articulation**. Most linguists, however, use these terms in a narrower sense, to refer to the simultaneous use of two places of obstruction only if the two overlapping articulations are equally important (i.e. if they contribute equally to the quality of the resultant sound). Coarticulation in this sense is found in some West African languages, for example, but not usually in English. If, on the other hand, one articulation is more important than the other, the more important one (i.e. the one that contributes most of the quality of the resultant sound) is usually called **primary articulation**, and the less important one (i.e. the one that merely adds a nuance to the quality of the resultant sound) is usually called **secondary articulation**. In common linguistic parlance, then, *coarticulation* and *primary/secondary articulation* are complementary although, strictly speaking, *coarticulation* is the more general, superordinate term.

We have already encountered one case of secondary articulation in this manual, namely in Lesson Three, when we classified the /w/ phoneme as a velar even though it is labialised, which means that it is produced with rounded lips. The velum, then, is the place of the primary articulation, and the lips are the place of the secondary articulation. It is unusual, however, that an English phoneme has a secondary articulation when it is pronounced in isolation. In other words, secondary articulations are not usually intrinsic to English phonemes, and the /w/ phoneme must therefore be regarded as an exception. In English, secondary articulations are almost always brought about by the influence of a neighbouring sound, as will be seen in the next section.

By the same token, it will be seen that a secondary articulation is usually not only the cause of allophonic variation, but also the effect of **assimilation**, i.e. the process whereby one sound becomes more like another. In fact, secondary articulation and allophonic variation are so closely interrelated with assimilation that the two sections on secondary articulation in this lesson can be seen as a continuation of the three sections on assimilation in the previous lesson. Like assimilation, a secondary articulation involves a speech organ that is not normally used in the production of a given sound, but still remains in a position needed for the articulation of a preceding sound, or begins to move to a position needed for the articulation of a following sound. Like assimilation, a secondary articulation can consequently be categorised as either progressive, i.e. influenced by a preceding sound, or regressive, i.e. influenced by a following sound, although the latter is much more common. And like assimilation, a secondary articulation can be influenced either by a sound belonging to a neighbouring word, or by a sound belonging to the same word, and in both cases it can usually be considered an aspect of **connected speech** because it makes the pronunciation easier, and is therefore instrumental in maintaining an isochronous rhythm. The difference between secondary articulation and assimilation is threefold: The former is more associated with the production of speech sounds whereas the latter is more associated with their quality. More importantly, the former (usually) affects only the place of articulation whereas the latter can affect any of the distinctive features. And, consequently, the former usually adds just a nuance to the quality of a phoneme whereas the latter can not only add a nuance, but also change the quality of a phoneme altogether, i.e. substitute one phoneme for another. We can say, then, that a secondary articulation is almost always effected by assimilation, but assimilation only sometimes effects a secondary articulation. The term *assimilation* therefore has a wider range of applications than the term *secondary articulation*.

In this manual, however, we have chosen to restrict the term *assimilation* to a process that changes the quality of a phoneme altogether, i.e. one that results in a complete substitution of phonemes, rather than using the term, like most linguists, also for a process that adds just a nuance to the quality of a phoneme, i.e. one that results merely in an alteration of phonemes, or in allophones. This choice may seem arbitrary, but it was made for clarity of presentation, and thus, ultimately, for better comprehension. We must make perfectly clear, however, that all the examples of secondary articulation given below are also examples of assimilation.

Main types of secondary articulation

We shall now discuss the main types of secondary articulation, namely labialisation, retroflexion, palatalisation, velarisation, and nasalisation. The last of these, nasalisation, does not quite belong here, as we shall see later. Before you continue reading, it may be advisable to reread the sections on the place of articulation in Lessons Two and Three.

Labialisation is a type of secondary articulation whereby a sound, usually a consonant, is produced with an unusual degree of lip-rounding in addition to the primary articulation. It is usually influenced by (the rounded lips of) a neighbouring /w/ or /ɔː, uː, ɒ, ʊ/. (Remember from Lesson Four that back vowels usually have lip-rounding in English.) Labialisation can be indicated in a phonetic transcription proper by a small *w*-like symbol, which is either placed under the symbol for the labialised sound, or raised and placed after it. Labialisation is usually regressive, i.e. influenced by a following sound, as is illustrated by the labialised alveolar /s/ in *soon* [sʷuːn], the labialised postalveolar

/r/ in *rude* [rʷuːd], the labialised palatoalveolar /ʃ/ in *shoe* [ʃʷuː], and the labialised velar /k/ in *quite* [kʷwaɪt]. But occasionally it is also progressive, i.e. influenced by a preceding sound, as is illustrated by the labialised alveolar /t/ in *boot* [buːtʷ]. (Compare the quality of these labialised sounds with that of the "purely" alveolar /s/ in *snake*, postalveolar /r/ in *red*, palatoalveolar /ʃ/ in *sherry*, velar /k/ in *Canada*, and alveolar /t/ in *tiger*, all of which are made without lip-rounding.)

Retroflexion is a type of secondary articulation whereby a sound, more specifically a vowel, is produced with a curled-back tongue tip approaching or touching the hard palate in addition to the primary articulation. Retroflexion is also referred to as *r*-colouring or **rhotacisation** [from Latin *rhotacismus*, Greek *rhôtakismós*, 'making an *r*-sound']. It is only important in rhotic accents, for example in most American accents, because it is influenced by a retroflex allophone of the /r/ phoneme, which rarely occurs elsewhere. Furthermore, as you know from Lesson Six, non-rhotic accents like RP have lost the /r/ phoneme almost entirely (except before a vowel). Retroflexion can be indicated in a phonetic transcription proper by a small, raised *r*-like symbol, which is upside down and placed after the symbol for the retroflexed (or *r*-coloured or rhotacised) vowel, and the retroflex /r/ that influences retroflexion can be transcribed as [ɻ]. Retroflexion is usually regressive, as is illustrated by the retroflexed /ɜː/ in *bird* [bɜːɹɻd] or *world* [wɜːɹɻld] in American English. If a retroflex /r/ is elided, which occasionally happens for example to simplify consonant clusters, the unarticulated sound may still exert its influence, and words like *bird* and *world* may then be pronounced with a retroflexed vowel nevertheless. (Compare the quality of the retroflexed /ɜː/ with that of the "normal" /ɜː/ in *bird* or *world* in RP.)

Palatalisation is a type of secondary articulation whereby a sound, usually a consonant, is produced with the body of the tongue coming near or touching the hard palate in addition to the primary articulation. In most cases, this involves a shift of the place of obstruction backwards. In the case of velars and the glottal, however, which are (normally) made in the back part of the mouth, it involves a shift forward. Palatalisation is often influenced by a neighbouring palatal, /j/, or by a front vowel, /iː, ɪ, e, æ/. It can be indicated in a phonetic transcription proper in several ways, most commonly by a small, raised *j*-like symbol after the symbol for the palatalised sound, or by an apostrophe. Palatalisation is usually regressive, as is illustrated by the palatalised alveolar /t/ in *tea* [tʲiː] and the palatalised velar /k/ in *keep* [kʲiːp]. (Compare the quality of these palatalised sounds with that of the "purely" alveolar /t/ in *tiger* and velar /k/ in *Canada*.) Palatalised consonants are sometimes described as "soft", and non-palatalised consonants as "hard". The use of these labels here is not related to the use of the same labels for describing the lenis and fortis articulation of consonants (as in "soft *s*" and "hard *s*"), but it must be equally discouraged.

Velarisation is a type of secondary articulation whereby a sound, almost always /l/, is produced with the back of the tongue coming near or touching the soft palate, or velum, in addition to the primary articulation. It is influenced by a following consonant (*any* consonant except /j/ in the same or in the next word) or pause, which means that it is always regressive. Velarisation can be indicated in a phonetic transcription proper by the diacritic [ˠ] after the symbol for the velarised sound, as in [lˠ], or, formerly and probably still more commonly, by a tilde placed through the symbol, as in [ɫ]. The velarised alveolar /l/, then, is found in words like *help* [heɫp], *milk* [mɪɫk], *cool* [kuːɫ], and *sail* [seɪɫ]. (Again, compare the quality of the velarised /l/ with that of the "purely" alveolar /l/ in *leopard*, which is made with the back of the tongue much further forward.)

Nasalisation is a process whereby a sound, usually a vowel, is produced with a lowered velum, which opens the passage to the nasal cavity, so that air escapes not only through the mouth (as is usually the case with vowels), but also through the nose. In English, nasalised sounds differ from "real" nasals, then, in that the latter involve a complete closure in the vocal tract, so that *no* air escapes through the mouth. (Other languages have nasals where the escape of some air through the mouth is intrinsic.) Nasalisation is influenced by a neighbouring nasal, /m, n, ŋ/, and can be indicated in a phonetic transcription proper by a tilde above the symbol for the nasalised sound. It is often regressive, as is illustrated by the nasalised /iː/ in *beam* [bĩːm], the nasalised /ɪ/ in *bin* [bĩn], and the nasalised /æ/ in *bang* [bæ̃ŋ]. But it can also be progressive, as is illustrated by the nasalised /æ/ in *mat* [mæ̃t], or regressive and progressive at the same time, as is illustrated by the nasalised /æ/ in *man* [mæ̃n]. (As before, compare the quality of these nasalised vowels with that of the "normal" /iː/ in *bee*, /ɪ/ in *fish*, and /æ/ in *apple*, all of which are made with the velum raised and air escaping only through the mouth.) Nasalisation is often grouped together with the various types of secondary articulation for the sake of convenience, but it is, strictly speaking, a different process because it affects the manner of articulation, not the place.

It has been shown here that secondary articulations (including nasalisation) usually occur only in specific environments. Consequently, the resultant pronunciation variants also usually occur only in specific environments, or we can say that the realisations of the underlying phonemes are rule-governed. The sounds discussed in this section, like virtually all the sounds discussed in this lesson, are therefore allophones in complementary distribution.

Exercises

EXERCISES

We have now covered all the features that we include in our broad phonetic transcription, and the exercises in this and the following lessons give further practice on all these features. Your transcriptions should not, however, include the narrower phonetic phenomena discussed in these lessons.

10.1 Transcribe the following text into IPA symbols

The story started nine months ago after all the trouble and unrest had faded away. Little did Amanda apprehend then that her life would dramatically change and for the better. Her training had been in theatre and performance; with these skills she had been able to land a dream position in a respectable company. There she had been given a number of understudies, minor parts, and two starring roles. In short she hadn't wasted a second in making a name for herself.

After appearing as a witch in Macbeth, Amanda asked for a short break "to recover from a particularly nasty bout of influenza," she explains. "I said goodbye to the theatre wishing that I could be back as soon as possible."

"All of a sudden I was snapped up from feeling terribly ill to the whirlwind of Hollywood by a film producer who had seen my final night in Macbeth."

151 words

10.2 Transcribe the spoken dialogue on the CD into IPA symbols

Track 21 and tracks 22–27

111 words

LESSON 11
MORE ALLOPHONES

In Lessons Five and Ten, we described allophonic variation in terms of processes that result in allophones (such as devoicing, aspiration, and the various types of secondary articulation). In the present lesson, on the other hand, we shall describe it in terms of particular phonemes that appear as different allophones. The phonemes chosen here are /t/, /r/, and /l/ because they are among the English sounds which are most variable, and consequently most important with respect to the learning and teaching of English pronunciation. But this is certainly not to mean that all other English sounds are much less variable (or much less important). On the contrary, you know from Lesson Five that the number of allophones of any given phoneme is, at least theoretically, virtually infinite. Many other sounds, then, could have been included in this lesson, and the description of /t, r, l/ and their most important allophones should therefore be seen as merely exemplary of the variability of the majority of English sounds.

t-sounds

Of the 12 most important allophones of the /t/ phoneme, the following 8 have already been described in previous lessons.

– What could be called a **neutral *t*** was first described in Lesson Three as a fortis alveolar plosive, and you later learnt in Lesson Ten when this sound is typically aspirated. It is the sound we hear word-initially in *tiger* [tʰaɪgə], or when /t/ is pronounced in isolation.
– The **unaspirated *t*** is a different realisation of the neutral *t*. It was described in detail in Lesson Ten. In that lesson, we looked at the environments in which the aspirated *t* typically occurs, and we said that the *un*aspirated *t* occurs in most other environments. It can be illustrated by the /t/ in *s*t*uff* [stʌf] and *s*t*ring* [strɪŋ]. (Remember that the absence of aspiration is not usually indicated by a diacritic.)
– The **glottal stop** was described in Lessons Two and Three. In some non-standard British accents, most notably Cockney, it is often used as an allophone of /t/ when it occurs after a vowel either word-internally, especially when followed by another vowel, /n/, or /l/, or word-finally, as in *bu*tt*er* [bʌʔə], *bu*tt*on* [bʌʔn̩], *bo*tt*le* [bɒʔl̩], and *bu*t [bʌʔ]. The use of a glottal stop in these environments is referred to as **glottal replacement**, or **T-glottalling**, or simply **glottalling**. Because of this particular use, the glottal stop in general is widely stigmatised by speakers of RP even though

other uses of the glottal stop (as a linking sound, for example, which we encountered in Lesson Six) are certainly entirely acceptable.
- The **alveolar flap**, or **alveolar tap**, was also described in Lesson Three. In American English, it is commonly used as an allophone of /t/ when it occurs after a vowel in a stressed syllable and before another vowel, as in *latter* [lærər], *writing* [ˈraɪrɪŋ], and *atom* [ærəm] (but not in *atomic* [əˈtʰɑːmɪk], for example, because here the /t/ occurs after a vowel in an *unstressed* syllable). Thus *latter*, *writing*, and *atom* often have the same pronunciation in American English as *ladder* [lædər], *riding* [ˈraɪdɪŋ], and *Adam* [ædəm]. Another way of describing this allophone, therefore, is to say that the /t/ has undergone a process of voicing, and now resembles a fast /d/. The words *latter*, *writing*, and *atom* could then be transcribed as [læṭər], [ˈraɪṭɪŋ], and [æṭəm].
- The **fronted** *t* was described in detail in Lesson Five, including the environments in which it occurs. It can be illustrated by the dental realisation of the normally alveolar /t/ in *eighth* [eɪt̪θ] and *not thin* [nɒt̪ θɪn].
- The **retracted** *t* was also described in detail in Lesson Five, again including the environment in which it occurs. It can be illustrated by the postalveolar realisation of the normally alveolar /t/ in *try* [t̠raɪ] and *fit right* [fɪt̠ raɪt].
- The **labialised** *t* was described in Lesson Ten, including the environments in which it occurs. It can be illustrated by the /t/ in *boot* [buːtʷ] and *twice* [tʷwaɪs].
- And the **palatalised** *t* was described in Lesson Ten as well, again including the environments in which it occurs. It can be illustrated by the /t/ in *tea* [tʲiː] and *text* [tʲekst].

The next four allophones of /t/ have *not* yet been described in this manual. We encounter them here for the first time.

- The **nasally released** *t* is produced with the usual complete closure at the alveolar ridge, which is maintained throughout the duration of the sound, so that no air escapes through the mouth, but with a lowered velum, so that air escapes through the nose instead. This kind of release is called **nasal release**, or **nasal plosion**, and it can be indicated in a phonetic transcription proper by a small, raised *n*-like symbol after the main symbol, as in [tⁿ]. A nasal release typically occurs in the production of a plosive when that plosive is followed by a nasal with the same place of articulation. This means that /t/ is usually nasally released when it is followed by /n/, as in *button* [bʌtⁿn̩], *eaten* [iːtⁿn̩], and *not now* [nɒtⁿ naʊ]. (Note that a nasal release is *not* a case of nasalisation, a process which was discussed in the previous lesson, because nasalisation involves the escape of air both through the mouth and through the nose.)
- The **laterally released** *t* is produced, initially, with the usual complete closure at the alveolar ridge, but the sides of the tongue are then lowered, so that air escapes around the sides of the central closure that still remains. This kind of release is called **lateral release**, or **lateral plosion**, and it can be indicated in a phonetic transcription proper by a small, raised *l*-like symbol after the main symbol, as in [tˡ]. A lateral release typically occurs in the production of /t/ and /d/ when they are followed by /l/,

as in *bottle* [bɒt˺l̩], *cattle* [kæt˺l̩], and *little* [lɪt˺l̩]. Note, here, that the central closure, i.e. the contact between the tongue tip and the alveolar ridge, is maintained throughout the duration of the /tl/ sequence.

- The **inaudibly released** *t*, or **unreleased** *t*, is also produced with the usual complete closure at the alveolar ridge, but the complete closure is maintained throughout the duration of the /t/ *and* an immediately following plosive or /m/, so that the air used for the production of both sounds is released at the end of the second sound. More generally, we can say that an **inaudible release** can occur in the sequence plosive plus plosive or plosive plus /m/. It can be indicated in a phonetic transcription proper by a small, raised right angle, [˺], after the symbol for the first sound in the sequence (i.e. the sound that is actually inaudibly released). An inaudibly released *t* can be illustrated by words like *catkin* [ˈkæt˺kɪn], *hatband* [ˈhæt˺bænd], and *atmosphere* [ˈæt˺məsfɪə].

- The **glottalised** *t* is produced with a tightly closed glottis (in effect, resulting in a simultaneous glottal stop), so that no more air can be pushed up from the lungs. The glottis remains closed throughout the duration of the /t/, thus trapping a body of air between it and the usual closure made for the /t/ higher up in the vocal tract, at the alveolar ridge. (We could say that the air is trapped between a lower, glottal closure and an upper, alveolar closure.) This air is then compressed by a sharp upward movement of the larynx (which contains the glottis), and released, by opening the upper closure, through the mouth. Thereafter, the glottis opens, so that new air can be pushed up from the lungs for the production of the next sound. Not just /t/ can undergo such a process of **glottalisation**, but also the other two fortis plosives, /p/ and /k/. (Note that the term *glottalisation* is used here in a rather specific sense. It is often used more broadly to refer to all kinds of activity in the glottis during sound production.) Glottalised fortis plosives differ from all other English sounds described in this manual in that they are not made with lung air. In other words, they are not produced by an egressive pulmonic air-stream mechanism. The air-stream used here is an **egressive glottalic air-stream**, and a sound produced by such an air-stream is referred to as a **glottalic** sound, or as an **ejective**. (Note that glottalic sounds can only be allophones in English whereas in many American Indian and African languages, such as Quechua, Amharic, and Hausa, they can also be phonemes.) A glottalic sound (such as the glottalised *t*) can be indicated in a phonetic transcription proper by a small, raised glottal stop symbol after the main symbol, as in [tʔ], or by a normal-sized glottal stop symbol before the main symbol, as in [ʔt], or by an apostrophe after the main symbol, as in [t']. (Remember, however, that an apostrophe is also commonly used to indicate palatalisation.) Glottalic sounds, or rather glottalic fortis plosives, typically occur after a vowel and before a consonant, as in *department* [dɪˈpɑːtʔmənt], *football* [ˈfʊtʔbɔːl], and *quite good* [kwaɪtʔ gʊd], or before a pause, usually at the end of words, as in *mat* [mætʔ] and *what* [wɒtʔ]. This kind of glottalisation is referred to as **glottal reinforcement**, or sometimes as **glottalling** (but the latter term is more commonly used as a synonym for glottal replacement). Glottalised fortis plosives, or glottalic fortis plosives, are common in everyday spoken

English. Without them, the language would probably sound pedantic or stilted, as can be illustrated by the pronunciation [dɪˈpɑːtʰmənt] for *department*. If the glottalisation, or the glottal reinforcement, is overdone, however, it sounds rather clipped, as though the speaker wanted to pronounce something very precisely, or to "spit" out the sound at the end of a word, which is sometimes done for humorous effect.

All the allophones of /t/ listed above usually occur in clearly defined environments, i.e. the choice between them is largely rule-governed, and they are therefore commonly regarded as contextual variants, or allophones in complementary distribution. But, as was pointed out in Lesson Five, speakers of a non-standard British accent who normally realise the /t/ in *bu*t*ter* as a glottal stop may occasionally realise it as an unaspirated *t* to sound more formal. Similarly, speakers of RP, who normally realise the /t/ in *bu*t*ter* as an unaspirated *t*, may occasionally realise it as a glottal stop to sound more colloquial. And any single speaker may at various times and for various reasons (or for no reason at all) realise the /t/ in *ea*t as an aspirated *t*, an unaspirated *t*, or a glottalised *t*. These examples show that the choice between several of the allophones of /t/ may also depend on such factors as language variety, social class, communicative situation, or simply on chance. In such cases, the allophones of /t/ must be regarded as free variants, or allophones in free variation.

r-sounds

We said in Lesson Three that no other consonant phoneme of English is as variable in its actual pronunciation as the /r/ phoneme. This statement seems to contradict what we said in Lesson Five and at the beginning of the present lesson, namely that the number of allophones of any given phoneme is virtually infinite, and it must therefore be further qualified: The /r/ *is* the most variable consonant phoneme of English in the sense that several of its allophones are, from a phonetic point of view, significantly different from one another, and it is only from a phonological point of view that they can be regarded as allophones of the same phoneme. This is underlined by the fact that the major pronunciation variants of /r/ can be represented in a phonetic transcription proper by separate symbols, rather than being indicated merely by diacritics. Of the 9 allophones of /r/ listed below, 5 (including what could be called a neutral *r*) are such major pronunciation variants. The remaining 4 are variants of the neutral *r*. The following 7 have already been described in previous lessons.

- The **neutral *r*** (neutral in RP, that is) was first described in Lesson Three as a lenis postalveolar approximant (or frictionless continuant), and you later learnt in Lesson Seven that it is non-syllabic. It is the sound we hear word-initially in *red*, or when /r/ is pronounced in isolation, and it can be represented in a phonetic transcription proper by an *r*-like symbol turned upside down and reversed, [ɹ], as in [ɹed].
- The **retroflex *r*** was also described in Lesson Three. More specifically, it is a lenis retroflex approximant, and it can be represented in a phonetic transcription proper by the symbol [ɻ]. It typically occurs in rhotic accents, for example in most American accents, after a vowel and before an alveolar consonant, as in *bi*r*d* [bɜːɻd] and

*wo*r*ld* [wɜːɹld] (transcribed more accurately as [bɜːʵɭd] and [wɜːʵɭd] if we want to indicate the retroflexion of the vowels influenced by the retroflex *r*). It does not occur in RP. (Note that there is another principally American allophone of /r/, referred to as a **molar *r***, or **bunched *r***, which is perceptually almost indistinguishable from a retroflex *r*, but has a different articulation.)

- The **rolled *r***, or **trilled *r***, was described in Lesson Three as well. More specifically, it is a lenis alveolar roll, or trill, and is represented in a phonetic transcription proper by the same symbol used for the underlying phoneme, [r]. It does not occur in RP, but it is typical of Scottish and Irish accents, and it is sometimes used in stylised speech, for example on stage or to convey jocular stereotypes. It is also common in the varieties of German spoken in the north of Germany, in Bavaria, and in Austria. The rolled *r* is sometimes called a **lingual roll**, or **lingual trill** [from Latin *lingua*, 'tongue'], as opposed to the uvular roll, or uvular trill, which will be described below.

- The **flapped *r***, or **tapped *r***, was the last *r*-sound described in Lesson Three. More specifically, it is a lenis alveolar flap, or tap, and it can be represented in a phonetic transcription proper by the symbol [ɾ]. (Note that this is the same sound that was described in the previous section as an allophone of the /t/ phoneme in American English.) It is similar to the rolled *r*, but it involves only *one* flap of the tongue tip against the alveolar ridge, rather than a vibration. It occurs in RP and in several other accents of British English, typically between two vowels, as in *ve*r*y Ame*r*ican* [veɾi əˈmeɾɪkən]. Because the flapped *r* resembles a fast /d/, it is sometimes (facetiously) spelt as *dd* by writers who want to represent spoken language as closely as possible, as in *veddy Ameddican*.

- The **devoiced *r*** was described in Lesson Five. It is a variant of the neutral *r*, and does not, therefore, have a separate symbol, but can be indicated by the diacritic [̥] added either to the symbol [r] or to the symbol [ɹ], depending on the degree of accuracy of the transcription. However, the devoiced *r* is no longer an approximant, like the neutral *r*, because the gap between the tongue tip and the rear of the alveolar ridge has become narrower, and the air now produces audible friction when forcing its way through. The devoiced *r* can therefore more specifically be described as a devoiced postalveolar fricative. We said in Lesson Five that it typically occurs after a fortis plosive, /p, t, k/, in stressed syllables. The example word given in that lesson, *try*, was transcribed as [tɹaɪ], but could also be transcribed more accurately as [tɹ̥aɪ] or, if we want to indicate the aspiration of the preceding plosive, [tʰɹ̥aɪ].

- The **syllabic *r*** was described in detail in Lesson Seven, including the environments in which it occurs. It is a lenis postalveolar approximant, like the neutral *r*, of which it is a variant, and it can be indicated by the diacritic [̩] added either to the symbol [r] or to the symbol [ɹ], depending on the degree of accuracy of the transcription. You already know from Lesson Seven that the syllabic *r* is very common in many rhotic accents, but rare in non-rhotic accents, such as RP.

- The **labialised *r*** was described in Lesson Ten, again including the environments in which it occurs. It is also a lenis postalveolar approximant (postalveolar because the rear of the alveolar ridge is still the place of the primary articulation), like the neutral *r*, of which it is a variant. It can be indicated by the diacritic [ʷ] added either to the symbol [r] or to the symbol [ɹ], depending on the degree of accuracy of the transcription. If the labialisation is overdone, i.e. if the lip-rounding is too strong, the labialised *r* begins to resemble a /w/. Such a sound is frequently used to satirise the (affected) speech of the upper classes, and it is sometimes (facetiously) spelt as *ww* by writers who want to represent it as closely as possible in traditional orthography, as in *I'm awfully sowwy*. Ironically, this is also the sound most English children make until they have learnt to articulate /r/ properly, and if adults make it, it is sometimes regarded as a language disorder.

The next two allophones of /r/ have *not* yet been described in this manual. We encounter them here for the first time.

- The **fricative *r*** is the second fricative among the *r*-sounds. It differs from the devoiced *r* only in that it has retained the intrinsic voicedness of /r/, and it can therefore more specifically be described as a voiced postalveolar fricative. It is another variant of the neutral *r*, and can be indicated by the diacritic [̞] added to the symbol [ɹ] (not usually to [r]). The fricative *r* only occurs after /d/, as in d*r*ead [dɹ̞ed], d*r*eam [dɹ̞iːm], and d*r*ive [dɹ̞aɪv].
- The **uvular *r*** is produced by moving the back of the tongue against the uvula. It is less technically also referred to as a **back *r***, or informally as **burr**. It is *not* a variant of the neutral *r*, but comes itself in two distinct variants. One variant is the **uvular roll**, or **uvular trill**. Unlike the lingual roll, which is produced by a vibration of the tongue tip against the alveolar ridge, the uvular roll is produced by a vibration of the back of the tongue against the uvula. It is a common sound in German (except in the varieties spoken in the north of Germany, in Bavaria, and in Austria), and a prestigious allophone of /r/ in French, which is why it is informally also referred to as the **Parisian *r***. It can be represented in a phonetic transcription proper by an *R*-like symbol, [ʀ]. The other variant is the **uvular fricative**. It is the third fricative among the *r*-sounds of English, and the friction here is produced by air forcing its way through a narrow gap between the back of the tongue and a tensed uvula. It can be represented in a phonetic transcription proper by an *R*-like symbol turned upside down, [ʁ]. Both variants of the uvular *r* are very rare in English. They are stigmatised by speakers of RP, and in the past were even regarded as language disorders. They are typical only of some accents of north-east England and south-east Scotland.

Any *r*-sound is technically termed a **rhotic**. Most of the nine rhotics listed here usually occur in clearly defined environments, i.e. the choice between them is largely rule-governed, and they are therefore commonly regarded as contextual variants, or allophones in complementary distribution. There are of course many more rhotics in English. One sound that is *not* considered a rhotic, however, is the bilabial roll, or bilabial trill, which we stereotypically produce to signal that we are freezing, or to imitate a car engine, as in *brrr*. This sound is transcribed as [ʙ].

l-sounds

The first instance of variation regarding *l*-sounds was encountered in Lesson Four, when we said that the duration of /l/ is usually shortened when followed by /p, t, k, tʃ, f, θ, s/ or /ʃ/ at the end of a syllable, exemplified by the shortened duration of the /l/ in *be*l*t* /belt/ as opposed to the "normal" duration of the /l/ in *be*ll*s* /belz/. The two *l*-sounds cannot differentiate words, and are phonetically similar, which means that they must be regarded as allophones. They are not usually counted among the most important allophones of /l/, but they remind us once again that the number of allophones of any given phoneme is virtually infinite. The most important allophones of /l/ are the five listed below, all of which (with one possible exception) have already been described in previous lessons.

- The **neutral *l*** (neutral in RP) was first described in Lesson Three as a lenis alveolar lateral (or lateral approximant), and you later learnt in Lesson Seven that it is non-syllabic. It is the sound we hear word-initially in *l*eopard* [lepəd], or when /l/ is pronounced in isolation, and it is represented in a phonetic transcription proper by the same symbol used for the underlying phoneme. The neutral *l* is sometimes described as palatalised because it is often produced not merely with the tip of the tongue touching the alveolar ridge, but also simultaneously with the whole front of the tongue coming near or touching the hard palate (but with the back of the tongue held low). Such a palatalised *l* is impressionistically called a **clear *l***. The raising of the front of the tongue gives the clear *l* a slight front-vowel quality, akin to an *i*-sound. In RP, the neutral *l*, or clear *l*, typically occurs only before a vowel or before /j/ (in the same or in the next word) *if* that vowel or /j/ follows immediately, i.e. without even the slightest pause in between (in all other environments, it yields to the velarised *l*, which will be listed below). Further examples of the neutral *l*, or clear *l*, can be heard in *l*ove* [lʌv], *si*ll*y* [sɪli], *fai*l*ure* [feɪljə], *mi*ll*ion* [mɪljən], *fa*ll *in* [fɔːl ɪn], and *fi*ll *it* [fɪl ɪt]. In many accents of Ireland (especially in the south) and Wales, it occurs in *all* environments whereas it virtually never occurs in many northern English, southern Scottish, and American accents. It also occurs in all environments in most German accents (including the most prestigious accent of Standard German) although /l/ in the accents of the north of Germany in particular is often even more front, or more *i*-coloured, than the English clear *l*. In several non-standard accents of German, /l/ is so much more front, or *i*-coloured, that *l*-sounds are frequently substituted with *i*-sounds, for example in words like *a*ll*es* and *Go*l*d*, which are then sometimes (facetiously) spelt as *ois* and *Goid* in an attempt to capture the accent as accurately as possible.
- The **devoiced *l*** was described in Lesson Five, including the environments in which it occurs. It is an alveolar lateral, like the neutral *l*, or clear *l*, and was illustrated in Lesson Five by the devoiced realisation of the normally voiced /l/ in *p*l*ease* [pl̥iːz]. We must add here, however, that /l/ can be devoiced not only after a fortis plosive in stressed syllables, but also after /f/ and especially after initial /s/, as in *f*l*y* [fl̥aɪ], *s*l*eep* [sl̥iːp], and *s*l*ender* [sl̥endə]. In RP, the devoiced *l* is usually also a neutral *l*, or clear *l*,

(as opposed to a velarised *l*) because phonologically, or phonotactically, the two-consonant cluster /p, t, k, f/ or /s/ plus /l/ at the onset of a syllable can only be followed by the vowel that forms the syllable centre, and such a cluster at the coda is simply not possible.

- The **fronted** *l*, or, more specifically, the **dental** *l*, was not mentioned explicitly in our discussion of fronting and dentalisation in Lesson Five because it is less common than the examples given there, but it surely deserves a mention here. The normally alveolar /l/ can be realised as a dental allophone (i.e. it can be articulated with the tongue tip and rims touching the teeth) if it is followed by the dental /θ/, as in *health* [helθ]. The place of the primary articulation, then, is the teeth, and the *l*-sound is therefore not an alveolar any more, but a lenis dental lateral. Because it is always followed by a consonant, the dental *l* is always velarised, i.e. the velum is the place of the secondary articulation, and the word *health* is thus transcribed more accurately as [heɫ̪θ].

- The **syllabic** *l* was described in detail in Lesson Seven, including the environments in which it occurs. It is a lenis alveolar lateral, like the neutral *l*, or clear *l*, and it was illustrated in Lesson Seven by such words as *table* [teɪbl̩], *proposal* [prəpəʊzl̩], and *shovel* [ʃʌvl̩]. What should be added here is that the syllabic *l* is typically velarised because it usually occurs at the end of a root, and is therefore often followed by a suffix consisting of or beginning with a consonant, or by a (slight) pause. The words *table*, *proposal*, and *shovel* are thus transcribed more accurately as [teɪbɫ̩], [prəpəʊzɫ̩], and [ʃʌvɫ̩].

- The **velarised** *l* was described in Lesson Ten, again including the environments in which it occurs (for the sake of simplification, we can say that it occurs in all the environments in which the neutral *l*, or clear *l*, cannot). It was illustrated in Lesson Ten by the words *help* [heɫp], *milk* [mɪɫk], *cool* [kuːɫ], and *sail* [seɪɫ], and in the present section by *health* [heɫ̪θ], *table* [teɪbɫ̩], *proposal* [prəpəʊzɫ̩], and *shovel* [ʃʌvɫ̩]. Further examples, involving influence of a following consonant in the next word, are *channel ferry* [tʃænɫ feri] and *fall down* [fɔːɫ daʊn]. Like the neutral *l*, or clear *l*, the velarised *l* is a lenis alveolar lateral (alveolar because the alveolar ridge is still the place of the primary articulation). More specifically, it is produced with the tip of the tongue touching the alveolar ridge, and simultaneously with the back of the tongue coming near or touching the velum (and possibly also with rounded lips). The raising of the back of the tongue (and the lip-rounding) gives the velarised *l* a slight back-vowel quality, akin to a *u*-sound. A *u*-sound is often described as a "dark" vowel probably because *u*-sounds occur in several "sad" words, like *doom* and *gloom*. The velarised *l* is therefore also impressionistically called a **dark** *l*. In many northern English, southern Scottish, and American accents, it occurs in *all* environments whereas it virtually never occurs in many accents of Ireland (especially in the south) and Wales. In several non-standard accents (particularly in Cockney) and in most Australian accents, the tip of the tongue does not quite touch the alveolar ridge, which frequently results in the substitution of a *u*-sound for the dark *l*, for example in words like *milk* and *people*, which are then transcribed as [mɪʊk] and ['piːpʊ].

All the allophones of /l/ listed here usually occur in clearly defined environments in RP, i.e. the choice between them is largely rule-governed, and they are therefore contextual variants in that accent, or allophones in complementary distribution. The same is true of the devoiced *l*, the fronted (or dental) *l*, and the syllabic *l* in most other accents. The neutral (or clear) *l* and the velarised (or dark) *l*, on the other hand, occur in *all* environments in some accents, and in these accents the two allophones are therefore *not* in complementary distribution.

When we say that all the allophones of /l/ listed here are allophones in complementary distribution in RP, we do not mean, of course, that *all* of them are mutually exclusive. On the contrary, we have seen that the devoiced *l* is usually a neutral (or clear) *l*, that the fronted (or dental) *l* is always a velarised (or dark) *l*, and that the syllabic *l* is typically also a velarised (or dark) *l*. What we mean, then, is that the allophones of /l/ form pairs within which there is mutual exclusivity. These pairs can be listed as follows:

neutral (or clear) *l*	vs.	velarised (or dark) *l*
devoiced *l*	vs.	voiced *l*
fronted (or dental) *l*	vs.	neutral (or clear) *l* (= alveolar)
syllabic *l*	vs.	non-syllabic *l*

In other words, the neutral (or clear) *l*, in RP, occurs in all the environments in which the velarised (or dark) *l* cannot, the devoiced *l* occurs in all the environments in which the voiced *l* cannot, the fronted (or dental) *l* occurs in all the environments in which the neutral (or clear) *l* (= alveolar) cannot, and the syllabic *l* occurs in all the environments in which the non-syllabic *l* cannot (except in very few cases where the non-syllabic *l* is preceded by a schwa, as was described in Lesson Seven). Such pairs can of course also be postulated for the allophones of /t/ and /r/, and the concept of complementary distribution has to be understood in this sense.

Finally, you know from Lesson Six, from the section on juncture, that allophones in complementary distribution may be the most reliable boundary signals, i.e. they often enable us to identify where one word ends, and the next word begins. This can also be illustrated in the context of the allophones of /l/. For example, the difference between *he lies* /hiː laɪz/ and *heal eyes* /hiːl aɪz/, in RP, lies mainly in the allophonic realisation of /l/ (and, admittedly, in the presence or absence of an ever so slight pause between the two words, which influences the realisation). In *he lies* [hiː laɪz], the /l/ is a neutral (or clear) *l*, which typically occurs immediately before a vowel, thus signalling that there is not necessarily a word boundary between /l/ and /aɪ/, and that the two phonemes may well belong to the same word. In *heal eyes* [hiːɫ aɪz], on the other hand, the /l/ is a velarised (or dark) *l*, which typically occurs before even the slightest pause, thus signalling that a word boundary between /l/ and /aɪ/ is very likely.

Exercises

11.1 Transcribe the following text into IPA symbols

"We need more oranges and apples before we can collect the soft fruit like strawberries and peaches," he bellowed down the phone.

Despite this rather unpleasant instruction coming up from the kitchen Carla and Sammy were in a good mood. They had both risen early, gone jogging and had a healthy breakfast. They were determined not to let Marco's foul mood upset their afternoon.

"Being identical twins has certain advantages," thought Carla: She had pretended to be her sister and vice versa on many occasions.

Now they planned to get their revenge on the angry cook. Sammy carefully wrapped four raw eggs in a spotted handkerchief and placed two more under her boss's shoes, which stood in the corner. The trap was set.

123 words

11.2 Transcribe the spoken dialogue on the CD into IPA symbols

Track 28 and tracks 29–33

110 words

Lesson 12
Intonation

In this final lesson, we shall examine intonation, a feature of suprasegmental phonology, or prosody. We have already come across other pronunciation features that cannot be segmented because they extend over units that are longer than just one sound. We discussed stress, for example, in Lessons Seven and Eight, and rhythm in Lesson Nine. Here, we shall begin our discussion by asking the question of what intonation is. We shall then briefly look at the concept of pitch, which, as you know from Lesson Two, is closely related to intonation. We shall proceed to identify the tone unit as the stretch of speech over which intonation acts. We shall categorise several intonation patterns, look at the structure of the tone unit, and, finally, discuss some of the functions intonation fulfils.

Intonation is a fundamental property of spoken language. Because of its complexity, however, our discussion can only be considered a basic introduction to this field, which necessarily omits or abbreviates some aspects that a more comprehensive book would discuss at greater length.

What is intonation?

Linguists have found many different ways to characterise **intonation**, which is also called **pitch contour** or **pitch movement**. In general, however, they agree on the following basic principles:

- All languages have intonation.
- Intonation is principally the variation of pitch, but also prominence, over a stretch of speech.
- Intonation has four functions. The **structural** function signals the grammatical or structural role of an utterance, determining, for example, whether it is a question, a request, or an instruction. The **accentual** function affects the prominence of a syllable, and thus plays a role in focusing stress on particular words in connected speech. The **attitudinal** function conveys the speakers' personal orientations towards what they say, or gives us clues about how the speakers feel – whether they are uninterested, excited, or ironic, for example. And the **discourse** function marks the turn-taking processes in an exchange between speakers.
- The set of intonation patterns, or contours, is limited and can be fully determined, but linguists are not in full agreement about the actual number of different contours.

- In order to analyse intonation, continuous speech can be broken down into smaller units, but there are different conventions about how to determine these units.

Pitch

Intonation, as was indicated above, is mainly shaped by the variation, or modulation, of the pitch of the voice. Prominence also plays a role, especially in marking the word that carries the main sentence stress. Our discussion, however, will be focused on pitch, rather than prominence.

You already know from Lesson Two that pitch is related to the frequency of the vibration of the vocal folds: The faster the vocal folds vibrate, the higher the pitch. Thus pitch is another way of referring to the **fundamental frequency** (F_0) of the voice. This frequency is also determined by the physical size, and consequently by the sex, of a speaker: In general, a male speaker usually has a lower pitch, at around 120 hertz, than a female speaker, who has an average pitch at around 210 hertz. You also know from Lesson Two that pitch is not a distinctive feature in English, so the absolute difference between the fundamental frequencies of individual speakers, or of men and women, is not significant in terms of segmental phonology.

Nonetheless, all speakers can use intonation to achieve the functions mentioned in the previous section, regardless of the absolute value of their own fundamental frequency. Thus an individual speaker can control the pitch of his or her voice, and in so doing may transmit information of one sort or another. Although no two speakers have the same fundamental frequency, it is the distinctive contrasts in a speaker's pitch level and the relative movements that are important to consider, rather than the absolute pitch frequency. In other words, the important question to ask when analysing intonation is whether a change in pitch carries linguistic, or communicative, significance.

The tone unit

We can normally break connected speech down into **utterances**, i.e. units that begin and end with a clear pause. While utterances may consist of only one syllable, such as *yes* or *no*, they are normally much longer, as in *The other day, while I was in town, I met Chris, who I hadn't seen for a couple of weeks*. Within an utterance, we can sometimes also identify smaller units, over which a single intonation contour extends. Such a stretch of speech we call a **tone unit**, or **tone group**. For example, the simple question (1) below, the longer question (2), and the statement (3) are all utterances.

(1) When?
(2) When did you say you would arrive?
(3) When he finally arrived, he discovered his friends had already left.

(1) and (2) each consist of a single tone unit whereas (3) is made up of two tone units. A tone unit, then, can extend over a stretch of speech as short as a single syllable, as in (1), or over a much longer stretch of speech, as in (2).

Intonation

As you know from Lesson One, intonation cannot be indicated by IPA symbols, and there is no other generally agreed system for writing intonation down. In this manual, therefore, we use conventional orthography, but without any punctuation, and we mark off tone units with double slashes, as in the following example:

// When he finally arrived // he discovered his friends had already left //

With the notions of utterance and tone unit, we have now introduced the last of the units of speech we consider in this manual: We can say that connected speech consists of utterances; an utterance is made up of one or more tone units; a tone unit is made up of one or more feet; a foot comprises one or more syllables; and a syllable consists of one or more phonemes.

Intonation patterns

Within a tone unit, one or more syllables are usually more prominent than others. The last prominent syllable in a tone unit is called the **tonic syllable**, or **nucleus**. The tonic syllable is the syllable on which the main pitch movement begins. The pitch movement may be restricted to the tonic syllable, but often it continues from the tonic syllable to the end of the tone unit. The tonic syllable, as well as being prominent, is said to carry **tonic stress**, or **nuclear stress**, and it is this tonic stress which determines the particular intonation pattern, or tone. The convention we adopt in this manual is that syllables which carry stress are written in capital letters, and tonic syllables are written in capital letters and are underlined.

We shall consider five different intonation patterns, or tones, in RP: **fall, rise, fall-rise, rise-fall,** and **high key** (where the whole intonation contour is at a raised pitch). These tones can be indicated by the symbols ↘ (for fall), ↗ (for rise), ↘↗ (for fall-rise), ↗↘ (for rise-fall), and ⇑ (for high key). The symbols are placed before the tone unit, as in the following examples:

↘	// WHERE do you LIVE //	(neutral question)
↗	// WHERE have you BEEN //	(angry parent to a child)
↘↗	// I'll BE there SOON //	(reassurance)
↗↘	// The FILM was WONderful //	(emphatic statement)
⇑	// HOW much did you PAY //	(question signalling surprise at the price)

Figures 5 and 6 illustrate a rise tone of a male voice and a fall-rise tone of a female voice, respectively, recorded by a spectrograph. Notice how the male voice has a much lower fundamental frequency, averaging around 120 hertz, than the female voice, which averages between 200 and 300 hertz. The contours also show that intonation is not a smooth phenomenon, but has many minor local perturbations. These smaller fluctuations play only a minor role in intonation as such, but undoubtably contribute to voice quality.

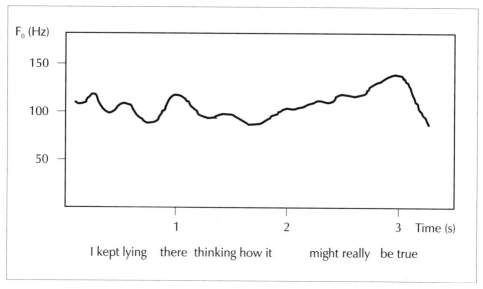

Fig. 5 Rise tone of a male voice.

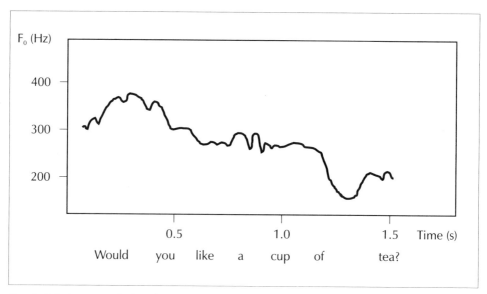

Fig. 6 Fall-rise tone of a female voice.

Tone unit structure

In Lesson Seven, we analysed the structure of the syllable, and noted that it has three components: onset, centre, and coda. In a similar way, the structure of the tone unit can be further analysed into four components. You already know that the **tonic syllable**

(TS), or **nucleus**, is the last prominent syllable in a tone unit. The **head** (H) is that part of a tone unit which extends from the first prominent syllable up to, but not including, the tonic syllable. The **pre-head** (PH) spans all the less prominent syllables before the head. And the **tail** (T) comprises all the syllables that occur between the tonic syllable and the end of the tone unit. We can mark off the four components of tone units with a vertical line, as in the following examples:

```
   ↘    //    WHERE do you | LIVE //
                    H         TS

   ↗    //    WHERE have you | BEEN //
                    H            TS

  ↘↗   //    I'll | BE there | SOON //
              PH      H          TS

  ↗↘   //    The | FILM was | WON- | -derful | //
              PH      H         TS        T

   ↕    //    HOW much did you | PAY //
                    H             TS
```

Functions of intonation

As was mentioned earlier in this lesson, intonation has four functions. A full description of all the different ways in which specific intonation patterns are used within these broad functional categories is beyond the scope of this manual. However, a number of key intonation patterns which are easily recognisable in English will be briefly discussed below.

Fall. Apart from being the most neutral tone in RP, the fall can signal finality and definiteness. It is surprising that many textbooks describe the rise as the standard tone for questions. In fact, it is the fall that is quite normal for neutral questions beginning with a question word. Examples:

> There were three people there.
> That's all I have to say.
> How are you? Where are you going? What time is it?

Rise. The rise is used for yes/no questions, for questions which are requests for a repetition of an answer, and for listing items (except the last item in a list, which is normally given a fall). When the speaker takes an authoritative or dominant role in the discourse, the rise is also commonly used, for example in questions in an aggressive interview, in instructions, or in commands. Examples:

> Do you live near here? Can I help you?
> Apples, oranges, bananas, and pears.
> When did your fever start?
> First turn left, then turn right.

Fall-rise. The fall-rise is generally used to confirm an equal participation in the discourse. Thus it is used to refer to shared information, to confirm information, to ask for permission, and to reassure. Examples:

> We're leaving at seven, aren't we?
> We can't afford it, it's too expensive.
> May I open the window?
> It'll be alright.

Rise-fall. The rise-fall is used to express strong personal impression. It can be used to convey a strong positive attitude, or to express surprise. Examples:

> That's a lovely view!
> What a goal!

High key. The high key is normally used to express surprise, strong disagreement, and sometimes strong agreement. Examples:

> Only 28? I thought you were at least 35!
> Actually, I think you're wrong!
> I quite agree!

These tones can all be identified in the spoken text in the practical section of Lesson Twelve. The analysis has been limited to marking the overall tone contour, without breaking the tone unit down into pre-head, head, tonic syllable, and tail. As the number of theoretically possible combinations of intonation contours that may be applied to any exchange is relatively high, we have transcribed only the spoken text.

Exercises

EXERCISES

12.1 Transcribe the following text into IPA symbols

Yet again he was late. She couldn't put up with it much longer. She was always on time; why couldn't he do the same? Travelling from Elephant and Castle at that time of night is no joke; waiting at the station was even worse. Yes she'd have to tell him it wasn't any good being left to wait for hours in the rain.

"You're here at last. I've been hanging around getting more and more infuriated with thinking about your terrible time-keeping. How would you enjoy it?"

"Yes sorry. I couldn't get away from the office. Actually, I would get here on time every week if it wasn't for the great mess that's always left for me to clear up. Then I have to settle the accounts and shut down the whole system. It takes forever."

"That's no excuse. We're supposed to have this time just for ourselves."

148 words

12.2 Transcribe the spoken dialogue on the CD into IPA symbols

Track 34 and tracks 35–40

108 words

12.3 Apply the intonation transcription convention to the spoken dialogue of 12.2

Appendix I: Solutions to the exercises

3.3

door	shore	saw	jaw	nor	chore	war	gore
four	more	paw	law	raw	bore	core	your
vote	tore	zoom	think	sing	there	horse	treasure
/d/	/ʃ/	/s/	/dʒ/	/n/	/tʃ/	/w/	/g/
/f/	/m/	/p/	/l/	/r/	/b/	/k/	/j/
/v/	/t/	/z/	/θ/	/ŋ/	/ð/	/h/	/ʒ/

reducing degree of obstruction	IPA symbol
plosives	/d/, /t/, /p/, /b/, /k/, /g/
affricates	/dʒ/, /tʃ/
nasals	/m/, /n/, /ŋ/
fricatives	/f/, /v/, /ʃ/, /s/, /z/, /θ/, /ð/, /h/, /ʒ/
laterals	/l/
approximants	/r/, /w/, /j/

3.4

	bilabial	labio-dental	dental	alveolar	post-alveolar	palato-alveolar	palatal	velar	glottal
plosives	paw bore /p/ /b/			tore door /t/ /d/				core gore /k/ /g/	
affricates						chore jaw /tʃ/ /dʒ/			
nasals	more /m/			nor /n/				sing /ŋ/	
slit fricatives		four vote /f/ /v/	think there /θ/ /ð/						horse /h/
groove fricatives				saw zoom /s/ /z/		shore treasure /ʃ/ /ʒ/			
laterals				law /l/					
approximants					raw /r/		your /j/	war /w/	

3.5a

		IPA symbol		distinctive feature
ro<u>p</u>e	ro<u>b</u>e	/p/	/b/	intensity
righ<u>t</u>	ri<u>d</u>e	/t/	/d/	intensity
ho<u>m</u>e	ho<u>p</u>e	/m/	/p/	intensity, manner
lin<u>k</u>	si<u>ng</u>	/k/	/ŋ/	intensity, manner
lea<u>v</u>e	lea<u>p</u>	/v/	/p/	intensity, place, manner
<u>w</u>ord	<u>b</u>ird	/w/	/b/	place, manner
<u>th</u>ink	<u>z</u>inc	/θ/	/z/	intensity, place
<u>y</u>east	<u>f</u>east	/j/	/f/	intensity, place, manner

3.5b

<u>h</u>ome	<u>R</u>ome	<u>c</u>omb
<u>r</u>ice	<u>v</u>ice	<u>n</u>ice
<u>y</u>our	<u>f</u>our	<u>j</u>aw
<u>sh</u>ip	<u>h</u>ip	<u>l</u>ip
<u>th</u>in	<u>sh</u>in	<u>ch</u>in
/h/	/r/	/k/
/r/	/v/	/n/
/j/	/f/	/dʒ/
/ʃ/	/h/	/l/
/θ/	/ʃ/	/tʃ/

<u>s</u>ource	<u>f</u>orce	<u>c</u>ourse	<u>h</u>orse
<u>t</u>ap	<u>m</u>ap	<u>n</u>ap	<u>g</u>ap
/s/	/f/	/k/	/h/
/t/	/m/	/n/	/g/

3.6a

dot	top	hot	path	log	post	girl
cat	age	stop	able	sport	thumb	break
few	vine	waste	north	song	zebra	wash
measure	bottle	mum	itch	than	five	wrong
/dt/	/tp/	/ht/	/pθ/	/lg/	/pst/	/gl/
/kt/	/dʒ/	/stp/	/bl/	/spt/	/θm/	/brk/
/fj/	/vn/	/wst/	/nθ/	/sŋ/	/zbr/	/wʃ/
/mʒ/	/btl/	/mm/	/tʃ/	/ðn/	/fv/	/rŋ/

Solutions to the exercises   129

3.6b

even	leave	very	cuff	fine	tough	awful
this	brother	choir	thin	seen	easy	breathe
ozone	witches	ducks	hens	foxes	bus	bust
weather	away	sow	pure	faith	mouth	morning

/vn/	/lv/	/vr/	/kf/	/fn/	/tf/	/fl/
/ðs/	/brð/	/kw/	/θn/	/sn/	/z/	/brð/
/zn/	/wtʃz/	/dks/	/hnz/	/fksz/	/bs/	/bst/
/wð/	/w/	/s/	/pj/	/fθ/	/mθ/	/mnŋ/

3.6c

new	thank	rabbit	car	kite	tablet	judge
church	switch	gin	dreamed	atlas	logging	stick
unit	ache	smash	treasure	ice	pleasure	eyes
finger	singer	cure	other	thought	broth	the

/nj/	/θŋk/	/rbt/	/k/	/kt/	/tblt/	/dʒdʒ/
/tʃtʃ/	/swtʃ/	/dʒn/	/drmd/	/tls/	/lgŋ/	/stk/
/jnt/	/k/	/smʃ/	/trʒ/	/s/	/plʒ/	/z/
/fŋg/	/sŋ/	/kj/	/ð/	/θt/	/brθ/	/ð/

4.3

h<u>ee</u>l	r<u>i</u>b	l<u>e</u>g	b<u>a</u>ck	th<u>u</u>mb	<u>a</u>rm	b<u>o</u>dy	j<u>a</u>w	f<u>oo</u>t	t<u>oo</u>th	g<u>i</u>rl	fing<u>e</u>r
h<u>ai</u>r	<u>ea</u>r	c<u>u</u>re	<u>ey</u>e	f<u>a</u>ce	b<u>oy</u>	n<u>o</u>se	br<u>ow</u>
			<u>i</u>ron	pl<u>ay</u>er	empl<u>oy</u>er	m<u>ow</u>er	sh<u>ow</u>er

/iː/	/ɪ/	/e/	/æ/	/ʌ/	/ɑː/	/ɒ/	/ɔː/	/ʊ/	/uː/	/ɜː/	/ə/
/eə/	/ɪə/	/ʊə/	/aɪ/	/eɪ/	/ɔɪ/	/əʊ/	/aʊ/
			/aɪə/	/eɪə/	/ɔɪə/	/əʊə/	/aʊə/

4.4a

| | close | | | | open | | | | mid | | |
1.	2.	3.	IPA	1.	2.	3.	IPA	1.	2.	3.	IPA
peak	bead	eat	/iː/	puck	bud	fuss	/ʌ/	peck	bed	rest	/e/
spook	boot	food	/uː/	pack	bad	chat	/æ/	perk	bird	work	/ɜː/
pick	bid	drink	/ɪ/	pot	bog	wash	/ɒ/	pork	bored	walk	/ɔː/
put	wood	cook	/ʊ/	park	bard	start	/ɑː/	upp<u>e</u>r	about	sofa	/ə/

	front				back				central		
1.	2.	3.	IPA	1.	2.	3.	IPA	1.	2.	3.	IPA
peak	bead	eat	/iː/	spook	boot	food	/uː/	perk	bird	work	/ɜː/
pick	bid	drink	/ɪ/	put	wood	cook	/ʊ/	puck	bud	fuss	/ʌ/
peck	bed	rest	/e/	pork	bored	walk	/ɔː/	upp<u>er</u>	about	sofa	/ə/
pack	bad	chat	/æ/	pot	bog	wash	/ɒ/				
				park	bard	start	/ɑː/				

4.4b

	centring				closing to /ɪ/				closing to /ʊ/		
1.	2.	3.	IPA	1.	2.	3.	IPA	1.	2.	3.	IPA
bear	pair	care	/eə/	bay	paste	waist	/eɪ/	boat	poke	toast	/əʊ/
beer	pier	fear	/ɪə/	by	pie	write	/aɪ/	bound	pound	house	/aʊ/
moor	poor	tour	/ʊə/	boy	poison	boil	/ɔɪ/				

It is useful to familiarise yourself with these vowel tables, and even to write down your own sets of sounds. Often it helps to think of a group or family of words with related senses that can act as a mnemonic. For instance, the group of animals *sheep, fish, hen, cat* would represent the four front vowels, as would *cheese, chips, bread, apples* if you chose food as the theme of your example words. *Snake, fly, oyster, goat, owl* or *steak, pie, joint, toast, mouth* could represent the closing diphthongs.

4.5

John sat by the open door; his broken foot rested on a short piece of wood. His brother Charles tried to creep past without waking him, but Charles's shoes had very slippery soles and his laces were undone: He slipped over, knocked the wood and woke up poor John. Both men were on the floor when Jill came in laughing loudly. She said she thought there had been some kind of accident. Now it was Charles who would have to spend the day resting on the sofa.

5.1

Sharon walked across the living room wondering what she should do about the news she had just received. She tried to appear calm and resist getting angry: Sharon's younger brother had phoned to arrange his stay with her next week. The problem was that she wanted to escape the hot city for the weekend and that would mean leaving George all alone without any company.

"He knows so few friends of mine, he doesn't like films or concerts and he hates places when they are empty," thought Sharon.

"There is nothing I can do about it except stay here this weekend – or perhaps if he uses Kate's boyfriend's flat instead. I'm sure Charles's place is big enough for two," she assured herself.

"Yes! Of course Charles wouldn't mind putting him up in the guest room with the single bed."

"Right. I'm going to ring him straight away."

[ʃærən wɔːkt¹ əkrɒs ðə lɪvɪŋ ruːm wʌndərɪŋ wɒt ʃiː² ʃʊd duː³ əbaʊt ðəi⁴ njuːz ʃi həd dʒʌst rɪsiːvd⁵ ʃi traɪd⁵ tuː³ əpɪə kɑːm ənd rɪzɪst getɪŋ æŋgri⁶,⁷ ʃærənz⁸ jʌŋgə⁹ brʌðə həd faʊnd⁵ tuː³ əreɪndʒ hɪz steɪ wɪð hɜː nekst wiːk ðə prɒbləm wɒz ðət ʃi wɒntɪd¹⁰ tuː³ ɪskeɪp ðə hɒt sɪti¹¹ fə ðə wiːkend ənd ðæt¹² wʊd miːn liːvɪŋ dʒɔːdʒ ɔːl əlaʊn wɪðaʊt eni¹¹ kʌmpəni¹¹

hi nəʊz¹³ səʊ fjuː frendz¹⁴ əv maɪn hi dʌzənt¹³ laɪk fɪlmz¹⁴ ɔː kɒnsəts¹⁵ ənd hi heɪts¹⁶ pleɪsɪz¹⁷ wen ðeɪ ɑː empti θɔːt ʃærən

ðeə ɪz nʌθɪŋ aɪ kən duː³ əbaʊt ɪt ɪksept steɪ hɪə ðɪs wiːkend ɔː pəɹhæps ɪf hi¹⁸ juːzɪz¹⁹ keɪts²⁰ bɔɪfrendz⁸ flæt ɪnsted aɪm ʃɔː tʃɑːlzɪz²¹ pleɪs ɪz bɪg ənʌf fɔː tuː³ ʃi² əʃɔːd hɜːself

jes əv kɔːs tʃɑːlz wʊdənt maɪnd pʊtɪŋ hɪm ʌp ɪn ðə gest ruːm wɪð²² ðə sɪŋgəl⁶ bed

raɪt aɪm gəʊɪŋ tə rɪŋ hɪm streɪt əweɪ]

---

1. Past-tense ending [t] after fortis consonants, except after /t/.
2. The pronouns *he, she, we, me* are transcribed with [ɪ], unless followed by a vowel or the semi-vowel /j/. Then we use intermediate [i].
3. Intermediate [u] before vowels.
4. The definite article *the* is usually transcribed [ðə], unless followed by a vowel. Then we use intermediate [i].
5. Past-tense ending [d] after vowels and lenis consonants, except after /d/.
6. When <ng> occurs in the middle of a morpheme, it is pronounced [ŋg].
7. In the word *angry*, the spelling <y> at the end of the word is represented by intermediate [i].
8. Possessive 's is transcribed [z] after vowels and lenis consonants, except after the lenis sibilants, /z, ʒ, dʒ/.
9. Even when <ng> occurs at the end of a morpheme, it is pronounced [ŋg] when it is followed by the comparative suffix *-er*.
10. Past-tense ending [ɪd] after /t/ or /d/.
11. As in note 7, intermediate [i] representing the spelling <y> at the end of a word.

¹² When *that* is demonstrative, it takes the full form [ðæt].
¹³ Third-person singular *-s* is transcribed [z] after vowels and lenis consonants, except after the lenis sibilants, /z, ʒ, dʒ/.
¹⁴ Plural *-s* is transcribed [z] after vowels and lenis consonants, except after the lenis sibilants, /z, ʒ, dʒ/.
¹⁵ Plural *-s* is transcribed [s] after fortis consonants, except after the fortis sibilants, /s, ʃ, tʃ/.
¹⁶ Third-person singular *-s* is transcribed [s] after fortis consonants, except after the fortis sibilants, /s, ʃ, tʃ/.
¹⁷ Plural *-s* is transcribed [ɪz] after sibilants, /s, z, ʃ, ʒ, tʃ, dʒ/.
¹⁸ Intermediate [i] before the semi-vowel /j/.
¹⁹ Third-person singular *-s* is transcribed [ɪz] after sibilants, /s, z, ʃ, ʒ, tʃ, dʒ/.
²⁰ Possessive *'s* is transcribed [s] after fortis consonants, except after the fortis sibilants, /s, ʃ, tʃ/.
²¹ Possessive *'s* is transcribed [ɪz] after sibilants, /s, z, ʃ, ʒ, tʃ, dʒ/.
²² In this manual, we use the lenis [ð] in our transcriptions of *with*.

5.2

[dʒɔɪs həd kʊkt¹ sʌpə bʌt heɪmɪʃ wɒntɪd² nʌθɪŋ tuː³ iːt hi niːdɪd² taɪm tə θɪŋk hi wʌndəd⁴ wɒt həd hæpənd⁴ tuː³ ɔːl ðə pɪktʃəz⁵ ənd bʊks⁶ hi həd pleɪst¹ səʊ keəfəli⁷ əraʊnd ðə flæt

dʒɔɪs ɔːlweɪz taɪdɪz⁸,⁹ θɪŋz⁵ əweɪ hi sed tə hɪmself

aɪ stækt¹ ɔːl ðə njuː bɪts⁶ ənd piːsɪz¹⁰ jʊ həd skætəd⁴ evriweə¹¹ ɪn ðə hɔːl ʃi¹² ɑːnsəd⁴ hɪz θɔːts⁶

ðəʊz wɜːks⁶ əv ɑːt dʒɜːnəlz⁵ ənd daɪəriz⁵,⁸,¹³ ɑː preʃəs tə miː¹² iːvən ɪf dʒɔɪs θɪŋks¹⁴ ðeə aʊt əv fæʃən naʊ ənd nɒt wɜːθ mʌtʃ hi mʌtəd⁴ kwaɪətli⁷ tə hɪmself

ɔːl mænə əv ɒbdʒɪkts⁶,¹⁵ frəm heɪmɪʃɪz¹⁶ feɪməs brʌðəz¹⁷ hjuːdʒ aʊtpʊt¹⁸ ɪn hɪz ʃɔːt taɪm əz ə faɪn ɑːtɪst naʊ tɜːnd⁴ pɒp sɪŋə¹⁹ klɒɡd⁴ ʌp evri⁷ ɪntʃ əv speɪs ɪn ðə kræmpt¹ flæt naʊ hi həd stɒpt¹ ənd lɪŋɡəd⁴,²⁰ ɪn frʌnt əv hɪz feɪvrɪt¹⁵ pɪktʃə hiː¹² ədɔːd⁴ ɪt hɪz fɪŋɡə²⁰ treɪst¹ ə feɪnt laɪn əkrɒs ðiː²¹ ɪmɪdʒ fə tuː¹⁹ lɒŋ¹⁹ hi həd weɪtɪd² fə sʌmθɪŋ tuː³ əkɜː ɪn hɪz laɪf

deɪvɪd ɡets¹⁴ ɒn wɪð θɪŋz⁵ ənd mænɪdʒɪz²² tuː³ endʒɔɪ laɪf səʊ dʌz²³ dʒɔɪs hiː¹² enviəsli⁷ θɔːt

ʃi¹² ɒptɪd² tə liːv hɪm ələʊn ənd həʊpt¹ hi wʊd rɪtɜːn tə ðə teɪbəl leɪtə fə aʊəz⁵ ʃi həd bɪn mɒbd⁴ baɪ ʌnrɪlentɪŋ kraʊdz⁵ əv ədmaɪərɪŋ¹³ fænz⁵ eɡd⁴ ɒn baɪ ə kreɪzd⁴ miːdɪə hɜː leɪtəst nɒvəl wept¹ naʊ sɒbd⁴ wɪð ɪməʊʃən red wʌn rɪvjuː heɪmɪʃ wəz sɪk wɪð envi⁷ dʒɔɪs wəz əʊvə ðə muːn]

---

¹ Past-tense ending [t] after fortis consonants, except after /t/.
² Past-tense ending [ɪd] after /t/ or /d/.
³ Intermediate [u] before vowels.
⁴ Past-tense ending [d] after vowels and lenis consonants, except after /d/.
⁵ Plural -s transcribed [z] after vowels and lenis consonants, except after the lenis sibilants, /z, ʒ, dʒ/.
⁶ Plural -s transcribed [s] after fortis consonants, except after the fortis sibilants, /s, ʃ, tʃ/.
⁷ Intermediate [i] when the spelling is <y> at the end of a word, such as *fairly*, *very*, or *lady*.

Solutions to the exercises 133

[8] Intermediate [i] because of the underlying spelling <y> in *tidy*.
[9] Third-person singular -s transcribed [z] after vowels and lenis consonants, except after the lenis sibilants, /z, ʒ, dʒ/.
[10] Plural -s transcribed [ɪz] after sibilants, /s, z, ʃ, ʒ, tʃ, dʒ/.
[11] Intermediate [i] because the underlying spelling is with a <y>: *every* in *everywhere*.
[12] The pronouns *he*, *she*, *we*, *me* are transcribed with [ɪ], unless followed by a vowel or the semi-vowel /j/. Then we use intermediate [i].
[13] The triphthong [aɪə] occurs here.
[14] Third-person singular -s transcribed [s] after fortis consonants, except after the fortis sibilants, /s, ʃ, tʃ/.
[15] Unstressed vowel occurring as [ɪ], rather than schwa, [ə].
[16] Possessive 's transcribed [ɪz] after sibilants, /s, z, ʃ, ʒ, tʃ, dʒ/.
[17] Possessive 's transcribed [z] after vowels and lenis consonants, except after the lenis sibilants, /z, ʒ, dʒ/.
[18] Unstressed vowel occurring as [ʊ], rather than schwa, [ə].
[19] When <ng> occurs at the end of a morpheme, it is simply pronounced [ŋ].
[20] When <ng> occurs in the middle of a morpheme, it is pronounced [ŋg].
[21] The definite article the is usually transcribed [ðə], unless followed by a vowel. Then we use intermediate [i].
[22] Third-person singular -s transcribed [ɪz] after sibilants, /s, z, ʃ, ʒ, tʃ, dʒ/.
[23] Third-person singular -s transcribed [z] after vowels and lenis consonants, except after the lenis sibilants, /z, ʒ, dʒ/.

6.1

Mary's loose change jangled in her pockets. A strongish cup of coffee was what she needed now. Every Thursday morning she goes to the gym and practises her aerobic technique and strengthens her tendons since she is training for a long distance race. More often than not she meets up with her ex-boss Jane, who belongs to the same sports club.

The caffeine started to work and Mary felt much better after the strenuous workout. Jane had arrived five minutes before Mary and was already sitting on a sofa and studying the menu while sipping on her mango juice cocktail when Mary had walked in and plonked herself down next to her.

"I feel better for that," Mary said brightly, pushing the tiny cup made of china across the tray and staring out of the café window at the store opposite.

She nudged Jane.

"I just saw Angela appearing from Jones's shoes across the road. I thought she was in Geneva, or somewhere in Switzerland," she whispered to her friend.

[meəriz[1,2] luːs tʃeɪndʒ dʒæŋgld[3,4] ɪn hə pɒkɪts[5] ə strɒŋɪʃ[6] kʌp əv kɒfi[7] wəz wɒt ʃi niːdɪd[8] naʊ evri[1] θɜːzdeɪ mɔːnɪŋ ʃi ɡəʊz[9] tə ðə dʒɪm ənd præktɪsɪz[10] hər[11] ərəʊbɪk tekniːk ənd streŋθənz[9,12] hə tendənz[13] sɪns ʃi[14] ɪz treɪnɪŋ fər[11] ə lɒŋ[6] dɪstəns reɪs mɔːr[11] ɒftən ðən nɒt ʃi miːts[15] ʌp wɪð hər[11] eks bɒs dʒeɪn huː bɪlɒŋz[6,9] tə ðə seɪm spɔːts[5] klʌb ðə kæfiːn staːtɪd[8] tə wɜːk ənd meəri felt mʌtʃ betər[11] aːftə ðə strenjuəs[16] wɜːkaʊt dʒeɪn həd əraɪvd[4] faɪv mɪnɪts[5] bəfɔː meəri ənd wəz ɔːlredi[1] sɪtɪŋ ɒn ə səʊfər[17] ənd stʌdiɪŋ[18] ðə menjuː waɪl sɪpɪŋ ɒn hə mæŋɡəʊ[3] dʒuːs kɒkteɪl wen meəri həd wɔːkt[19] ɪn ənd plɒŋkt[19] həself daʊn nekst tə hə

aɪ fiːl betə fə ðæt meəri sed braɪtli[1] pʊʃɪŋ ðə taɪni[1] kʌp meɪd əv tʃaɪnər[17] əkrɒs ðə treɪ ənd steərɪŋ[11] aʊt əv ðə kæfeɪ wɪndəʊ ət ðə stɔːr[11] ɒpəzɪt

ʃi nʌdʒd[4] dʒeɪn

aɪ dʒʌst sɔːr[17] ændʒələr[17] əpɪərɪŋ[11] frəm dʒəʊnsɪz[20] ʃuːz[13] əkrɒs ðə rəʊd aɪ θɔːt ʃi wəz ɪn dʒəniːvər[17] ɔː sʌmweər[11] ɪn swɪtsələnd ʃi wɪspəd[4] tə hə frend]

1   Intermediate [i] when the spelling is <y> at the end of a word, such as *fairly*, *very*, or *lady*.
2   Possessive *'s* transcribed [z] after vowels and lenis consonants, except after the lenis sibilants, /z, ʒ, dʒ/.
3   When <ng> occurs in the middle of a morpheme, it is pronounced [ŋg].
4   Past-tense ending [d] after lenis consonants, except after /d/.
5   Plural *-s* transcribed [s] after fortis consonants, except after the fortis sibilants, /s, ʃ, tʃ/.
6   When <ng> occurs at the end of a morpheme, it is simply pronounced [ŋ].
7   Intermediate [i] for the spelling <ee> at the end of a word when the syllable is unstressed.
8   Past-tense ending [ɪd] after /t/ or /d/.
9   Third-person singular *-s* transcribed [z] after vowels and lenis consonants, except after the lenis sibilants, /z, ʒ, dʒ/.
10   Third-person singular *-s* transcribed [ɪz] after the sibilants, /s, z, ʃ, ʒ, tʃ, dʒ/.
11   Linking *r*.
12   When <ng> occurs at the end of a morpheme, it is pronounced [ŋ]; this is so in the consonant cluster [ŋθ] at the end of the morpheme [streŋθ] in the word *strengthens*.
13   Plural *-s* transcribed [z] after vowels and lenis consonants, except after the lenis sibilants, /z, ʒ, dʒ/.
14   The pronouns *he, she, we, me* are transcribed with [ɪ] unless followed by a vowel or the semi-vowel /j/. Then we use intermediate [i].
15   Third-person singular *-s* transcribed [s] after fortis consonants, except after the fortis sibilants, /s, ʃ, tʃ/.
16   Intermediate [u] for the spelling <u> in <uous>.
17   Intrusive *r*.
18   Intermediate [i] when the spelling is <y> at the end of a word, and this is so in the underlying form *study*.
19   Past-tense ending [t] after fortis consonants, except after /t/.
20   Possessive *'s* transcribed [ɪz] after sibilants, /s, z, ʃ, ʒ, tʃ, dʒ/.

6.2

[debrə[r1] əʊpənd[2] hər[3] aɪz[4] ənd ðen blɪŋkt[5] əgen[6]

ðeə mʌst bɪ sʌmθɪŋ rɒŋ ɔːr[3] aɪm driːmɪŋ ʃɪ mɜːməd[2] tə həself

ʃɪ siːmd[2] tə bɪ hʌngri[7,8] θɜːsti[8] ənd taɪəd[2] ɔːl təgeðər[3] ət wɒnts ɒn ðə siːlɪŋ ʃɪ kəd meɪk aʊt ə smɔːl traɪæŋgl[7] daɪrektli[8] əbʌv hər[3] ɒv ə dɑːkər[3] ɒrɪndʒ əgeɪnst[9] ðə rest əv ðə rʌsti[8] kʌləd[2] peɪnt

haʊ ə jʊ fiːlɪŋ tədeɪ ekəʊd[2] ə vɔɪs frəm ðə səʊfər[r1] ɪn ðə kɔːnər[3] əv ðə ruːm

wel ðeəz[10] ə tɪŋglɪŋ[7] ɪn maɪ təʊz[4] maɪ fɪŋgəz[4,7] ə stɪŋɪŋ[11] ənd maɪ hedz[10] bʌzɪŋ laɪk kreɪzi[8] maɪ dʒɔː[r1] ənd nek stɪl eɪk bət əʊvərɔːl[3] aɪm betə ðən jestədeɪ ʃɪ rɪplaɪd[2] ʌnkən'vɪnsɪŋli[8] debrəz[12] dɒktər[3] ɒftən vɪzɪtɪd[13] dʒʌst ɑːftər[3] iːvnɪŋ mɪəltaɪm ənd ɑːskt[5] ə nʌmbər[3] əv kwestʃənz[4] bɪfɔːr[3] əsesɪŋ weðər[3] ɔː nɒt tə prɪskraɪb[14] eni[8] njuː pɪlz[4] ɔː tæbləts[15] hɪ tʊk hɪz taɪm hɪ lɪŋgəd[2,7] hɪ laɪkt[5] tə drɔː[r1] aʊt ði[16] ægəni[8]

ɔːlraɪt tuː ekstrə[r1] ɪndʒekʃənz[4] əv mɔːfiːn hɪ dɪsaɪdɪd[13] bət fə nəʊ lɒŋgə[17] ðən θriː deɪz[4]

dɪspaɪt hə hʌngər[3,7] ənd θɜːst debrə wəz rɪliːvd[2] wen ði[16] ɒd ʃeɪp əbʌv hə rɪsiːdɪd[13] ɪntə ðə rest əv ðə siːlɪŋ ənd ʃɪ drɪftɪd[13] ɒf ɪntuː[18] ənʌðə diːp sliːp]

---

[1] Intrusive *r*.
[2] Past-tense ending [d] after lenis consonants, except after /d/.
[3] Linking *r*.
[4] Plural -*s* transcribed [z] after vowels and lenis consonants, except after the lenis sibilants, /z, ʒ, dʒ/.
[5] Past-tense ending [t] after fortis consonants, except after /t/.
[6] [əgeɪn] is also possible.
[7] When <ng> occurs in the middle of a morpheme, it is pronounced [ŋg].
[8] Intermediate [i] when the spelling is <y> at the end of a word, such as *fairly*, *very*, or *lady*.
[9] This may also be pronounced [əgenst].
[10] Short form of auxiliary *is* is transcribed [z] after vowels and lenis consonants, except after the lenis sibilants, /z, ʒ, dʒ/.
[11] When <ng> occurs at the end of a morpheme, it is simply pronounced [ŋ].
[12] Possessive *'s* transcribed [z] after vowels and lenis consonants, except after the lenis sibilants, /z, ʒ, dʒ/.
[13] Past-tense ending [ɪd] after /t/ or /d/.
[14] Unstressed [ɪ] in the prefix *pre-*.
[15] Plural -*s* transcribed [s] after fortis consonants, except after the fortis sibilants, /s, ʃ, tʃ/.
[16] The definite article *the* is usually transcribed [ðə], unless followed by a vowel. Then we use intermediate [i].
[17] Even when <ng> occurs at the end of a morpheme, it is pronounced [ŋg] when it is followed by the comparative suffix -*er*.
[18] Intermediate [u] before vowels.

7.1

[dʒəʊzɪf wəz siːtɪd ɒn hɪz bælkəni ɪn ðə fiːbḷ¹ ɪluːmɪˈneɪʃn̩² əv ðə nɪəli ɪkˈstɪŋgwɪʃt³ sʌn ðə deɪ wəz nəʊ lɒŋgə hɒt ənd ɪgˈzɒtɪk³ bɜːdz mɪŋgl̩d¹ wɪð ðə daɪɪŋ reɪz swuːpɪŋ ɑːftə klaʊdz əv hɒvr̩ɪŋ⁴ mɪdʒɪz hɪ lʊkt aʊt əʊvə ðə rɪvə reɪdʒɪŋ ɪn ðə væli fɪld wɪð hjuːdʒ rɒks bɪləʊ ðə rɔːr⁵ əv gʌʃɪŋ wɔːtə defn̩d⁶ hɪz ɪəz ənd ə faɪnt spreɪ ˈpɜːmɪeɪtɪd⁷ ðə kuːl eə nɔːməli hɪ mɪksɪz ə drɪŋk sɪts ʌnpəˈtɜːbd ənd wɪʃɪz əweɪ ði aʊəz bʌt ðɪs iːvn̩ɪŋ⁸ hæpn̩d⁹ tʊ bɪ ʌnlaɪk eni ʌðər⁵ iːvn̩ɪŋ⁸

aɪv ˈfɪnɪʃt tʃæptə sevn̩¹⁰ hɪ θɔːt ənd rɪtn̩¹¹ ðə bɪˈgɪnɪŋ əv sekʃn̩² tuː

hɪ wəz suÉˈpriːmli pliːzd sɪns hɪz deɪli efəts fər⁵ ə gʊd fjuː mʌnθs həd ɒf(t)n̩⁶,¹² endɪd ɪn dɪsəˈpɔɪntmənt ənd frʌsˈtreɪʃn̩² fə sʌm riːzn̩¹³ ðə rɔːr¹⁴ aɪˈdɪəz hɪ wəz tɔɪɪŋ wɪð həd fɔːmd ðəmselvz ɪntu ə ˈkɒŋkriːt ənd kənvɪnsɪŋ həʊl ðət rɪəli wɜːkt

ɔːl aɪ hæv¹⁵ tə du ɪz kiːp ɒn gəʊɪŋ laɪk ðɪs ɪn ðɪs ˈpɜːfɪkt sɪtjueɪʃn̩²,¹⁶,¹⁷ ənd aɪl bɪ ˈfɪnɪʃt baɪ dʒuːn nekst jɪə]

1. Syllabic [l̩] for the spelling <le> at the end of a word.
2. Syllabic [n̩] because of the preceding palatoalveolar fricative [ʃ].
3. Compare the lenis sequence /ɪgz/ for <ex> in *exotic* with the fortis sequence /ɪks/ for <ex> in *extinguished*.
4. May be pronounced with either a syllabic [r̩] as indicated, or with a short schwa [hɒvərɪŋ].
5. Linking *r*.
6. Syllabic [n̩] in the unstressed syllable, following the labiodental fricative /f/.
7. Intermediate [i] in the syllable spelt <iate>.
8. Syllabic [n̩] in the unstressed syllable, following the labiodental fricative /v/.
9. Syllabic [n̩] in the unstressed syllable, following the bilabial plosive /p/.
10. Syllabic [n̩] in this environment after the labiodental fricative /v/.
11. Syllabic [n̩] in this environment after the alveolar plosive /t/.
12. There is omission of the alveolar plosive /t/ in the consonant cluster /ftn/. Omitted sounds are enclosed in parentheses, ( ). You will learn more about omission of sounds in Lesson Nine, but the transcription of *often* is best learnt like this.
13. Syllabic [n̩] in this environment after the alveolar fricative /z/.
14. Intrusive *r*.
15. Strong form of *have* because it is stressed.
16. The palatoalveolar fricative [ʃ] may be pronounced here: [sɪtʃueɪʃn̩].
17. Intermediate [u] in the syllable spelt <uate>.

7.2

[əʊpn̩ɪŋ¹ ðə bɒtl̩² ˈmɪrɪəm³ kʊdn̩t⁴ ʌndəˈstænd⁵ waɪ ðər⁶,⁷ əpɪəd tʊ bi⁸ klaʊdi ˈsedɪmənt drɪftɪŋ ʌp frəm ðə bɒtm̩⁹ əv ði ɪkˈskwɪzɪtli¹⁰ sentɪd trænzˈluːsn̩t¹¹ ˈlɪkwɪd ʃi həd bɪn¹² əˈʃɔːd¹³ baɪ ðə seɪlzmən ðət ə njuː metl̩¹⁴ fɪltreɪʃn̩¹⁵ sɪstəm həd əʊvəˈkʌm¹⁶ ɜːliə prɒbləmz əlaʊɪŋ waɪn tə bi⁸ prəˈdjuːst ðət wəz iːzi tə drɪŋk streɪt frəm ðə bɒtl̩² ɒn ðɪs ədvaɪs ʃi həd pɜːtʃəst nɒt dʒʌst wʌn bət θriː keɪsɪz əv ðə faɪnəst əʊk mətʃjɔːd¹⁷ red naʊ ʃi wəz wʌndr̩ɪŋ¹⁸ əz ʃi kærɪd ɒn pɔːrɪŋ weðə jet əgeɪn ʌnsəˈspektɪŋli ʃi həd bɪn rɪpt ɒf baɪ ən ʌnˈskruːpjʊləs¹⁹ ɪndəˈvɪdʒʊəl ðə faɪn l̩¹⁴ grɪti drɒp splæʃt ɪntu ə sevn̩θ²⁰ glɑːs ˈmɪriəm saɪd ənd həʊpt nəʊbədi wʊd nəʊtɪs ðə kʌlə liːst əv ɔːl ðə teɪst əv hɜː preʃəs ˈvɪntɪdʒ

1. Syllabic [n̩] is probably nearly always used in this context, is given as the pronunciation in most dictionaries, and here conforms to our guideline from Lesson Seven: The syllabic [n̩] is especially frequent when /n/ is preceded by an alveolar plosive or fricative in unstressed syllables.
2. Syllabic [l̩] for the spelling <le> at the end of a word.
3. Stress marked because it falls on "lighter" monophthong, rather than the diphthong.
4. Normally pronounced in its weak form with the syllabic nasal [n̩]. Also conforming to note 1 above.
5. Stress normally falls on the second word in compounds with *under-*, but stress is sometimes used to distinguish two senses of a word. For example, *underground*, which may be an adjective meaning 'below the surface of the earth' /ʌndəˈgraʊnd/ or a noun meaning 'people in a society who are trying new and often shocking or subversive ways of living' /ˈʌndəgraʊnd/. This exemplifies a contrastive stress distinction in English: Nouns tend to have stress on the first syllable, verbs and adjectives on the second (in this case it is the third syllable that carries stress because schwa is always unstressed).
6. In this context, *there* is an indefinite adverb, and would normally be pronounced [ðə] when followed by a consonant, or [ðər] with a linking *r* when followed by a vowel. When *there* occurs as a demonstrative adverb, it is pronounced [ðeə] when followed by a consonant, as in *it's over there near the door* [ɪts əʊvə ðeə nɪə ðə dɔː], or [ðeər] with a linking *r* when followed by a vowel, as in *there it is* [ðeər ɪt ɪz]. (See also Lesson Eight on weak forms.)
7. Linking *r*.
8. The speaker seems to use intermediate [i] here.
9. Syllabic [m̩] in this environment after the alveolar plosive /t/.
10. Stress on second syllable.
11. The ending <ent> is normally transcribed with syllabic [n̩], especially after alveolar plosives or fricatives.
12. This pronunciation of *been* with intermediate [i] rather than [ɪ] seems to be becoming standard in RP.
13. You may hear a slight palatal glide from the palatoalveolar fricative [ʃ] to the back vowel [ɔː]: [ʃʲɔː]. It is quite possible that you might also perceive this sequence as the diphthong /ʊə/ also preceded by a short glide: [ʃʲʊə]. The interpretation you arrive at is probably dependent on your own articulation of the word *assured*.
14. Syllabic [l̩] for the spelling <al> at the end of a word.
15. Syllabic [n̩] because of the preceding palatoalveolar fricative.
16. Stress on final syllable as in note 3 above.
17. The speaker here pronounces the fortis affricate, [tʃ], in the word *matured*. You may perceive the vowel as a long back monophthong [ɔː], or as a centring diphthong [ʊə].
18. It seems that a syllabic [r̩] is pronounced here, rather than a consonant cluster [ndr] or a weak syllable with schwa [ndər].
19. Intermediate [u] occurs here in the weak syllable represented by the spelling <pu>.
20. Syllabic [n̩] in this environment after the labiodental fricative /v/.

8.1

[ðər¹,² ɪz lɪtl̩³ taɪm tə luːz kʌm ɒn⁴ wi məs⁵ hʌri ðə treɪn liːvz ɪn hɑːf ən⁶ aʊə

daʊnt ˈpænɪk wil⁷ iːzɪli get ðeə⁸ baɪ tæksi aɪv dʒəst rʌŋ fə wʌn naʊ

aɪ həd təʊld dʒefri wid⁷ bi ðər²,⁸ ɒn taɪm fə wʌns dʒʌdʒɪŋ frm̩⁹ ðə ˈtræfɪk ðɪs mɔːnɪŋ wi
ʃʊd¹⁰ bi liːvɪŋ mɔːrˀ ə les naʊ jə nevə naʊ wɒt kn̩¹¹ hæpn̩¹² ɒn ðə weɪ tə ðə steɪʃn̩¹³

jə naʊ wɒt dʒefri sez ðəʊ hi dɪsaɪdɪd ðət hi wəd du ɪgˈzæktli wɒt hi ˈɔːlweɪz wɒntɪd ɒn ðɪs
ˈhɒlɪdeɪ səʊ naʊ rʌʃ naʊ hæsl̩³ naʊ ˈpreʃəraɪzɪŋ

jes bət ɪf wɪə nɒt¹⁴ ðeə⁸ baɪ ten ðæts¹⁵ prɪsaɪsli haʊ hil⁷ bi fiːlɪŋ ənd ʌnprɪdɪktəˈbɪlɪti əv ðə
ˈtræfɪk ɪz ðə flɔːʳ¹⁶ ɪn jə plænz

duː¹⁷ stɒp medl̩ɪŋ³ wɪð dʒefriz əfeəz aɪm ʃɔː hi kən mænɪdʒ ˈpɜːfektli wel ɒn ɪz¹⁸ əʊn]

---

1. Weak form of *there* because it is an indefinite adverb, rather than a demonstrative adverb.
2. Linking *r*.
3. Syllabic [l̩] for the spelling <le> at the end of a word.
4. The preposition *on* has no weak form.
5. Word-final alveolar plosive /t/ is usually absent before consonants in unstressed *must*. You might transcribe this sequence with stressed *must*: [mʌst hʌri].
6. Single segment of /n/ is also possible here, in which case it would be transcribed with syllabic [n̩].
7. Normally, when a pronoun combines with an auxiliary verb, it is pronounced with either intermediate [i] or intermediate [u].
8. Strong form of *there* because it is a demonstrative adverb, rather than an indefinite adverb. When *there* occurs as a demonstrative adverb, it is pronounced [ðeə] when followed by a consonant, as in *it's over there near the door* [ɪts əʊvə ðeə nɪə ðə dɔː], or [ðeər] with a linking *r* when followed by a vowel, as in *there it is* [ðeər ɪt ɪz].
9. The preposition *from* is probably very short in this environment, and may be transcribed with syllabic [m̩].
10. Rather than the lexical participle *leaving* carrying stress, it is more likely that the modal auxiliary *should* is stressed, thus taking a strong form.
11. The auxiliary verb *can* is probably very short in this environment, and may be transcribed with syllabic [n̩].
12. Syllabic [n̩] in unstressed syllable, following bilabial plosive /p/.
13. Again, syllabic [n̩] in unstressed syllable. This time following palatoalveolar fricative /ʃ/.
14. The full form supposes that *not* is stressed.
15. Strong form of *that* because it is a demonstrative adjective.
16. Intrusive *r*.
17. Strong form of *do* because it is emphatic.
18. A much reduced form of *his* is likely here.

Solutions to the exercises

8.2

[ɪt wɒznt[1] ʌnˈtɪl ðə ʃɒp faɪnli[2] kləʊzd ðət ðə mɪsɪŋ stɒk wəz nəʊtɪst dʒɔːdʒ went streɪt tə ðə ˈmænɪdʒə tə tel hə ðæt[3] θruː sʌm kəʊˈɪnsɪdn̩s[4] twenti faɪv paʊndz wɜːθ əv kəmpjuːtə pərɪfr̩l̩z[5] həd nɒt bɪn teɪkn̩[6] əkaʊnt ɒv[7] ðɪs wəz ðə θɜːd deɪ ðət ˈsʌmθɪŋ həd dɪsəpɪəd ənd naʊ sæli wəz bɪˈkʌmɪŋ səspɪʃəs

ðeəz[8] mɔː tə ðɪs ðən miːts ði aɪ ʃi[9] wɪspəd tʊ dʒɔːdʒ ʌndə hə breθ aɪ dəʊn(t)[10] wɒnt tə brɪŋ ðə lɔː[11] ɪntə ðɪs bət aɪ meɪ hæv[12] nəʊ ɒlˈtɜːnətɪv ɪf θɪŋz kiːp ˈvænɪʃɪŋ wɪˈðaʊ(t)[13] treɪs dʒɔːdʒ wəz ˈwʌrid[14] ðət hi wəz prɒbəbli ðə praɪm ˈsʌspekt (ə)speʃəli[15] əz hi həd əʊnli stɑːtɪd wɜːkɪŋ ðeər[16] ə mʌnθ əɡəʊ]

---

[1] The auxiliary verbs are usually used in their strong forms when they occur in negations with *not*. Here, *was* is a copula, rather than an auxiliary verb, but the rule still applies that negative forms are usually strong.

[2] It is possible that the alveolar nasal is perceived as syllabic [n̩].

[3] Strong form of *that* occurs here probably because the speaker pauses before speaking the *that*-clause, making it the end of a longer stretch of speech. Strong forms are normally used at the end of a clause or sentence.

[4] The spelling <ence> is normally transcribed with syllabic [n̩], especially after alveolar plosives and fricatives.

[5] There are two consecutive syllabic consonants here, [r̩] followed by [l̩].

[6] Here, the speaker uses a syllabic [n̩] in the unstressed syllable.

[7] Strong form of *of* because it occurs sentence-finally.

[8] It is quite possible that you will perceive this sequence as [ðeːz]. The vowel is strong, rather than weak, and is either a lengthened monophthong or a diphthong with a relatively short glide.

[9] The speaker uses an intermediate [i] in the pronoun.

[10] There is omission of the alveolar plosive /t/, this time in word-final position, but in the middle of the consonant cluster /ntw/ running across the word boundary. Omitted sounds are enclosed in parentheses, ( ). You will learn more about omission of sounds in Lesson Nine.

[11] The speaker here avoids an intrusive *r*. We could transcribe this phonetically as [lɔːʔɪntə].

[12] The verb *have* takes a strong form here because it is a lexical verb, rather than an auxiliary.

[13] The speaker omits the word-final alveolar plosive /t/, or replaces it with a glottal stop, [ʔ].

[14] Although this is a participle form of the verb *worry*, and therefore the second syllable cannot be stressed, you might like to mark stress to make the correct stress placement clearer.

[15] The speaker omits the /ə/ from the beginning of the word *especially*.

[16] The word *there* has a demonstrative function, pointing to the place where George works, so it takes a full form, and in this instance a linking *r* precedes the word *a*.

9.1

[ɜːli ɒn 'θɜːzdeɪ¹ mɔːnɪŋ dʒʌs(t)² bɪfɔːr³ eɪt əklɒk ðə fɜːs(t)² ten⁴ gruːps əraɪvd redi tə stɑːt ðeə njuː treɪnɪŋ reɪ'ʒiːm⁵ wɪðɪn⁵ fɔːr³ aʊəs⁶ fjuː əv ðə pə'tɪsɪpənts wər eɪbl̩ tə rɪ'zɪst ðə tempteɪʃn̩ əv sɪtɪŋ iːvn̩ ðəʊ ði əʊnli speɪs left ʌn'klʌtəd⁷ wɪð ɪ'kwɪpmn̩t wəz ðə friːzɪŋ kəʊld stəʊm⁸ flɔː

ðeɪ wər³ ɔːl km̩pliːtli səpraɪz(d)⁹ tə faɪn(d)⁹ ðət ðeə mʌn(θ)s¹⁰ əv prepəreɪʃn̩ həd bɪn juːsləs mentl̩ 'stæmɪnərˡ¹¹ ən fɪsɪkl̩ ə'dʒɪlɪti wə rɪkwaɪəd fə ðɪs kaɪnd əv 'eksəsaɪz bət 'nəʊwʌn ɪk'spektɪd sətʃ gruːəlɪŋ tɑːsks tə bi əsaɪn(d)¹² frəm ðə stɑːt naʊ ðə len(k)θ¹³ əv ðə hɔːl wəz lɪtəd wɪð jʌŋ stjuːdn̩ts pʌzl̩d ɪgzɔːstɪd ənd dɪprest

fræŋkli ðə həʊl θɪŋ ɪz ə təʊtl̩ ʃæmbl̩z t(ə)deɪz¹⁴ bɪn ə km̩pliːt¹⁵ raɪtɒf səd ðeə treɪnə

tə'mɒrəʊ aɪ æn'tɪsɪpeɪt mɔːr³ ənd əl get_təm¹⁶ wɜːkn̩¹⁷ nɒn'stɒp wəz hər³ əʊnli aɪ'dɪərˡ¹¹ əv haʊ tu ɪmpruːv ðeər³ ɔːfl̩ pəfɔːmn̩s]

---

1. Some speakers might use intermediate [i] instead of the diphthong.
2. Elision of word-final /t/ in the consonant cluster /stb/. This occurs later in the middle of the cluster /stt/ in *first ten*.
3. Linking *r*.
4. Possible regressive assimilation of place: Word-final alveolar nasal, /n/, in the word *ten* becomes the velar nasal, [ŋ], under the influence of the following velar plosive [g] in the word *groups*. Either form would probably be syllabic in fast connected speech with the elision of /e/: [t(e)n̩] or [t(e)ŋ̍].
5. Stress on the second syllable.
6. Possible regressive assimilation of intensity: Word-final lenis alveolar fricative, /z/, in the word *hours* becomes the fortis alveolar fricative, [s], under the influence of the following fortis labiodental fricative, [f], in the word *few*. Here, we transcribe it with the symbol [s], rather than the narrow transcription of [z̥]. Since our transcription is a broad phonetic one, we do not include the devoiced diacritic, [̥], but we discussed this feature in Lesson Five.
7. Prefix *un-* does not carry stress.
8. Possible regressive assimilation of place: Word-final alveolar nasal, /n/, in the word *stone* becomes the bilabial nasal, [m], under the influence of the following labiodental fricative [f] in the word *floor*.
9. Elision of word-final /d/ in the consonant cluster /zdt/, and later in the consonant cluster /ndð/.
10. Possible elision of /θ/ in the consonant cluster /nθs/.
11. Intrusive *r*.
12. Elision of word-final /d/ in the consonant cluster /ndf/.
13. Elision of /k/ in the consonant cluster /ŋkθ/. And internal regressive assimilation of place: Velar nasal, /ŋ/, assimilates to alveolar nasal, [n], under the influence of the following dental fricative [θ].
14. Elision of schwa in the syllable [tə]. Normally, in this context, the elided segment would be replaced by aspiration and would be transcribed phonetically as [tʰdeɪ].
15. Elision of schwa in the syllable [kəm]. This is compensated for by making the bilabial nasal syllabic: [m̩].

Solutions to the exercises

[16] Possible progressive assimilation of manner: Word-initial dental fricative /θ/ in the word *them* assimilates to the preceding alveolar plosive [t] in *get*. The two sounds are then articulated as one sound, indicated by the horizontal swung line connecting them.
[17] Possible elision or reduction of /ɪ/ with substitution by the syllabic consonant, and regressive assimilation of place: Syllabic velar nasal, /ŋ/, in the word *working* assimilates to the following alveolar nasal, [n], in the word *non-stop*.

9.2

[dʒɒn pɔɪntɪd tʊ ðə dɪstn̩t[1] hɪlz ə lɒŋ laɪŋ[2] gəʊɪŋ ɒf ɪntə ðə həraɪzn̩[3]

ðæts weə wɪər[4] eɪmɪŋ tə get tu[5] bɪfɔː ˈsʌnse(t)[6] tənaɪt hi[7] mʌtəd

ɪt hædn̩t bɪn[8] ə gʊd[9] mɔːnɪŋ ɪn ðə fɜːs(t)[10] pleɪs hɪʃ‿ʃɜːt[11] həd gɒt snægd ɒn ə waɪl(d)[12] bræmbl̩ ðen hi[7] həd brəʊkn̩ maɪks bræn(d)‿nju:[13] kʌmpəs hiː[14] wɒzn̩t ət ɔː(l)[15] pliːzd ən tə kæp ɪt ɔːl[16] hi həd pækt ðə rɒm[17] mæp

hɪʃ‿ʃuːz[11] wə taɪt hɪs[18] fiːt eɪkt hɪs[18] pæk wəz hevi[19] hɪz[18] bæk kəmpleɪnd

maɪk traɪd tə tʃɪə hɪm ʌp[20] bət (h)ɪs[18,21] tʃæti dʒəʊks əʊnli siːm(d)[22] tə meɪk dʒɒn iːvm̩[23] mɔː[24] ˈɒbstɪnət maɪk ˈɪrɪteɪtɪd hɪs[18] praɪd wɪθ[25] hɪz ˈlaɪthɑːtɪd hæpɪnəs dʒɒn wʊd fɑː rɑːðə bi mɪzrəbl̩

jes haɪkɪŋ wəz ˈdefn̩ɪtli nɒt hɪs[18] kʌp əf[26] tiː]

---

[1] May also be transcribed with a weak schwa and nasal [ə̆n], where [˘] signals 'extra short', though you do not need to use this diacritic in your transcriptions.
[2] Regressive assimilation of place: Word-final alveolar nasal, /n/, in the word *line* becomes the velar nasal, [ŋ], under the influence of the following velar plosive [g] in the word *going*.
[3] This may also be heard as having a weak schwa in the final syllable: [həraɪzən].
[4] Linking *r*. If you listen carefully, you might perceive this as the voiced labiodental approximant [ʋ], a sound sometimes used by RP speakers. This could then be understood as an instance of the rarely occurring non-contiguous assimilation, with all the initial sounds in *where we're aiming* becoming similar as [weə wɪə ʋeɪmɪŋ].
[5] Here, the intermediate [u] marks a difference in the grammatical function of the two words *to* and *to* in the phrase *aiming to get to*. The first *to* is adverbial while the second *to* is prepositional and is at the end of a unit of meaning, and so it takes a fuller form.
[6] Elision of word-final /t/ in *sunset*.
[7] This speaker uses intermediate [i] in all forms of pronouns.
[8] There seems to be a shorter /iː/ vowel here, so unstressed [i] is given in the transcription.
[9] The speaker avoids regressive assimilation here. Often this sequence would be pronounced [gʊb mɔːnɪŋ].
[10] Elision of word-final /t/ in the consonant cluster /stpl/.
[11] Regressive assimilation of voice and place: The speaker replaces word-final voiced alveolar fricative, /z/, in the word *his* with the following voiceless palatoalveolar fricative, [ʃ], in the

word *shirt*. The two identical sounds are then merged into one prolonged pronunciation, indicated by the lowered horizontal swung line. The same process occurs below in the case of *his shoes*.

12 Elision of word-final /d/ in the consonant cluster /ldbr/.

13 Elision of word-final /d/ in *brand* means that the nasal in *brand* and the following nasal in *new* are pronounced as one slightly longer than normal alveolar nasal. This is indicated by the lowered horizontal swung line. There is strong motivation for this elision because the words occur as a standard collocation, and are even listed together in some dictionaries as a lexical item.

14 A strong form is used here to emphasise that it is Mike who wasn't at all pleased.

15 Here, there is elision of the word-final lateral, /l/, in *all*, especially because in this position it would be a dark *l*, [ɫ], somewhat similar to the dark vowel [o], close in quality to the preceding monophthong /ɔː/. You will learn about the dark *l* in Lesson Eleven.

16 In this case, the lateral sounds "fuller", and there is probably contact between the tongue tip and the roof of the mouth.

17 There is some tendency towards regressive assimilation of place: Word-final velar nasal, /ŋ/, in the word *wrong* is assimilated to the following bilabial nasal, [m], in the word *map*.

18 This speaker has a strongly devoiced word-final /z/, and, in fact, seems to pronounce two of the four instances of *his* in this sequence as [hɪz̥] while the first is assimilated to the following [ʃ]. Altogether these might be taken as possibly another case of non-contiguous assimilation. The final instance in *his back*, where the following sound is lenis, seems to be slightly less devoiced, however, so it is transcribed with [z].

19 The speaker seems to pronounce *heavy* with a short [ɪ], despite the rule whereby endings spelt as <y> are pronounced with intermediate [i].

20 You might notice strong aspiration here at the end of the word *up*. You do not have to transcribe this, but we could do so thus: [ʌpʰ].

21 Probable elision of word-initial glottal fricative, /h/, which is common in weak forms of pronouns beginning in <h> when not in sentence-initial position.

22 Elision of word-final /d/ in *seemed*. We might alternatively interpret this as a lengthened [t] resulting from assimilation: The speaker, as already mentioned, has quite strong word-final fortis articulation, so in this context there could be regressive assimilation of the regular past-tense morpheme realised as the lenis alveolar plosive, /d/, in the word *seemed* (because it follows the lenis nasal /m/) to the fortis plosive [t] under the influence of the following [t] in *to*. Then the /t/ would be considered lengthened thus: [siːmd̥‿tə].

23 Regressive assimilation of place: The speaker replaces word-final syllabic alveolar nasal, [n̩], in the word *even* with the syllabic bilabial nasal, [m̩], under the influence of the following bilabial nasal, [m], in the word *more*.

24 This speaker avoids the linking *r* here.

25 In keeping with the female speaker's tendency to devoice, the fortis [θ] is clearly heard here.

26 In keeping with the female speaker's tendency to devoice, the fortis [f] is clearly heard here.

10.1

[ðə stɔːri staːtɪd naɪm‿mʌn(θ)s¹,² əgəʊ ɑːftər³ ɔːl ðə trʌbl̩ ən ʌnˈrest⁴ həd feɪdɪd əweɪ lɪtl̩ dɪd əmændər⁵ æprɪˈhend ðen ðət hə laɪf wʊ(d)⁶ drəmætɪkli tʃeɪndʒ ænd⁷ fə ðə betə hə treɪnɪŋ həb‿bɪn⁸ ɪn θɪətər³ ən pəfɔːməns wɪð‿ðiːz⁹ skɪlz ʃi həd bɪn eɪbl̩ te lænd ə driːm pəzɪʃn̩ ɪn ə rɪˈspektəbl̩ kʌmpəni ðeə ʃi həd bɪn gɪvn̩ ə nʌmbər³ əv ˈʌndəstʌdiz maɪnə paːts ən tuː staːrɪŋ rəʊlz ɪn ʃɔːt ʃi hædn̩t weɪstɪd ə seknd̩ ɪm‿meɪkɪŋ¹ ə neɪm fə həself

ɑːftər³ əpɪərɪŋ əz ə wɪtʃ ɪm‿məkbeθ¹ əmændər⁵ ɑːs(k)t¹⁰ fər³ ə ʃɔːt breɪk tə rɪˈkʌvə frəm ə pətɪkjəli naːsti baʊt əv ɪnfluˈenzə¹¹ ʃi ɪkspleɪnz aɪ seg‿gʊ(b)‿baɪ¹²,¹³ tə ðə θɪətə wɪʃɪŋ ðət aɪ kəb‿bɪ⁸ bæk əs‿suːn¹⁴ əz ˈpɒsɪbl̩

ɔːl əv ə sʌdn̩ aɪ wəs‿snæpt¹⁴ ʌp frəm fiːlɪŋ terɪbli ɪl tə ðə ˈwɜːlwɪnd əv ˈhɒliwʊd baɪ ə fɪlm prədjuːsə hʊ həd siːn maɪ faɪnl̩ naɪt ɪm‿məkbeθ¹]

---

1. Probable regressive assimilation of place: Word-final alveolar nasal, /n/, in *nine* is articulated furher forward, similar to the following bilabial nasal, [m], in *months*. Then the two sounds are pronounced as one, indicated by the lowered horizontal swung line. This also occurs below in *in making* and *in Macbeth*.
2. Elision of /θ/ in the consonant cluster /nθs/.
3. Linking *r*.
4. The prefix *un-* does not carry stress.
5. Intrusive *r*.
6. Probable elision of word-final /d/ in the word *would*. The sequence at the word boundary between *would* and *dramatically* may also be realised as two sounds pronounced as one, but with greater duration, and would then be transcribed with a lowered horizontal swung line connecting them: [wʊd‿drəˈmætɪkli].
7. Here, the form of *and* is likely to be full because it is emphatic.
8. Regressive assimilation of place: The word-final alveolar plosive /d/ in *had* is replaced with the following bilabial plosive [b] in *been*. Then the two sounds are articulated as one prolonged sound, indicated by the lowered horizontal swung line. This also occurs below in the sequence *could be*.
9. The sequence at the word boundary between *with* and *these* may be seen as the two identical sounds pronounced as one, but with greater duration, and thus is transcribed with a lowered horizontal swung line connecting them.
10. Probable elision of /k/ in the consonant cluster /sktʃ/.
11. Intermediate [u] in second syllable.
12. Regressive assimilation of place: Word-final alveolar plosive /d/ in *said* is replaced with the following velar plosive [g] in *goodbye*. Then the two sounds are articulated as one prolonged sound, indicated by the lowered horizontal swung line.
13. Complete elision of /d/, or assimilation to [b] in *goodbye*, similar to note 8.
14. Regressive assimilation of intensity: Word-final lenis /z/ in *as* is replaced with the following fortis [s] in *soon*. Then the two similar sounds are merged into one prolonged sound, indicated by the lowered horizontal swung line. This also occurs below in *was snapped*.

10.2

[də juː[1] fænsi gəʊɪŋ tə ðə sɪnəmə[2] tənaɪt ðəz ðæt[3] njuː mærɪˈneləʊ ʃəʊɪŋ ət ði rˈlektrɪk

ʃɔː waɪ nɒt aɪ hævn̩(t)[4] siːn enɪθɪŋ diːsn̩(t)[4] fə(ʔ)[5] eɪdʒɪz

dʒæk wɒtʃt hə lɑːs(t)[6] θrɪlə(ʔ)[7] ɒn ðə ˈteləvɪʒn̩[8] ði ʌðə deɪ jə[9] nəʊ haʊ hə[10] gəʊz ɒn en(d)ləsli[11] əbaʊ(t)[12] ðə klʌtʃ əv tem[13] praɪzɪz ʒiz[14] wʌn əʊvə ðə jɪəz

əʊ[15] jes nevə stɒp(s)[16] sɪŋɪŋ hə preɪzɪz ðə ˈnjuːspeɪpəz ə pæk(t)[4] fʊl əv ðə skændl̩ ðɪs məʊs(t)[4] riːsn̩t wʌn həz kɔːzd tuː

enɪweɪ ˈsʌmθɪŋ ɪkstrɔːdn̩ri fər[17] ə tʃeɪndʒ əd[18] biː[19] wɜːθ traɪɪŋ

raɪt aɪl rɪŋ ðə ˈtɪkɪʔ[20] ˈhɒtlaɪn[21] ən tʃek əveɪləˈbɪlɪti ðen wi kʊd prəhæps[22] siː ɪ(f)[23] seərər[24] ən ænə wɒntɪd tə kʌm əlɒŋ wɪ kəd]

---

[1] Intermediate [u] occurs here.
[2] The speaker here uses an RP pronunciation with word-final schwa. Many speakers would use the long monophthong [ɑː] instead.
[3] The vowel here is short, but since *that* is demonstrative, it should be [æ], rather than schwa. You may also perceive this sequence as [ðeəzæt].
[4] Here, the speaker probably elides word-final /t/ in the consonant cluster /nts/, and then in the same line in the cluster /sntf/ in *decent for*. (Also below in the consonant clusters /ktf/ in *packed full* and /str/ in *most recent*.)
[5] The female speaker avoids using a linking *r*. Instead, we hear a very weak glottal stop, [ʔ], to give emphasis to *ages*.
[6] The male speaker definitely elides word-final /t/ in the consonant cluster /stθr/. There is only movement of the tongue forward from alveolar to dental position.
[7] The male speaker, too, avoids using a linking *r*. Instead, we hear a slightly stronger glottal stop than the one used by the female speaker.
[8] The prefix *tele-* normally carries stress on the first syllable.
[9] Here, the speaker uses a very noticeably short schwa in the word *you*, rather than short [ʊ].
[10] Here, the speaker uses a very noticeably short schwa in the word *he*, rather than either short [ɪ] or intermediate [i].
[11] Elision of /d/ in the consonant cluster /ndl/.
[12] The male speaker definitely elides word-final /t/, and may replace it with a weak glottal stop, [ʔ]: [əbaʊʔ].
[13] Regressive assimilation of place: The speaker articulates word-final alveolar nasal, /n/, in *ten* as the bilabial nasal, [m], under the influence of the following [p] in *prizes*.
[14] Possible progressive assimilation of intensity, resulting here in a lenis sound: The speaker may replace word-initial fortis palatoalveolar fricative, /ʃ/, in *she* with the lenis palatoalveolar fricative, [ʒ], under the influence of the word-final lenis alveolar fricative, [z], in *prizes*. This is a relatively unusual process (after all, you learnt in Lesson Nine that assimilation of intensity across word boundaries always results in a fortis sound), and it is not absolutely clear whether this assimilation occurs here. You may perceive the palatoalveolar segment as either voiced or voiceless.
[15] You might hear the slight aspiration at the beginning of this diphthong. In fact, acoustic analysis shows that the aspiration continues across the schwa segment of the diphthong: [ʰəʰʊ].

Solutions to the exercises   145

16 Elision of word-final /s/ in the middle of the consonant cluster /pss/.
17 Here, the speaker does use a linking *r*.
18 Very reduced form of *would*.
19 The speaker uses an intermediate [i] here.
20 The speaker probably uses a glottal stop, [ʔ], instead of an alveolar plosive.
21 The speaker probably uses a laterally released plosive in the word *hotline*: The alveolar plosive [t] is followed by the homorganic lateral, [l]. The plosive is formed, but not released. Instead, the release of the closure occurs through the following segment when the sides of the tongue drop to form the articulation for the lateral. We could transcribe this sequence as [tˡl], where the diacritic [ˡ] indicates a lateral release. (You will learn more about laterally released plosives in Lesson Eleven.) Alternatively, the speaker might use a glottal stop instead of an alveolar plosive. Either way, there seems to be no release before the lateral.
22 The speaker pronounces the word as transcribed, which is a common blend of the two correct forms [pəhæps] and [pr̥hæps].
23 You may perceive elision of the fortis labiodental fricative, /f/.
24 Here, the speaker seems to use intrusive *r*, connecting the words *Sarah* and *and*.

11.1

[wi niːd mɔːrˈ¹ ˈɒrɪndʒɪz ənd æpl̩z bɪfɔː wi kŋ² kəlek(t)³ ðə sɒf(t)³ fruːt laɪk strɔːbr̩iz⁴ n̩ piːtʃɪz hi ˈbeləʊd⁵ daʊn ðə fəʊn

dɪspaɪt ðɪs rɑːðərˈ¹ ʌnˈpleznt⁶ ɪnˈstrʌkʃn̩ kʌmɪŋ ʌp frəm ðə kɪtʃn̩ kɑːləʳ⁷ ən sæmi wərˈ¹ ɪn ə gʊb⁸ muːd ðeɪ həb‿bəʊθ⁹ rɪzn̩ ɜːli gɒn dʒɒgɪŋ ən hæd ə helθi brekfəst ðeɪ wə dɪˈtɜːmɪnd nɒt tə let ˈmɑːkəʊz⁵ faʊl muːd ʌpˈset ðeərˈ¹ ɑːftəˈnuːn

biːɪŋ aɪˈdentɪkl twɪnz həs‿sɜːtn̩¹⁰ ədˈvɑːntɪdʒɪz θɔːt kɑːlə ʃi həb¹¹ prɪˈtendɪd tə bi hə sɪstərˈ¹ ən(d)¹² vaɪs vɜːsəʳ⁷ ɒn meni əkeɪʒn̩z

naʊ ðeɪ plæn(d)¹³ tə get ðeə rɪˈvendʒ ɒn ði æŋɡri kʊk sæmi keəfli ræpt fɔː rɔːʳ⁷ egz ɪn ə spɒtɪd ˈhæŋkətʃiːf ən pleɪs(t)¹⁴ tuː mɔːrˈ¹ ʌndə hə bɒsɪs¹⁵ ʃuːz wɪtʃ stʊd ɪn ðə kɔːnə ðə træp wəs‿set¹⁰]

---

¹ Linking *r*.
² Possible regressive assimilation of place: The alveolar nasal, /n/, is replaced with the velar nasal, [ŋ], under the influence of the following velar plosive [k] in *collect*. Either form would probably be syllabic in fast connected speech.
³ Elision of /t/ is likely in the consonant cluster /ktð/. Elision of /t/ in the consonant cluster /ftf/ is very likely because the sequence would then be reduced to two identical sounds, and the words would be pronounced [sɒf‿fruːt].
⁴ Syllabic [r̩] is often pronounced in the word *strawberry*.
⁵ Stress falls on the first syllable even though the second syllable is a diphthong; [əʊ] is often unstressed in this position.
⁶ The prefixes *un-* and *i-* (also occuring as *im-*, *in-*, *ir-*) are usually unstressed.
⁷ Intrusive *r*.

[8] Possible regressive assimilation of place: The alveolar plosive /d/ is replaced with the bilabial plosive [b] under the influence of the following bilabial nasal, [m].
[9] Again, possible regressive assimilation of place: The alveolar plosive /d/ is articulated as the following bilabial plosive [b]. The two sounds are then articulated as one prolonged sound, indicated by the lowered horizontal swung line.
[10] Possible regressive assimilation of intensity: The lenis alveolar fricative, /z/, becomes devoiced, [s], under the influence of the following fortis alveolar fricative, [s]. The two identical sounds are then merged into one prolonged sound, indicated by the lowered horizontal swung line.
[11] Possible regressive assimilation of place: The alveolar plosive /d/ is replaced with the bilabial plosive [b] under the influence of the following bilabial plosive [p].
[12] Possible elision of /d/ in the unstressed *and*.
[13] Possible elision of /d/ in the consonant cluster /ndt/.
[14] Possible elision of /t/ in the middle of the consonant cluster /stt/.
[15] Possible regressive assimilation of intensity: The lenis alveolar fricative, /z/, becomes devoiced, [s], under the influence of the following fortis palatoalveolar fricative, [ʃ].

11.2

[ˈeniweɪ aɪ faɪn(d)¹ ðə həʊl ekspləneɪʃn̩ kmpliːtli ʌnbəliːvəbl̩² aɪ miːn huːˈevə hɜːd əv sʌtʃ ə rɪˈdɪkjʊləs³ endɪŋ tu ə pleɪŋ⁴ gʊd əʊl(d)⁵ dɪˈtektɪv θrɪlə

jɔːr⁶ ən ɔːfl̩ ˈskeptɪk aɪ ɪˈmædʒɪn(d)⁷ ˈsʌmθɪŋ dɪfrənt mɔːr⁸ ækjərət aɪv ədmɪtɪd ðæt⁹ bət aɪ θɪŋk jə rɒŋ¹⁰ tə sədʒest ɪts ʌtə nɒnsəns

haʊ kn̩ juː¹¹ seɪ ðæt⁹ səʊ kɑːmli wen streɪt ɑːftəwədz jʊ ˈkrɪtɪsaɪz(d)¹ ði æktəz fə biːɪŋ ɪnˈsensətɪv ən kriˈeɪtɪŋ¹² ə kɒmədi aʊt əv ə trædʒədi¹³

jes bət wɒt¹⁴ əbaʊt ðə siːn weə¹⁵ æntəni lets ðə hɔːsɪz ɪsˈkeɪp ðen hi ɪmself straɪdz ɒf wɔːks ɔːl deɪ əʊnli luːzɪŋ hɪz weɪ ɪn ði end¹⁶ ðæt wəz dʌn ɪkˈsepʃn̩li wel

aɪ səpəʊz jə raɪt ðeə bət]

[1] There is probable elision of the plosive, though you may perceive the [d] because it is expected in this word.
[2] The standard pronunciation is with the vowel in the second syllable reduced to [ɪ], but here the speaker pronounces *unbelievable* with a schwa, [ə].
[3] The weak vowel in the third syllable is actually slightly more close and back than schwa, and so it is transcribed as [ʊ]. However, schwa would also be acceptable in your transcription.
[4] There is regressive assimilation of the alveolar nasal, /n/, to the velar nasal, [ŋ], under the influence of the following velar plosive [g].
[5] Some weak elision of word-final /d/ in the middle of the consonant cluster /ldd/.
[6] In this line, the female speaker uses the linking *r* twice (see note 8). In the sequence *you're an awful sceptic*, the vowel in *you're* [jɔːr] is relatively long, but it is certainly a monophthong, rather than a diphthong. In more careful speech, the centring diphthong [ʊə] may be used.
[7] Some weak elision of word-final /d/ in the consonant cluster /nds/.

Solutions to the exercises

8   We hear a second linking *r* in the sequence *more accurate*.
9   The vowel in *that* is not reduced because the word is demonstrative.
10 In *you're wrong*, there is no linking *r* because the word-final vowel in *your* [jə] is followed by the postalveolar approximant, [r], in *wrong*.
11 Intermediate [u] in *you* because of emphasis.
12 Here, the male speaker uses the intermediate [i] in an interesting way: If you listen carefully, you can hear the [i] vowel in the word *creating* and then at the end of the word *comedy*. We can expect this form in these positions, but he then uses the more careful RP form of [ɪ] at the end of the sentence in the word *tragedy*.
13 Careful RP form of [ɪ] at the end of the sentence in the word *tragedy*, rather than the more common intermediate [i] for words with spelling ending in <y>.
14 If you listen carefully to the sequence [jes bət wɒt], you will hear the elision of the word-final /t/ in *but*, or it is possibly realised as a glottal stop, [ʔ]. The consonant at the end of *what* is a tap, [ɾ], rather than the alveolar plosive [t]. This is quite typical of rapid connected British English in such sequences.
15 The female speaker seems to use a very short diphthong and avoids a linking *r*. Instead, she appears to use a very brief glottal stop, which we might transcribe as [weəʔ æntəni].
16 Here, the female speaker uses a glottal stop twice in the sequence *way in the end*: [weɪʔ ɪn ðiʔ end]. The stop is so noticeable that it would probably be transcribed in the form shown, rather than in superscript as a linking sound. Generally, we would expect to hear a linking semi-vowel in such a sequence: [weɪʲ ɪn ðiʲ end].

12.1

[jet əgen hi¹ wəz leɪt ʃi kʊdn̩t pʊt ʌp wɪð ɪp² mʌtʃ lɒŋgə ʃi¹ wəz ˈɔːlweɪz ɒn taɪm waɪ kʊdn̩t hiː³ du ðə seɪm trævlɪŋ frəm ˈelɪfənt n̩ kɑːsl̩ ət ðæ(t) taɪm⁴ əv naɪt ɪz nəʊ dʒəʊk weɪtɪŋ ət ðə steɪʃn̩ wəz iːvn̩ wɜːs jeʃ‿ʃɪd⁵,⁶ hæf⁷ tə tel (h)ɪm⁸ ɪt wɒzn̩t eni gʊb‿biːɪŋ⁹ lef(t) tə⁴ weɪt fər¹⁰ aʊəz ɪn ðə reɪn

jʊə¹¹ hɪər¹⁰ ət lɑːst aɪv bɪn hæŋɪŋ əraʊnd getɪŋ mɔːr¹⁰ ən mɔːr¹⁰ ɪnˈfjʊərieɪtɪd¹² wɪθ‿θɪŋkɪŋ¹³ əbaʊtʃɔː¹⁴ ˈterɪbl̩ ˈtaɪmkiːpɪŋ haʊ wʊd ju ɪndʒɔɪ ɪt

jes sɒri aɪ kʊdn̩(t)¹⁵ get əweɪ frəm ði ˈɒfɪs ˈæktʃʊəli aɪ wəg‿get¹⁶ hɪər¹⁰ ɒn taɪm evri wiːk ɪf ɪt wɒznt fə ðə greɪp¹⁷ mes ðəts ˈɔː(l)weɪz¹⁸ lef(t)‿fə¹⁹ miː tə klɪər¹⁰ ʌp ðen aɪ hæv tə setl̩ ði əkaʊnts ənd ʃʌt²⁰ daʊn ðə həʊl sɪstəm ɪt teɪks fərevə

ðæts nəʊ ɪksˈkjuːs wɪə səpəʊs(t)²¹ tə hæv ðɪs taɪm dʒʌs(t)²² fər¹⁰ aʊəˈselvz]

1. Probable intermediate [i] preceding the semi-vowel [w].
2. Possible regressive assimilation of place: The alveolar plosive /t/ is replaced with the bilabial plosive [p] under the influence of the following bilabial nasal, [m].
3. Emphasis on *he*, so full form is given.
4. Elision of word-final /t/. This also occurs below in *left to*.
5. Possible regressive assimilation of place: The alveolar fricative [s] is replaced with the following palatoalveolar fricative [ʃ]. The two identical sounds are then merged into one prolonged pronunciation, indicated by the lowered horizontal swung line.
6. Relatively emphatic, so probably with intermediate [i].
7. Even though *have* is emphatic here, it is likely that there is regressive assimilation of intensity: The lenis labiodental fricative, [v], is replaced with fortis labiodental fricative, [f], under the influence of the following fortis alveolar plosive, [t]. Alternatively, we could transcribe this as [hæv̥ tə], showing devoicing.
8. Probable elision of /h/.
9. Possible regressive assimilation of place: The alveolar plosive /d/ is replaced with the following bilabial plosive [b]. The two sounds are articulated as one prolonged sound, indicated by the lowered horizontal swung line.
10. Linking *r*.
11. Emphasis in sentence-initial position would mean that the vowel in *you're* is realised as a full diphthong.
12. Typically, intermediate [i] in the suffix *-iate*.
13. Tendency for regressive assimilation of voice: Word-final lenis dental fricative, /ð/, is replaced with the following fortis dental fricative, [θ]. The two identical sounds are then merged into one prolonged pronunciation, indicated by the lowered horizontal swung line.
14. Yod coalescence: Word-final /t/ and word-initial /j/ merge together to form the affricate [tʃ].
15. Possible elision of word-final /t/ in the consonant cluster /dntg/.
16. Possible regressive assimilation of place: The alveolar plosive /d/ is replaced with the following velar plosive [g]. The two sounds are articulated as one prolonged sound, indicated by the lowered horizontal swung line.
17. Possible regressive assimilation of place: The alveolar plosive /t/ is replaced with the bilabial plosive [p] under the influence of the bilabial nasal, [m].

Solutions to the exercises   149

[18] Possible elision of the lateral, especially because in this position it would be a dark *l*, [ɫ], close in quality to the preceding monophthong [ɔː] in the syllable <al>.
[19] Possible elision of /t/ in the consonant cluster /ftf/. The two remaining identical sounds are then merged into one prolonged pronunciation, indicated by the lowered horizontal swung line.
[20] It is probable here that there would be no audible release of the word-final alveolar plosive [t] because it is followed in the next word by the word-initial alveolar plosive [d]. The whole phrase *shut down* would most likely be voiced from the first vowel in *shut*. Thus we could transcribe the phrase as [ʃʌd̚ daʊn], where the diacritic [̚] indicates an inaudible release.
[21] Possible elision of /t/ in the middle of the consonant cluster /stt/.
[22] Possible elision of /t/ in the consonant cluster /stf/.

12.2

[wʊdʒu¹ laɪk ənʌðə kʌp əv tiː ɒr² aɪ km̩³ meɪk səm kɒfi aɪ(v)⁴ pʊt ðə ketl̩ ɒn

(ə)⁵ nəʊ θæŋks wʌnz ɪˈnʌf wɒ(t)⁶ dɪ(d)⁷ jə¹ θɪŋk əv ðə fɪlm⁸ wɪ sɔː ˈjestədeɪ

wel æktʃəli⁹ aɪ hævn̩(t)⁶ dɪˈsaɪdɪd weðər¹⁰ aɪ laɪkt ɪt ɔː nɒt ɪts kwaɪt ə dɪsˈtɜːbɪŋ vɜːʃn̩ əv ə veri sɪmpl̩ stɔːri

æbsəˈluːtli aɪ əgriː laːs(t)¹¹ naɪt aɪ kʊdn̩t ge(t)¹² tə sliːp ət ɔː(l)⁸,¹³ aɪ kep(t)¹¹ laɪɪŋ ðeər¹⁰ æŋkʃəs(l)i¹³ θɪŋkɪŋ əbaʊ(t)¹⁴ haʊ ɪp¹⁵ maɪ(t)¹⁴ rɪəli bi truː

dʒɒn sez ænəʳ¹⁶ ənd hi ˈɑːgjuːd fə(ʔ)¹⁷ aʊəz əbaʊt weðə ðə mɪstri truːli wɒs‿sɒlvd¹⁸

jes aɪ wʌndə bəd‿ðen¹⁹ əgen ðeɪ kn̩ nevər¹⁰ əgriː ɒn ˈeniθɪŋ rɪmembə lɑːst jɪə]

---

[1] In the sequence *would you*, the female speaker uses yod coalescence: The alveolar plosive /d/ and the palatal approximant, /j/, merge to form the affricate [dʒ]. Later, in the male speaker's sequence *what did you*, there is no coalescence: The [d] is followed by [j] although the plosive may be articulated (and perceived) as a tap, [ɾ].
[2] Linking *r* connects a very short monophthong [ɒ] to the following diphthong [aɪ].
[3] The nasal here is undoubtedly syllabic (although it is very short). There may even be regressive assimilation of [n̩] to [m̩] under the influence of the following [m].
[4] There is a very faint residue of the elided [v], which would signal the expected present perfect tense here.
[5] Possibly a very short schwa representing *oh*.
[6] Probable elision of word-final /t/.
[7] Very weak word-final [d].
[8] The male speaker's lateral in *film* (and later in *all*) is actually articulated as a dark back vowel. The tongue makes no contact with the roof of the mouth. The sound has been transcribed here as a lateral even though it would be closer to transcribe this as [o].
[9] Either weakening of diphthong [ʊə] to [ə] or elision of intermediate [u] in the unstressed syllable: [æktʃ(u)li].
[10] Linking *r*.
[11] Elision of word-final /t/ in the consonant cluster /stn/. This also occurs later in the consonant cluster /ptl/ in *kept lying*.
[12] Elision of word-final /t/.

13 The male speaker here elides the lateral in the word *all*. This also occurs below in the word *anxiously*. This may be because his laterals tend to be articulated as dark vowels, possibly owing to influence of such articulation by non-standard speakers.
14 Here, the word-final alveolar plosive /t/ is either elided or articulated as a short glottal stop, [ʔ].
15 Regressive assimilation of place: The speaker articulates alveolar plosive /t/ as the bilabial plosive [p] under the influence of the following bilabial nasal, [m].
16 Intrusive *r*.
17 Unusually, the female speaker avoids a linking *r* in the phrase *for hours*. Instead, she seems to use a short glottal stop, [ʔ].
18 Regressive assimilation of intensity: The speaker articulates the lenis /z/ as a fortis [s]. Then the two identical sounds are merged into one prolonged sound, indicated by the lowered horizontal swung line.
19 Again, regressive assimilation of intensity, but this time resulting in a lenis sound: The speaker articulates fortis /t/ as lenis [d] under the influence of the following lenis [ð]. The sounds are almost articulated as one sound, so they are joined by the lowered horizontal swung line. You learnt in Lesson Nine that assimilation of intensity across word boundaries usually results in a fortis sound; here, however, this is not the case.

12.3

↘↗ // Would you LIKE another cup of TEA // ↘ // Or i can MAKE some coffee //

↘ // I've PUT the KETTle on //

↘ // NO thanks // ↘↗ // ONE'S enOUGH //

↘ // What did you THINK of the FILM we saw yesterday //

↘ // Well actually i haven't deCIded // ↘ // whether i LIKed it or NOT //

↘ // It's quite a diSTURBing version // ↘↗ // of a VERy simple STORy //

↘ // AbsoLUTEly // ↕ // I agree // ↘ // last NIGHT i COULDn't get to SLEEP at all //

↘ // I kept LYing there ANxiously thinking // ↗ // how it might really be TRUE //

↗↘ // John says Anna and he argued for HOURS //
↘↗ // about WHETHer the mystery truly WAS solved //

↗↘ // YES // ↘ // i WONder //

↘ // But then aGAIN // ↘ // they can NEVer agree on ANything //

↗ // ReMEMber last YEAR //

Appendix II: Glossary of linguistic terms

accent The pronunciation features of a language variety.

accentual function of intonation The affect of intonation on the prominence of a syllable, which plays a role in focusing stress on particular words in connected speech.

acoustic phonetics The study and description of the physical properties of speech sounds, and their transmission.

affricate A manner of articulation. Affricate sounds consist of two homorganic elements: the first is plosive, the second fricative. Affricates have a complete closure of the vocal tract, but the air is released slowly enough to produce friction, which we hear as a hissing *s*-like sound. There are two affricates in English: one fortis, /tʃ/, and one lenis, /dʒ/.

air-stream mechanism The type of air movement used to produce speech sounds.

allomorph One of at least two variant realisations of a morpheme.

allophone One of at least two variant realisations of a phoneme. Allophones do not contrast meaning. They occur either in complementary distribution or in free variation.

alveolar A place of articulation. Alveolar sounds are made with the tongue tip coming near or touching the bony ridge behind the upper teeth, called the alveolar ridge. The sound we transcribe as /t/ is alveolar.

anaptyxis The insertion of a vowel between two consonants, like the schwa in *please*, [pəliːz]. See also *epenthesis*.

aph(a)eresis An elision at the beginning of a word. For example, the historical elision of the initial consonants in *k̲nife*, *k̲night*, and *w̲rong*.

aphesis A special case of aph(a)eresis, when the elided initial sound is a vowel. For example, when *a̲lone* becomes *lone*.

apical A type of articulation that involves the tip of the tongue. Dental, alveolar, and postalveolar sounds are apical.

apocopation, apocope An elision occurring at the end of a word.

applied linguistics The practical application of linguistic findings, for example to foreign language teaching.

approximant A manner of articulation. An approximant is generally made with a wider gap between the speech organs than is the case in the production of fricatives. The speech organs approach each other, but they do not touch each other and there is no audible friction. The sound transcribed as /r/ is an approximant.

articulatory phonetics The study and description of how the speech organs, also called vocal organs or articulators, in the vocal tract are used in order to produce, or articulate, speech sounds.

aspiration The audible puff of breath, or the brief *h*-sound, resulting from the sudden release of air in the articulation of a plosive.

assimilation An aspect of connected speech, where one sound, usually a consonant, becomes more like, or identical with, a neighbouring sound regarding one or more of the distinctive features. The opposite of dissimilation.

attitudinal function of intonation The ability of intonation to express speakers' personal attitudes towards what they say, for example whether they are uninterested, excited, or ironic.

auditory phonetics The study and description of the perception of speech sounds by the listener.

back vowel A vowel articulated with the back of the tongue raised highest.

back-clipping A special case of clipping, when a syllable or part is taken from the end of a word.

backed See *retraction*.

backness One of the three criteria for the description of vowel phonemes. Frontness and backness refer to the part of the tongue that is raised highest.

bilabial A manner of articulation. Bilabial sounds are made with both lips. The sound we transcribe as /b/ is a bilabial.

cardinal vowel A set of vowel sounds that illustrate the extremes of vowel quality the vocal tract is able to produce. Cardinal vowels are not sounds of any particular language.

central vowel A vowel articulated with the centre of the tongue raised highest. An intermediate position between the two extremes of front and back vowels.

centre A part of a syllable which is produced with little or no obstruction of air, and is therefore usually formed by a vowel. Also called peak or nucleus.

centring diphthong A diphthong that moves towards schwa. There are three centring diphthongs in English: /ɪə/, /eə/, and /ʊə/.

checked syllable See *closed syllable*.

checked vowel The vowel that forms the centre of a closed, or checked, syllable.

clear *l* A non-syllabic lenis alveolar lateral. The sound we hear word-initially in *leopard*, or when /l/ is pronounced in isolation. It is represented in a phonetic transcription proper by the same symbol used for the underlying phoneme. Contrasts with dark *l*.

click A sound produced by the air being sucked in as a result of movements against the back part of the roof of the mouth. Click sounds do not exist in English.

click language A language that has click sounds.

clipping The omission of whole syllables or entire parts of words.

close vowel A vowel articulated with the tongue high, close to the palate.

closed syllable A syllable that ends in a consonant. Sometimes also called a checked syllable.

closed word class A category of words whose number is limited and largely fixed. Closed word classes are determiners (including articles), pronouns, prepositions (including particles), conjunctions, auxiliary verbs, numerals, and interjections.

closing diphthong A diphthong that moves towards a close vowel. There are five closing diphthongs in English: /eɪ/, /aɪ/, /ɔɪ/, /əʊ/, and /aʊ/.

cluster A sequence of consonants pronounced consecutively, without an intervening vowel or pause.

coarticulation The simultaneous use of two places of obstruction, especially when these two places of obstruction are equally important. Also called double articulation.

coda A structural element in a syllable that follows the centre, and is produced with greater obstruction of air. A coda is, therefore, always formed by one or more consonants.

competence The individual speaker's internalised knowledge of the language. Stands in contrast to performance, which is the actual language use of an individual speaker. A term proposed by the American linguist Noam Chomsky. See also *langue* and *parole*.

complementary distribution A systematic relationship between two or more linguistic units (mostly allophones or allomorphs), where one unit can only occur in an environment in which none of the other units can. The units are mutually exclusive. See also *free variation*.

compression The reduction of vowels and the elision of sounds in unstressed syllables. See also *elision*, *reduction*, and *weak form*.

consonant A class of sound produced by an obstruction of an air-stream either in the pharynx or in the vocal tract. All consonants generally have two things in common: Phonetically, they are made with an obstruction of air, and phonologically, they typically occur at the margins of syllables. Contrasts with vowel.

content word See *lexical word*.

contextual variant A linguistic unit in complementary distribution with other units.

continuant A broad classification of the manner of articulation of speech sounds. Continuants are made without a complete closure of the speech organs. All speech sounds apart from plosives and affricates are continuants.

contoid A phonetic class of sounds that are produced with an obstruction of air. All consonants except the frictionless continuants are contoids. Contrasts with vocoid.

dark *l* A velarised lenis alveolar lateral produced with the tip of the tongue touching the alveolar ridge, and simultaneously with the back of the tongue coming near or touching the velum. The dark *l* occurs in all the environments in which the neutral *l* or clear *l* cannot. It is transcribed as [ɫ]. See also *velarisation*.

dental A manner of articulation. Dental, or interdental, sounds are made with the tongue tip and rims between the upper and lower teeth or against the upper teeth. The two dentals in English, /θ/ and /ð/, are often popularly called "teeaitch" because of their spelling.

dentalisation Occurs when fronting results in a dental sound, articulated with the tongue tip and rims touching the teeth. Dental articulation can be indicated in the IPA by the diacritic [̪] under the relevant symbol.

descriptive linguistics The objective and systematic study of language. Descriptive linguists observe and analyse language as it is used naturally in any given speech community to discover the rules and regularities of the underlying language system. Contrasts with prescriptive linguistics.

devoicing Occurs when an intrinsically voiced sound is articulated with less voice than usual or with no voice at all.

diacritic Mark added to indicate slight alterations to the usual value of a phonetic symbol.

dialectology The study and description of regional variation within a language.

diphthong A vowel sequence starting with a monophthong, whose quality then changes towards, but never quite reaches, another monophthong through a gliding movement of the tongue. Also called gliding vowel or vowel glide. A diphthong is conventionally analysed as one vowel phoneme. The vowel sequence we transcribe as /eɪ/ is a diphthong.

discourse function of intonation The role of intonation to signal the turn-taking processes in an exchange between speakers.

dissimilation The process whereby one sound becomes less like a neighbouring sound or a sound in close proximity, often to achieve greater ease of pronunciation, and also greater clarity. The opposite of assimilation.

distinctive feature The three features of intensity, place, and manner of articulation determine the consonant sounds of a language.

distribution The range of environments in which a linguistic unit can occur.

dorsal A type of articulation that involves the body of the tongue. Palatal and velar sounds are dorsal.

double articulation See *coarticulation*.

duration The absolute or actual time taken in the articulation of a sound. It is a purely phonetic feature since it plays no role in determining the phonological function of a sound in the language system. Duration is one component of stress (together with loudness, pitch, and sound quality).

egressive glottalic air-stream One of the four air-stream mechanisms. Air is pushed up from the space between the vocal folds. A sound produced in this way is called ejective or glottalic.

egressive pulmonic air-stream One of the four air-stream mechanisms. The majority of sounds used in human languages are produced with air that is pushed up from the lungs through the windpipe, or trachea, leaving the body through the mouth and sometimes through the nose. Virtually all English sounds are produced by an egressive pulmonic air-stream mechanism.

ejective A sound produced by air being pushed up from the space between the vocal folds, i.e. by an egressive glottalic air-stream. Also called glottalic.

elision The omission of one or more sounds in connected speech. The opposite of instrusion.

empty word See *grammatical word*.

epenthesis Insertion of a sound in word-internal position. An inserted vowel like the schwa in *please* [pəliːz] is an epenthetic vowel. See also *anaptyxis*.

epiglottal A manner of articulation. An epiglottal sound is made by a movement of the epiglottis against the lower pharynx. Such sounds do not exist in English.

fall An intonation contour that falls.

falling diphthong A diphthong in which the first element is longer and louder than the second. English diphthongs are usually falling diphthongs.

fall-rise An intonation contour that first falls, then rises.

fixed stress In many languages, word stress is fairly predictable. These languages are said to have fixed stress, or to be fixed-stress languages.

flap A manner of articulation. A flap, or tap, involves a single flap by one articulator against another. There are no flapped phonemes in English, but there are some pronunciation variants produced in this way. The sound we transcribe as [ɾ] is a flap.

foot The distance beginning with (and including) a strong stress and ending right before (and excluding) the next strong stress.

fore-and-aft clipping The omission of whole syllables or entire parts of words from the beginning and end of a word.

fore-clipping The omission of whole syllables or entire parts of words from the beginning of a word.

form word See *grammatical word*.

fortis An intensity of articulation. Fortis consonants are made with stronger breath force, or higher tension, than lenis consonants.

free stress In some languages, word stress is difficult to predict; it is rule-governed only to a very limited extent. These languages are said to have free stress, less commonly also movable stress, or to be free-stress languages.

free variation Occurs when two or more linguistic units (mostly allophones or allomorphs) can replace one another without there being any rule governing their distribution. See also *complementary distribution*.

fricative A manner of articulation. Fricatives are made when air is forced through a very narrow gap between two speech organs, producing audible friction. The fricatives fall into two subcategories: slit fricatives, where air is released through a narrow horizontal opening, and groove fricatives, where the tongue is slightly hollowed. The sound we transcribe as /f/ is a slit fricative whereas /s/ is a groove fricative. See also *sibilant*.

frictionless continuant A phonetic class of sounds. Laterals and approximants are categorised as frictionless continuants because neither group involves audible friction.

front vowel A vowel articulated with the front of the tongue raised highest.

fronting The articulation of a sound further forward in the mouth than the underlying phoneme, usually under the influence of the surrounding sounds.

frontness One of the three criteria for the description of vowel phonemes. Frontness and backness refer to the part of the tongue that is raised highest.

function word, functor See *grammatical word*.

fundamental frequency (F_0) A quantitative acoustic measurement mainly of the number of times the vocal folds vibrate per second, measured in hertz (Hz). Fundamental frequency, or pitch, is affected by the physical size, and consequently by the sex, of a speaker. In general, a male speaker has a lower pitch, at around 120 hertz, than a female speaker, who has an average pitch of around 210 hertz. See also *pitch*.

glide See *semi-vowel*.

gliding vowel See *diphthong*.

glottal A sound that is produced in the larynx when air passes through the glottis. The only English phoneme that is articulated in this way is the fortis /h/. The glottal stop is of course also a glottal, but it is not an English phoneme.

glottal closure A sound produced by the closure of the glottis. The vocal folds are firmly pressed together, and the air-stream is stopped completely. A glottal closure can produce only one sound: a glottal stop.

glottal plosive See *glottal stop*.

glottal replacement The use of a glottal stop as an allophone of /t/ when it occurs after a vowel either word-internally, especially when followed by another vowel, or word-finally. Also called T-glottalling, or simply glottalling.

glottal stop The sound made when the glottis is closed, i.e. the vocal folds are firmly pressed together, and the air-stream is stopped completely. Also called glottal plosive.

glottalic See *ejective*.

glottalisation A process whereby a plosive is produced with a tightly closed glottis (resulting in a simultaneous glottal stop), so that no more air can be pushed up from the lungs. The glottis remains closed for the duration of the plosive, thus trapping a body of air between it and the usual closure made higher up in the vocal tract. All three fortis plosives can undergo glottalisation.

glottalling See *glottal replacement*.

glottis The space between the vocal folds, located behind the Adam's apple in the larynx.

grammatical word A word that primarily fulfils a grammatical function, and has little or no lexical content. Also referred to by a number of other terms, such as *empty word*, *form word*, *function word*, *functor*, *structural word*, and *structure word*. Grammatical words comprise determiners (including articles), pronouns, prepositions (including particles), conjunctions, auxiliary verbs, and a few adverbs, such as *not* and *there*.

graphology The study and description of the writing system of a language.

head In intonation, the part of a tone unit that extends from the first prominent syllable up to, but not including, the tonic syllable.

hiatus The articulatory break, or gap, between two consecutive vowels belonging to different syllables or words linked through the insertion of an additional sound. See also *liaison*.

high key An intonation contour that has an overall raised pitch.

homograph A word that has the same spelling as another word, but differs in meaning (and possibly also in pronunciation).

homophone A word that has the same pronunciation as another word.

homorganic Speech sounds that are articulated in the same place, in other words, with the same speech organs, are homorganic. Affricates consist of two homorganic sounds.

hypercorrection, hyperurbanism An over-correction of one's language, resulting from an attempt to adjust one's speech to a prestige norm.

implosive A sound produced by the glottis making the air move inwards.

ingressive glottalic air-stream One of the four air-stream mechanisms. Air is moved inwards by the glottis.

ingressive velaric air-stream One of the four air-stream mechanisms. Air is sucked in as a result of movements against the back part of the roof of the mouth. A sound produced in this way is called click, and a language that has click sounds is often referred to as a click language.

intensity of articulation One of the three distinctive features used for the description of consonants. The force with which the air-stream is pushed up from the lungs.

interdental See *dental*.

International Phonetic Alphabet The most widely used phonetic alphabet, and one that provides suitable symbols for the sounds of any language.

intonation A suprasegmental feature of spoken language. The variation of pitch and prominence over longer stretches of speech.

intrusion The insertion of a sound that is not represented in the spelling and has no historical justification. By far the most common example is the intrusive *r*, but there is also the intrusion of a glottal stop, and the intrusion of semi-vowels. The opposite of elision.

intrusive *r* The link between two consecutive vowels belonging to different words or, less commonly, to different syllables within the same word through the insertion of an /r/ that has no historical justification. The intrusive *r* – especially the word-internal one – is widely stigmatised by language purists, who regard it as a non-standard pronunciation, or simply as incorrect.

IPA Abbreviation for the International Phonetic Alphabet and the International Phonetic Association.

isochronism, isochronous rhythm, isochrony See *stress-timing*.

isosyllabicity, isosyllabic rhythm, isosyllabism See *syllable-timing*.

juncture The phonological and phonetic features that mark the boundaries between syllables, words, and clauses. More broadly, the term also refers to the transition between these units. Such a broad concept of juncture overlaps considerably with the concept of liaison, and, in fact, some linguists include liaison as a part of juncture.

labial A type of articulation that involves the lips. Bilabial and labiodental sounds are labial.

labialisation A process whereby a sound, usually a consonant, is produced with an unusual degree of lip-rounding. It is usually influenced by the rounded lips of a neighbouring sound. Labialisation is indicated in a phonetic transcription proper by a small *w*-like symbol, which is either placed under the symbol for the labialised sound, or raised and placed after it.

labiodental A manner of articulation. Labiodental sounds are made by a movement of the lower lip against the upper teeth. The sound transcribed as /f/ is a labiodental.

labiovelar A more precise label for the English velar phoneme /w/ because it is pronounced with rounded lips.

laminal A type of articulation that involves the blade of the tongue. Palatoalveolar sounds are laminal.

langue A speech community's shared knowledge of a language. Stands in contrast to parole, which is actual language use. A term proposed by the Swiss linguist Ferdinand de Saussure. See also *competence* and *performance*.

larynx Hollow muscular organ situated in the upper part of the trachea, or windpipe, behind the Adam's apple. Also called the voice box.

lateral A manner of articulation. Laterals, or more specifically lateral approximants, are made with air that escapes around the sides of a partial closure of the speech organs, but the narrowing of the air passage does not produce friction. English has only one lateral, /l/, where the tip of the tongue touches the centre of the alveolar ridge.

lateral plosion, lateral release   Occurs when an alveolar plosive initially has the usual complete closure at the alveolar ridge, but the sides of the tongue are then lowered, so that air escapes around the sides of the central closure that remains. A lateral release typically occurs in the production of /t/ and /d/ when they are followed by /l/.

lax   A feature of intensity used by American linguists to describe vowels which are articulated with relatively weak breath force. The label corresponds with the term *lenis*, which is used to describe the intensity of consonant articulation. Contrasts with tense.

lect   The language variety spoken in a particular speech community or the way a language is used by a particular speaker. See also *dialectology*.

length   The relative time a sound is sustained as perceived by the listener. For example, the middle sounds in the words *fool* and *full* are commonly described as a long *u* and short *u*, respectively. The difference here is one of length. Length is a phonological concept because the long *u* and short *u* have different functions within the English sound system.

lenis   An intensity of articulation. Lenis consonants are made with weaker breath force, or lower tension, than fortis consonants.

lexical stress   See *word stress*.

lexical word   A word that has more lexical content, or meaning, than a grammatical word. Lexical words comprise nouns, full (or lexical) verbs, adjectives, and the vast majority of adverbs. Also called content word.

liaison   A transition, or link, between sounds or words. See also *hiatus*.

linking r   A link between words through the articulation of a normally unarticulated word-final /r/, which is articulated only when preceded by a vowel in the same word, and followed by an initial vowel in the next word. A case of liaison.

linking sound   A sound that is absent in a word when that word is pronounced in isolation, but present in the same word in certain phonetic environments in connected speech, usually for ease of pronunciation.

liquid   Laterals and approximants are sometimes referred to as liquids because of their "flowing" sound quality. It is a traditional term no longer in common use, and should be avoided.

loudness   A phonetic property of spoken language and of individual sounds. It is related to the breadth, or amplitude, of the vibration of the vocal folds. Loudness is one component of stress (together with pitch, duration, and sound quality).

manner of articulation   One of the three distinctive features used for the description of consonants. It refers to the type or degree of closure of the speech organs at the place of articulation.

mid vowel   A vowel articulated with the tongue between close and open positions.

minimal pair   A pair of words that differ in meaning and in only one sound. Each of the two contrasting sounds in such a minimal pair is a distinct phoneme.

monophthong   A vowel sound during the articulation of which the speech organs do not change their position. Also called pure or plain vowel.

morph   An actual, concrete form, or realisation, of a morpheme.

morpheme   The smallest unit of meaning within the words of a language.

morphology   The study and description of the structure of words.

morphonology, morphophonemics, morphophonology   The overlap between morphology and phonology.

movable stress   See *free stress*.

nasal   A manner of articulation. A nasal is made with a complete closure in the vocal tract while the velum, or soft palate, is lowered, so that air escapes through the nose. In the production of English nasals, usually *all* the air escapes through the nose. Other languages have nasals where some air also passes through the mouth. The sound transcribed as /m/ is a nasal. Contrasts with oral.

nasal plosion, nasal release   Occurs when an alveolar plosive is produced with the usual complete closure at the alveolar ridge, which is maintained throughout the duration of the sound, so that no air escapes through the mouth, but with a lowered velum, so that air escapes through the nose instead. This kind of release is indicated in a phonetic transcription proper by a small, raised *n*-like symbol after the main symbol. A nasal release typically occurs in the production of a plosive when that plosive is followed by a nasal with the same place of articulation.

nasalisation   A process whereby a sound, usually a vowel, is produced with a lowered velum, which opens the passage to the nasal cavity, so that air escapes not only through the mouth (as is usually the case with vowels), but also through the nose. Nasalisation is influenced by a neighbouring nasal, and can be indicated in a phonetic transcription proper by a tilde above the symbol for the nasalised sound.

neutral vowel   See *schwa*.

non-continuant   A broad classification of the manner of articulation of speech sounds. Non-continuants are produced with a complete closure of the speech organs (both mouth and nose). Plosives and affricates are non-continuants.

non-contrastive distribution   A property of allophones. Refers to the fact that allophones do not contrast meaning, as phonemes do.

non-rhotic accent   An accent in which the /r/ phoneme is articulated only before a vowel, not before a consonant or pause. Also called an *r*-less accent, or a non-*r*-pronouncing accent. Contrasts with rhotic accent.

non-*r*-pronouncing accent   See *non-rhotic accent*.

nuclear stress   See *tonic stress*.

nucleus See *centre* and *tonic syllable*.

onset A structural element in a syllable which precedes the centre, and is produced with greater obstruction of air. An onset is always formed by one or more consonants.

open syllable A syllable that ends with the centre.

open vowel A vowel articulated with the tongue low.

open word class A category of words whose number is, in principle, unlimited because new words are continually added. Open word classes are nouns, full (or lexical) verbs, adjectives, and, to a great extent, adverbs.

opening diphthong A diphthong that moves towards a more open vowel. There are no opening diphthongs in English.

oral A manner of articulation. An oral sound is produced with the velum raised, so that the passage to the nasal cavity is blocked, and the air escapes only through the mouth. Contrasts with nasal.

palatal A place of articulation. A palatal sound is produced when the body of the tongue comes near or touches the palate. There is only one palatal in English, /j/.

palatalisation A process whereby a sound, usually a consonant, is produced with the body of the tongue coming near or touching the hard palate in addition to another place of articulation. Palatalised consonants are sometimes described as "soft", and non-palatalised consonants as "hard". Palatalisation can be indicated in a phonetic transcription proper by a small *j*-like symbol.

palatoalveolar A place of articulation. A palatoalveolar sound is made with the tongue tip touching the alveolar ridge, and with a simultaneous raising of the blade of the tongue towards the hard palate. The sound transcribed as /ʒ/ is palatoalveolar. See also *laminal*.

paragoge An intrusion in word-final position.

paralinguistic feature A linguistic feature of lesser importance in the communication of meaning. Tone of voice is a paralinguistic feature.

parole Actual language use. Stands in contrast to langue, which is a speech community's shared knowledge of a language. A term proposed by the Swiss linguist Ferdinand de Saussure. See also *competence* and *performance*.

peak See *centre*.

performance The actual language use of an individual speaker. Stands in contrast to competence, which is an individual speaker's internalised knowledge of the language. A term proposed by the American linguist Noam Chomsky. See also *langue* and *parole*.

pharyngal, pharyngeal A place of articulation. A pharyng(e)al sound is made when the root of the tongue is pulled back in the pharynx. There are no such sounds in English.

pharyngeal cavity, pharynx   The throat.

phone   An actual, concrete speech sound. The realisation of a phoneme by an individual speaker.

phoneme   The smallest distinctive, or contrastive, unit in the sound system of a language. A phoneme is an abstract linguistic unit representing a speech sound that has a function within the sound system of a language, or as part of the speakers' langue or competence. Phonemes are abstract, idealised sounds that are never pronounced and never heard. A phoneme of a language is identified through a minimal pair.

phoneme inventory   The complete set of phonemes in a sound system. Also called phonemic system.

phonemic symbol   A phonetic symbol that, strictly speaking, represents a phoneme, rather than a phone.

phonemic system   See *phoneme inventory*.

phonetic alphabet   A set of phonetic symbols.

phonetic symbol   A symbol used to represent a speech sound in a one-to-one correspondence.

phonetic transcription   The process of writing down spoken language as accurately as possible using phonetic symbols. And the resultant written text.

phonetics   The study and description of concrete utterances and concrete, individual speech sounds.

phonographic relationship   A one-to-one correspondence between speech and writing.

phonology   The study and description of the sound system of a language.

phonotactics   The part of phonology that deals with the rules governing the possible positions and combinations of phonemes.

pitch   A phonetic property related to the frequency of the vibration of the vocal folds. The faster the vocal folds vibrate, the higher the pitch. Pitch shapes the intonation of connected speech, and can distinguish meaning at a suprasegmental level, but cannot change the function of an individual sound within the sound system of English. Pitch is one component of stress (together with loudness, duration, and sound quality). See also *fundamental frequency*.

pitch contour   The specific rises and falls in pitch which shape a particular kind of intonation pattern. Also called pitch movement.

pitch movement   See *pitch contour*.

place of articulation   One of the three distinctive features for the description of consonants. The place of articulation names the speech organs that are primarily involved in the production of a particular sound.

plain vowel   See *monophthong*.

plosive A manner of articulation. A plosive, or stop, is a sound that has a complete closure at some point in the vocal tract, builds up the air pressure while the closure is held, and then releases the air explosively through the mouth. The sound transcribed as /p/ is a plosive.

postalveolar A place of articulation. A postalveolar sound is made with the tongue tip approaching or touching the rear of the alveolar ridge or the area just behind it. There is only one postalveolar in English, /r/.

pre-head In intonation, the part of a tone unit that spans all the less prominent syllables before the head.

prescriptive linguistics A tradition which *prescribes*, rather than *describes*, correct usage that all educated people should use in speaking and writing. Prescriptive linguistics does not fully recognise ongoing language change and stylistic variation. Contrasts with descriptive linguistics.

primary articulation An articulation of greater importance than any other simultaneous articulation. Contrasts with secondary articulation, which merely adds a nuance to the quality of the resultant sound.

prominence The combination of greater loudness, higher (or sometimes lower) pitch, greater duration, and sound quality that makes a particular sound, or a syllable centre, stand out perceptually in relation to its surrounding sounds. Prominence is a concept of auditory phonetics. It correlates with stress in articulatory phonetics.

prosody See *suprasegmental phonology*.

prosthesis, prothesis An intrusion in word-initial position. This does not usually occur in English.

pure vowel See *monophthong*.

r-colouring See *retroflexion*.

Received Pronunciation The most prestigious accent of Standard British English, associated with the dialect spoken in the south-east of England. Also called RP.

reduced vowel See *schwa*.

reduction An aspect of connected speech that involves the modification of a vowel to /ə/ or /ɪ/, or the elision of one or more sounds, or both. Also called weakening.

retraction The articulation of a sound further back in the mouth than the underlying phoneme, usually under the influence of the surrounding sounds. Retracted sounds are also, though less commonly, called backed.

retroflex A manner of articulation. A retroflex sound is produced when the tip of the tongue is curled back to approach or make contact with the front part of the roof of the mouth, or hard palate, just behind the alveolar ridge. There are no retroflex phonemes in RP or any other accent of English. There is, however, a retroflex pronunciation variant in most American accents, in Irish English, and in accents of south-west England, transcribed as [ɻ].

retroflexion A process whereby a vowel is produced with a curled-back tongue tip approaching or touching the hard palate in addition to another articulation. Also called *r*-colouring or rhotacisation. Retroflexion can be indicated in a phonetic transcription proper by a small, raised *r*-like symbol, which is upside down and placed after the symbol for the retroflexed vowel.

r-full accent See *rhotic accent*.

rhotacisation See *retroflexion*.

rhotic Pertaining to or characterised by *r*-sounds. Also: Any *r*-sound.

rhotic accent An accent that has not lost the /r/ phoneme in the course of the centuries, and in which an /r/ is pronounced whenever it occurs in the spelling. Also called an *r*-ful accent, or *r*-pronouncing accent. Contrasts with non-rhotic accent.

rhyme A structural element in a syllable comprising the centre and the coda (if there is one). Together, these elements account for the rhyming potential of syllables.

rhythm In spoken language, the recurrence of prominent elements at what are perceived to be regular intervals of time. Depending on the particular language, such prominent elements are usually either stresses or syllables. The type of rhythm is a characteristic suprasegmental feature of the pronunciation of any given language, and therefore forms the basis for one of the fundamental categorisations of the languages of the world. See also *stress-timing* and *syllable-timing*.

rise An intonation contour that rises.

rise-fall An intonation contour that first rises, then falls.

rising diphthong A diphthong in which the second element is more prominent. Rising diphthongs rarely occur in English.

r-less accent See *non-rhotic accent*.

roll A manner of articulation. A roll, or trill, involves an intermittent closure of the speech organs in the vocal tract. In other words, a roll is produced when one articulator vibrates against another. There are no rolled phonemes in RP or any other accent of English, but some dialects have a rolled pronunciation variant.

RP Abbreviation for Received Pronunciation.

r-pronouncing accent See *rhotic accent*.

schwa One of the seven English short vowels. The centre of the tongue is raised between mid-close and mid-open position, and the lips are in a neutral shape. The schwa occurs solely in unstressed syllables. Since most unstressed syllables contain a schwa, this vowel is the most frequently occurring sound in English. Also called a neutral vowel or a reduced vowel.

secondary articulation An articulation which is of lesser importance than another simultaneous articulation, called primary articulation. In English, the main types of secondary articulation are labialisation, retroflexion, palatalisation, and velarisation.

segmental phonology The segmentation of language into individual speech sounds provided by phonetics. Segmental phonology is not concerned with the production, the physical properties, or the perception of these sounds, but in the function and possible combinations of sounds within the sound system.

semi-vowel In a broad sense, all frictionless continuants, /l, r, j, w/. They are consonants from a phonological point of view, and (almost) vowels from a purely phonetic point of view. In a narrower sense, only /j, w/. Also called glides.

sentence stress The stress or prominence carried by a word within an utterance.

sibilant Any of the alveolar and palatoalveolar fricatives, /s, z, ʃ, ʒ/. These fricatives have a sharper s-like sound than other fricatives. Also called groove fricatives. Sometimes the affricates, /tʃ, dʒ/, are also included in the group of sibilants. See also *fricative*.

silent letter A letter in the written form of a word that is not pronounced.

soft palate See *velum*.

sonority The intrinsic relative loudness, or "carrying-power", of a phoneme. According to a common sonority hierarchy, vowels are more sonorous than consonants.

sound quality The quality characterised by a sound's distinctive features. A speech sound has the same sound quality irrespective of the loudness, pitch, or duration with which it is pronounced.

standard, standard variety The form of a language generally associated with educated speakers. Even though it may have a regional origin, it is regarded as regionally neutral in that it can be found anywhere in a country. Thus a standard is a sociolect, rather than a dialect.

stop See *plosive*.

stress The combination of a number of articulatory features which make a speech sound, syllable, or word more prominent than others. Loudness, pitch, duration, and sound quality are the main components of stress. See also *prominence*.

stressed syllable Within a word, the syllable which carries stress. A stressed syllable can contain any vowel as its centre except /ə/, and the vowel always has its "full", original sound quality. Contrasts with unstressed syllable.

stress-timing A type of rhythm whereby strong stresses tend to occur at relatively equal intervals of time, irrespective of the number of lesser-stressed syllables or words between them. English, Russian, and modern Greek are stress-timed languages. Also called isochronous rhythm, isochrony, or isochronism. See also *rhythm*.

strong form The pronunciation variant of a given word which contains a strong vowel, and from which no sounds have been elided. Contrasts with weak form.

strong syllable A syllable that has a strong vowel as its centre, irrespective of whether it is stressed or unstressed. Contrasts with weak syllable.

strong vowel A vowel that has its full, original sound quality, except /ə/, which is always weak. Contrasts with weak vowel.

structural function of intonation The ability of intonation to express a grammatical or structural role of an utterance, for example whether an utterance is a question, a request, or an instruction.

structural word, structure word See *grammatical word*.

suprasegmental phonology The study and description of those features of pronunciation that cannot be segmented because they extend over more than one segment, or sound. Such features include stress, rhythm, and intonation. These features together are also referred to as prosody.

syllabic consonant A consonant forming the centre of a syllable, instead of a vowel. It has the phonological characteristics of a vowel, but retains the phonetic characteristics of a consonant. A syllabic consonant is indicated by a small vertical line, [ ], under the relevant symbol. There are five consonants that can be transformed into syllabic consonants: /l, n, m, ŋ, r/.

syllabication, syllabification The division of words into syllables.

syllable A linguistic unit that is typically larger than a single sound and smaller than a word. Phonetically, a syllable must have a centre, also called peak or nucleus, which is produced with little or no obstruction of air, and is therefore usually formed by a vowel. Phonologically, the English syllable has the maximal structure CCCVCCCC (with 'C' representing a consonant, and 'V' representing a vowel), the minimal structure V, or any structure in between.

syllable-timing A type of rhythm whereby all syllables tend to occur at relatively equal intervals of time, irrespective of whether they are stressed or unstressed. French, Spanish, and Japanese are syllable-timed languages. This type of rhythm is also characteristic of the pronunciation of some second-language varieties of English, owing to the influence of local mother tongues. Also called isosyllabic rhythm, isosyllabicity or isosyllabism. See also *rhythm*.

syncopation, syncope Elision in the middle of a word, most commonly referring to the elision of vowels. The term can also refer to the (historical) elision of consonants, and to the elision of whole syllables. Syncope is sometimes represented in the spelling by an apostrophe, as in *t'day* and *t'night*.

syntax The study and description of sentence patterns and structures.

tail In intonation, the part of a tone unit that comprises all the syllables occurring between the tonic syllable and the end of the tone unit.

tap See *flap*.

tense A feature of intensity used by American linguists to describe vowels which are articulated with relatively much breath force. The label corresponds with the term *fortis*, which is used to describe the intensity of consonant articulation. Contrasts with lax.

T-glottalling See *glottal replacement*.

timbre See *tone of voice*.

tonal quality See *tone of voice*.

tone group See *tone unit*.

tone language A language in which a change of pitch can change the function of a sound. Over half the languages of the world are tone languages.

tone of voice The "colour" of a voice, produced by the specific pattern of vibration of the vocal folds, which, in turn, causes a specific combination of soundwaves, without affecting the sound quality. Also called voice quality, tonal quality, or timbre. Sometimes regarded as a paralinguistic feature.

tone unit A stretch of speech over which a single intonation contour extends. A tone unit may be either a part of an utterance, or a whole utterance. Also called tone group.

tonic stress The stress carried by the tonic syllable, which determines the particular intonation contour. Also called nuclear stress.

tonic syllable In an utterance, the syllable on which the main pitch movement begins. The pitch movement may be restricted to the tonic syllable, but often it continues from the tonic syllable to the end of the tone unit. Also called nucleus.

trill See *roll*.

triphthong A sound sequence that consists of three vowels. There are five triphthongs in English. Unlike a diphthong, a triphthong is not analysed as one phoneme. It is interpreted as a closing diphthong followed by a schwa. The sequence /aʊə/, then, is a triphthong consisting of two phonemes.

unstressed syllable Within a word, a syllable which is unstressed. Unstressed syllables contain mainly /ə, ɪ, ʊ/ or a syllabic consonant as their centre. Contrasts with stressed syllable.

utterance A unit of spoken language that begins and ends with a clear pause, usually has a complete syntactic structure, and a complete meaning. An utterance may be as short as a single word, or as long as a complex sentence.

uvular A place of articulation. A uvular sound is made by moving the root or back of the tongue against the uvula, which is the appendage that hangs down from the velum. There are no uvular phonemes in English.

velar A place of articulation. A velar sound is made by placing the back of the tongue against or near the velum, or soft palate. The sound transcribed as /k/ is a velar.

velarisation A process whereby a sound, almost always /l/, is produced with the back of the tongue coming near or touching the velum, or soft palate, in addition to another place of articulation. It is influenced by a following consonant or pause, and can be indicated in a phonetic transcription proper by a tilde placed through the relevant symbol, as in [ɫ]. See also *dark l*.

velum   The back part of the roof of the mouth. Also called the soft palate.

vocal cords, vocal folds   Two folds of muscle and connective tissue located behind the Adam's apple in the larynx, or voice box. They are opened and closed during the production of speech.

vocoid   A phonetic class of sounds that are produced without any obstruction of air. All frictionless continuants and all vowels are vocoids. Contrasts with contoid.

voice box   See *larynx*.

voice onset time   The time that elapses between the onset of speaking and the point at which the vocal folds begin to vibrate. Also called VOT.

voice quality   See *tone of voice*.

voiced   A feature of sounds produced with the glottis narrow, so the vocal folds are together, and the air-stream forces its way through, causing the vocal folds to vibrate. Contrasts with voiceless.

voiceless   A feature of sounds produced with the glottis open, so the vocal folds are apart, and air passes through without causing the vocal folds to vibrate. Contrasts with voiced.

VOT   Abbreviation for voice onset time.

vowel   A class of sound produced with no obstruction of air, and typically occurring at the centre of a syllable. Contrasts with consonant.

vowel chart, vowel diagram   A triangle or quadrilateral within which vowels are schematically represented on the basis of the two criteria closeness/openness and frontness/backness. It approximately reflects the space in the centre of the mouth, where the vowels are articulated.

vowel dispersion   The even distribution of the vowels of a language within a vowel chart. Most languages of the world have vowel dispersion.

vowel glide   See *diphthong*.

weak form   A pronunciation variant of a word that contains a weak vowel, or from which one or more sounds have been omitted, or both. Weak forms can occur only in non-prominent positions. Thus they are always unstressed. Contrasts with strong form.

weak syllable   A syllable that has a weak vowel as its centre. Contrasts with strong syllable.

weak vowel   A vowel that results from a reduction (as is often the case with /ə/ and /ɪ/) or one that occurs solely in unstressed syllables (i.e. mainly /ə/, but also [i], [u]). The syllable of which it forms the centre is called a weak syllable. Contrasts with strong vowel.

weakening   See *reduction*.

word stress The stress carried by a syllable within a word. Word stress in many languages is governed by rules that apply to almost the entire vocabulary, and is therefore fairly predictable. In other languages, word stress is more difficult to predict since it is rule-governed only to a very limited extent. Also called lexical stress.

yod coalescence The merging of /t, d, s/ or /z/ with /j/ – either across word boundaries or within a word – to form /tʃ, dʒ, ʃ/ or /ʒ/, respectively.

zero coda A structural feature of a syllable that has no coda.

zero onset A structural feature of a syllable that has no onset.

NEUERSCHEINUNG FEBRUAR 2011

narr VERLAG   francke VERLAG   attempto VERLAG

Björn Rothstein

Wissenschaftliches Arbeiten für Linguisten

narr studienbücher
2011, 218 Seiten
€[D] 19,90 / SFr 30,50
ISBN 978-3-8233-6630-0

Wenn es um „linguistisches Arbeiten" geht, bestehen bei den Studierenden oftmals große Unsicherheiten bezüglich Inhalt, Form und Methode. Dieses Studienbuch vermittelt Schritt für Schritt die notwendigen Arbeitstechniken, um erfolgreich sprachwissenschaftliche Studien durchführen, präsentieren und verschriftlichen zu können. Klassische Bereiche wie Themenfindung, Informationsbeschaffung, Besonderheiten wissenschaftlicher Textsorten und bibliographische Konventionen werden genauso thematisiert wie die Probleme, vor denen Studierende üblicherweise im Bereich der Linguistik stehen: Lektüre und Überprüfung von linguistischen Texten, Argumentationstechniken, Beweisführungen und die Datenerhebung, -verwaltung und -notation.
Zahlreiche Schaubilder und Beispiele veranschaulichen den Text. Für die praktische Anwendbarkeit sorgen die am Ende jedes Kapitels angefügten Checklisten.

Narr Francke Attempto Verlag GmbH+Co. KG · Dischingerweg 5 · D-72070 Tübingen
Tel. +49 (07071) 9797-0 · Fax +49 (07071) 97 97-11 · info@narr.de · **www.narr.de**

NEUERSCHEINUNG HERBST 2010

Ruth Albert / Nicole Marx

Empirisches Arbeiten in Linguistik und Sprachlehrforschung

Anleitung zu quantitativen Studien von der Planungsphase bis zum Forschungsbericht

narr studienbücher
2010, 202 Seiten,
€[D] 19,90/SFr 30,50
ISBN 978-3-8233-6590-7

Das Studienbuch bietet eine systematische Anleitung für Studierende, die eine quantitativ vorgehende empirische Untersuchung im Bereich Linguistik/Sprachlehrforschung planen. Jeder einzelne Schritt wird ausführlich erklärt: vom Finden einer genau definierten Untersuchungsfrage über die Methoden der Datenerhebung (Beobachtung, Befragung, Experiment und Nutzung von Textkorpora) und -auswertung sowie deren statistischer Aufbereitung bis zum Schreiben des Forschungsberichts. Zu allen Kapiteln gibt es Übungsaufgaben mit Lösungshinweisen und ausführliche Hinweise auf weiterführende Literatur.

Narr Francke Attempto Verlag GmbH+Co. KG · Dischingerweg 5 · D-72070 Tübingen
Tel. +49 (07071) 9797-0 · Fax +49 (07071) 97 97-11 · info@narr.de · **www.narr.de**

NEUERSCHEINUNG

narr VERLAG   francke VERLAG   attempto VERLAG

Laurenz Volkmann

Fachdidaktik Englisch: Kultur und Sprache

narr studienbücher
2010, XIV, 282 Seiten,
€[D] 19,90/SFr 30,50
ISBN 978-3-8233-6593-8

Das Studienbuch positioniert sich zwischen den zahlreichen methodikorientierten Einführungen zur Englischen Fachdidaktik (die entweder Sprachdidaktik oder Literaturdidaktik zum Gegenstand haben) und Büchern zum interkulturellen Lernen, Landeskunde und Cultural Studies. Leitfrage ist: Wie kann die »Kultur« eines anderen Landes repräsentativ und exemplarisch unterrichtet werden? Wie prägt das Verständnis von Kultur und Sprache den Unterricht und welche Themen, Texte und Methoden sind hier zu favorisieren? Konkret geht es dabei dann um Themenbereiche wie
- die Zusammenhänge von Sprache und Kultur beim Erlernen und Verwenden einer Fremdsprache
- die Grundsatzfrage, wie weit sich der Englischunterricht nach wie vor auf die »Kernländer« des Englischen, GB und die USA, beschränken soll?
- die verschiedenen Formen der kommunikativen Kompetenz, interkulturellen und interkulturell-kommunikativen Kompetenz sowie transkulturellen Kompetenz
- die wachsende Rolle des Englischen als Sprache internationaler Kommunikation (lingua franca)
- die Veränderungen von Bewusstsein, Verhalten und Kommunikation durch die Neuen Medien und die resultierenden Folgen für den Englischunterricht

JETZT BESTELLEN!

Narr Francke Attempto Verlag GmbH+Co. KG · Dischingerweg 5 · D-72070 Tübingen
Tel. +49 (07071) 9797-0 · Fax +49 (07071) 97 97-11 · info@narr.de · **www.narr.de**

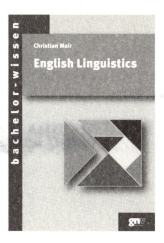

Christian Mair

English Linguistics

An Introduction

bachelor-wissen
2008, 272 Seiten,
€[D] 14,90 / Sfr 27,90
ISBN 978-3-8233-6393-4

This book is a compact and easy-to-use introduction to English linguistics which
- is tailored to the needs of students of English at German, Austrian and Swiss universities,
- contains graded exercises to motivate students to carry out independent research, and
- bridges the gap between linguistics and the literary and cultural-studies components of the typical BA in English Studies

bachelor-wissen *English Linguistics* goes beyond the usual introduction in offering accompanying web resources which provide additional material and multi-media illustration.

 Narr Francke Attempto Verlag GmbH + Co. KG
Postfach 25 60 · D-72015 Tübingen · Fax (0 7071) 97 97-11
Internet: www.narr.de · E-Mail: info@narr.de